LIVING ON A DEADLINE

LIVING ON A DEADLINE

DEADLINE

A History of the Press Association

Chris Moncrieff

First published in Great Britain in 2001 by
Virgin Books Ltd
Thames Wharf Studios
Rainville Road
London W6 9HA

A catalogue record for this book is available from the British
Library.

ISBN 1 85227 917 6

Typeset by TW Typesetting, Plymouth, Devon
Printed and bound in Great Britain by Mackays of Chatham PLC

Contents

Acknowledgements

Many young journalists, understandably, regard the Press Association as a jumping-off place for what they view as the more glamorous areas of the media world. I take the reverse view.

I regard the PA as far and away the most important part of what is still called Fleet Street. What appeals to me about the PA is that it has no axe to grind, it express no views about any of the topics about which it writes, it runs no editorials, it does not campaign.

There are no nail-biting anxieties of the kind experienced, for instance, by Sunday paper reporters, that their 'exclusive' story may suddenly, and infuriatingly, cease to remain exclusive only an hour or two before publication time.

And when, in 1994, I was retired, having reached the age of 64, I was overjoyed when the then editor-in-chief, Colin Webb, asked if I would stay on, on a retainer basis. I can tell you, I needed no second bidding.

I have to say that I could not have written this book without a lot of help, always willingly given, by a lot of kind people, who were happy to share their reminiscences with me, fill in the blank areas, correct mistakes and often to lend me documents and cuttings that they cherished.

I have also drawn heavily on *Reporter Anonymous*, by the late George Scott, a history of the Press Association published in its centenary year, 1968.

In writing this personal view of the Press Association I received enormous help from the present chief executive and editor-in-chief, Paul Potts, former chief executive Robert Simpson, the editor, Jonathan Grun, two former editors-in-chief, David Chipp and Colin Webb, as well as from a former associate editor, Reg Evans. The former executive editor Brian Robins also readily offered his help, which I would have greatly valued. Alas, tragically for his family and his many friends, he died suddenly before this could happen. However, his widow, Rene, kindly made available to me much important material that Brian had kept.

I have received no less invaluable help from many others, a lot of them past and present PA stalwarts including Ian Yates, Richard Winfrey, Jack Purdham, Tim Moynihan, James Maguire, Jack Dodd, Harry Aspey, Geoffrey Meade, Chris Mead, David Giles, Martin Keene, Peter Willoughby, Mark Hird, Mike Riches, Nelson Fairley, Peter Went, Bill Martin, Hilda Richards, Ray Smith, Ron Bell, Peter Archer, Paul Fuller, Peter Woodman, Richard Savill, Alan Jones, Bob Hutchinson, Rob Gibson, Martin Cleaver, Tony Smith, Paddy Hicks, Bob Roberts, Anjali Kwatra and James Hardy.

Terry Manners, associate editor of the PA, who has since left, performed a magnificent job in editing the original manuscript.

I would also like to thank Richard Peacock and all his staff at the PA News Library for their unfailing patience and good cheer at my constant raids on their territory.

There are also special thanks to Dr Margaret Scammell, Senior Lecturer in Media and Communications in the Department of Social Psychology at the London School of Economics and Political Science, for her help and encouragement, and to Alex Leys for enormous help with the saga of UK News.

Now we come to the 'last but not least' bit: my good lady wife Maggie, for her help, encouragement and patience. She has also heroically kept on clearing the weeds and mowing the grass while all this has been going on.

Finally I would like to pay tribute to the generations of PA journalists who are not mentioned in this book but whose loyalty and commitment to all that is good in journalism have helped the Press Association to be the great company that it is.

Foreword

When an MP first arrives in the Commons, there's a great deal to learn from more experienced colleagues. If you are lucky to have a wise head giving advice, it won't be long before the political reporters of the Press Association – and their importance – are pointed out.

For those like myself who entered Parliament in 1983, the Press Association was personified by the distinctive and seemingly ever-present figure of Chris Moncrieff, the PA's then political editor. Although many political journalists were more famous in the wider world, you quickly learnt that few were more important than Chris – and that none was more careful to ensure he did not abuse his position or the influence it gave him.

What marked out Chris – and continues to mark out his successors and the PA itself – is their pride in trying to report the news quickly, accurately and fairly. So it seems right to me, and I'm sure to MPs of all parties, that Chris has been asked to write a new history of the PA.

It's a fascinating story of how the PA grew from the musings of four Victorian newspaper men, in the back of a horse-drawn cab, about how news could be provided to their provincial papers to become a unique national institution, owned by and serving its customers.

The PA today is very different from the organisation those newspapermen could possibly have imagined. But by providing copy to every national and regional daily paper in the British Isles – along with hundreds of broadcasting stations – the PA is more than meeting the ambitions of its architects.

The history of the PA charts the immense changes in newspapers and journalism over the last 130 years. The birth and death of individual newspapers and of competitors to the PA itself, the arrival of radio and TV news, and, in recent years, the opportunities and challenges of new technology are all reflected here.

It also, of course, reflects the history of our country. In war and peace, at times of great national crisis and celebration, the PA has played a key role in keeping the country informed. So much so that many of the great news dramas of our times have been illustrated, in the papers or on TV, by a PA picture showing the world the exact moment when the news, good or bad, became official.

This helps highlight the special place the PA retains in our journalism. Even in the world of fierce competition and 24-hour rolling TV news, the words 'It's running on PA' still matter.

Tony Blair

10 Downing Street
April 2001

Prologue: The First Word . . .

THE PRESS ASSOCIATION is the backbone and the flesh of British journalism. But it does not wear the jazzy clothes. Every day since its birth in 1868 – with a very few insignificant blips – the PA has poured out words and (in the last fifty years or so) pictures that, as often as not, have provided the essential material for every morning and evening newspaper in the British Isles – and, more recently, for radio and television as well. Throughout the media industry, the PA has a reputation for speed, accuracy, fairness and flexibility. It does not have any political views. It writes no opinionated editorials – or editorials of any kind whatsoever. It does not campaign or crusade. It simply gathers the news and the pictures and distributes them as fast as modern communications systems will allow, which is virtually instantaneously.

The doors of the Press Association never close. The news desk is staffed continuously, morning, noon and night, and has been so right from the start. Reporters and other journalists hired by the PA must be prepared to work at all hours of the day and night, often in uncomfortable and sometimes dangerous conditions.

Whenever the PA gets a story, it is used straightaway. There is no waiting for the next edition, the next news bulletin or the weekend in the case of a Sunday newspaper. Every second of every day is a deadline for the Press Association. Working for the PA is *living* on a deadline.

And, although many journalists regard the PA as a springboard for what they see as more glamorous jobs on national newspapers, radio or television, there is little doubt that the Press Association has more influence on what appears in the media – written, sound or visual – than any other single entity of the media industry.

It is often claimed that the BBC Radio 4's *Today* programme sets the agenda, particularly the political agenda, for the day. Up to a point, that may be true.

But what is also certainly true is that politicians and other figureheads clamour to get their words on the PA. This is not simply to save them from making a score of telephone calls around Fleet Street papers and elsewhere, but it's because they know the PA will give them a fair run – but only, of course, if the item is newsworthy. All judgments made on PA are editorial judgments. Never political. Michael Heseltine, the former Conservative Deputy Prime Minister, knows more about how to deal with the press than most. And he has always been fully seized of the power and importance of the Press Association.

Once, when he expressed a view about the way a document had been treated by the PA, he said, 'You know as well as I do that whatever the Press Association does will be followed by the rest of the press that day.' He could not have expressed it more accurately. In the unattractive language of commerce, the PA would be described as a market leader.

The PA has more than a hundred masters to serve: these are the newspapers and agencies that subscribe to its now manifold services. Every single one of them has its own agenda and idiosyncrasies. They all have different deadlines. Some want large wodges of copy; others require a summarised version of events, and plenty of 'snippets'. All have to be catered for.

On a really momentous story, such as the declaration of war or the death of Diana, Princess of Wales, the PA will issue a 'flash', giving the news in the smallest number of words. A major train crash, for instance, would be heralded by a 'rush', just one grade lower; as would the death of an important figure or the result of a highly newsy court case. In circumstances of lesser news value but still of importance, a 'snap' would be issued, which gives the basic elements of the story – for instance, a House of Commons vote – in a single, all-embracing, stand-alone sentence. Of course, none of these examples are hard and fast. The category of the alert depends on individual cases. But in each case when an alert is issued it is preceded, just seconds ahead, by an audio or visual warning in newsrooms up and down the land.

The PA was born in the days when news by pigeon post was still an option, and indeed the transmission of football scores from stadiums to newspaper offices by pigeon was operated within living memory. The PA once had a modest pigeon loft in the Midlands, but its existence was short-lived and calamitous.

However, the PA used to 'telegraph' racing results through a series of men using a form of semaphore ticktack system between the winning post and the reporter at base: often a distance of several miles. It looked, on the face of it, to be a high-risk procedure but it always seemed to work. There have been occasions, too, when PA reporters, believe it or not, have taken to the saddle themselves, and galloped back with the news, as from Aix to Ghent. This happened when a racing reporter found this the only way to get the result through to the PA in the days before sophisticated communications. Nowadays, of course, the PA has managed to keep abreast of advances in new technology and new media, although, in the early days of computers, trade union objections held the PA back for several years.

However, despite these setbacks, the PA has moved fairly smoothly from the days of crackling wireless signals to sexy, sultry Ananova, the world's first virtual newscaster; and from dropping packets of pictures by parachute on to wasteland to be picked up by newspaper messengers to a system whereby pictures are distributed virtually direct from the camera to the recipient.

But, just because the PA moves remorselessly ahead into what Harold Wilson, often misquoted, called 'the white heat of technological revolution', it does not mean that all the old, tried and tested methods and practices are discarded by the wayside. For instance, although tape recorders and similar electronic devices are of inestimable value to a reporter, shorthand is still better and it is certainly quicker, even in the new millennium.

The Press Association is one of the few places in the media world where you will still find reporters with immaculate shorthand. The PA now has an electronic feed of what is said in the House of Commons. It is recorded and can be replayed. But reporters who rely on their shorthand alone – and most of them still do – get their stories out that much more quickly than those who resort to the tape. And shorthand is, of course, essential in long-running and dramatic court cases. The coverage of the 1995 Rosemary West mass-murder trial, for which the PA received an award, was a case in point.

It is one of the great values of PA that its reporters stay on when others have darted off. This is especially true of the House of Commons. After Question Time (the first hour), there is a massive exodus from the Press Gallery. When the turmoil has subsided, the only people normally left behind, apart from representatives from *Hansard*, are the PA reporters. That means that pretty well the entire news media of the world rely utterly on PA for everything that happens in the chambers of the House of Commons – and House of Lords – for the bulk of each day's sitting.

Time was when the PA was regarded as the 'agency of record', where celebrities thought they simply had to speak for their words automatically to appear on the tapes. It was never like that. But there are still those, politicians mainly, who seem to think they have a God-given right for their utterances to be promulgated on the PA. They regard the PA as some form of Post Office. And they are told firmly that this is not and never has been the case, and that they have to compete for space on the tape. Newsworthiness is the key.

Once, in the 1980s, the old Liberal Party actually applied a measuring tape to the PA outpourings and complained that compared with the exposure the Conservatives and Labour were getting, and bearing in mind the number of MPs each party had, the Liberals were about a foot and a half short of their 'entitlement'. It was a bizarre and ridiculous misunderstanding of what the PA was, and is, all about.

They were quietly told that it did not work like that. The PA, although endeavouring to be fair at all times, is under no obligation, legal or otherwise, as are some of the broadcasters on certain occasions, to allot a 'quota' for each political party. And it would be ludicrous if that were the situation. Newsworthiness must always be the criterion.

But PA is far more than simply a backup for the national and provincial newspapers and the electronic media. Nor does it sit back and wait for stories to fall into its lap. It digs and delves for exclusive stories, and indeed was responsible for two of the most momentous stories of recent years. The resignation of Margaret Thatcher, for instance, was a Press Association exclusive. And the PA reported the death of Diana, Princess of Wales, some sixteen minutes before the official announcement – and sixteen minutes is an eternity in journalism.

So those who claim – and some still do – that the day of the scoop has long gone are totally at odds with the facts. The PA provides background on big crime cases and analysis and interpretation of political events. A comprehensive NewsFeatures department distributes up-to-the-minute feature articles, invariably with a topical context. There is a fully fledged weather-forecasting service. What is more, the PA has entered the field of broadcasting and television and has pioneered the opportunities and scope of new-media technicalities. The PA's TV and other listings, updated daily on a rolling basis, are used in scores of newspapers and magazines.

And the PA's sports department – which has moved out of London and is now based in Leeds – provides the most comprehensive coverage and data of all, ranging from wall-to-wall football coverage to curling and everything in between. Every single goal scored in the main football divisions, and some of the lower ones as well, is recorded on the PA tapes within seconds.

Nowadays, PA's reporters travel the globe. But this was not always the case. The 'joke' always used to be: Anything south of Dover belongs to the international news agency, Reuters. And that, in practical terms, was pretty well true. Press Association was the 'home' news agency and was for years virtually confined to these shores. Overseas stories – including those with an overwhelming British interest, such as a touring member of the royal family, or the Prime Minister, or the England cricketers fighting for the Ashes in Australia – were all covered as a matter of course by Reuters, although they often called on PA to provide expert staff to help them.

Gradually, the situation changed. With Reuters modifying their own emphasis on news gathering for the British market, it became clear that the PA needed to spread its own wings. Reuters had their eyes on the global market, rather than the particular. Therefore, for instance, when it came to overseas cricket coverage, Reuters were unable to furnish the detail and the scale that the British papers demanded. It became obvious, too, that, after Britain's entry into what was then called the Common Market in 1972, it was essential that the PA had its own man and its own office in Brussels.

However, it was not until 1977 that the PA had a permanent presence in Brussels, which was fast becoming a rich source of British-interest stories. Reuters, whose markets were much broader than the PA's, could not, by its very nature, focus on these stories in the detail and depth that the PA's clientele required. The PA therefore simply told Reuters that they were going to staff Brussels – and that is what happened.

It paid off magnificent dividends and the occupants of that post have been used not only for European Union stories (their prime reason for being there) but also as 'firemen' covering all sorts of other British-interest stories that blow up from time to time in Europe and beyond, including New York, where the PA opened a bureau in 2001.

Nowadays, PA reporters roam the globe. They went to war in the Falklands, in the Gulf, in Bosnia and Kosovo. The prime minister of the day never goes anywhere, at home or abroad, without at least one accompanying Press Association representative. And the same applies to the royal family. PA sports reporters also follow the mainstream sports – football, cricket, tennis et al. – to the four corners of the earth, wherever a British interest is at stake. Not so many years ago, the PA was seconding sports writers to help Reuters with the Olympic Games. Now, the PA covers the Olympics in its own right.

And, at general election times, the PA has no peer. Where possible, a year is spent preparing for what is one of the most complicated and momentous operations in the journalists' calendar. Others have tried to compete with the PA's rapid results-gathering operation, not without success. But, overall, the PA probably has the best record of any in this field.

The organisation of general election coverage is a massive task. The moment one general election is over, the PA has to start thinking about the next one. All this is interspersed with organising coverage of the local elections, which is a no less daunting operation.

Up to the beginning of World War Two – when PA moved into 85 Fleet Street – the organisation employed an army of messenger boys, smartly turned out in uniform, who used to race around London, mostly on foot, delivering telegrams to post offices. Their journeys to specified post offices were strictly timed and, if the boys took noticeably longer than the prescribed time and without a plausible excuse to explain themselves, then punishment was meted out.

The picture operation – at first a joint exercise with Reuters – did not get under way until after the war. Some of the finest photographers, many returning from the forces, were recruited. A few turned up for work at the outset still in military uniform.

And, on the Internet, the PA had one of the most up-to-date and frequently updated websites of anybody. It included, for a time, a Westminster area, which enabled surfers to 'visit', watch and listen to the House of Commons live and in action. All this coincided with the 'birth' of the green-eyed virtual newscaster, Ananova, a cyberspace beauty and a pioneer in this exciting

new technological world. Ananova, a 'woman' of infinite potential, was sold to Orange, the mobile-telephone giant.

It is all a very far cry from those gas-lit days in 1868 when the
Press Association was born. The romantic version is that it was
conceived by four frock-coated gentlemen in a befogged London
hansom cab struggling through a pea-souper en route for Brixton.
Everybody likes to think that that is true – and it probably is true at
least in part. But what is more likely is that newspapers throughout
the country were getting tired of the operations of the cavalier,
untrustworthy, inaccurate and often downright stroppy private
telegraph companies, who were sending them what today would be
regarded as highly dodgy and sometimes dangerous news stories.

It was an act of nationalisation in 1870 – to which both the
Conservative and Liberal administrations had contributed and
by which the Post Office took over the telegraphs from the
private telegraph companies – that really put the Press Association in business.

From those Victorian days until now, the Press Association
has been pouring out millions of words a week. But only a fool
would suggest that it has all been plain sailing. The media world
is ferociously competitive and the PA has had its moments of
glory, its alarms and excursions, and its setbacks, too. But those
setbacks, mercifully, have been few and far between. On one or
two occasions, but hardly more, the service has been halted
through industrial disputes, to which, in most cases, the Press
Association has not been a party. Thankfully, those stoppages of
service have been brief. There has never been an occasion when
the entire editorial staff walked out. Although, on one unceleb-
rated occasion, a new subeditor walked out of the office and
joined a picket line at the front entrance on the very day he
joined the Press Association.

Nor has the Press Association been immune from attempts by
would-be rivals to put it out of business. There have been sallies
from Exchange Telegraph, British United Press and the Central
News over the years.

But probably the most threatening of all was the establishment of UK News, a Leicester-based operation, which seemed
set, at one stage, to be in danger of acquiring large chunks of
PA's traditional clientele. The management did not underestimate the peril in which the PA stood at that time. The staff were
bluntly told, 'There is no room in the market for more than one
of us.' It was therefore a battle to the death.

All this happened at a crucial period when the PA was on the point of moving from 85 Fleet Street – the last national news organisation to quit 'The Street' – into its new, hi-tech offices at 292 Vauxhall Bridge Road, in the Victoria area of London, in 1995. Happily for the PA and thanks to some delicate and tricky negotiations by senior executives, led by the editor-in-chief Paul Potts, the business came back and UK News foundered.

PA can now look forward to a bumpy road ahead. Because every road in the media world is beset with boulders, pitfalls and obstacles of one sort or another. No ride is ever smooth. But there is no reason why the PA should not continue to march ahead in the face of all these hazards which may be thrown in its path. Let us hope so.

Meanwhile, it has been a fascinating story so far . . .

1 Birth in the Fog

THE BRITISH ECONOMY was booming. Louis Pasteur had discovered bacteria and Joseph Lister had developed antiseptic. It was the 1860s and more than 20 million people now lived in Queen Victoria's Britain. The social elite enjoyed cycling tours, amateur theatricals, shooting, fox hunting, gambling and garden parties and were schooled at home or in the most select institutions. The less fortunate, however, still lived in crowded conditions where diseases such as cholera and TB were rife. By 1868, the nation was just emerging from one of the worst cholera epidemics in its history, mainly due to poor housing conditions, lack of clean water, no drainage, sewerage or street cleaning. But things were looking up for the working class. The Reform Act the previous year had given the vote to uneducated industrial workers – and that meant Benjamin Disraeli's government had to educate them properly, particularly so that they could read their ballot papers. The growing British public was now developing a thirst for information and knowledge and with it grew a demand for newspapers across the country.

It was against this backcloth, in the shadow of the flickering gas lamps and hansom cabs of Queen Victoria's England, that the Press Association, Britain's first major and now premier national news agency, was born. That year, Fleet Street, London EC4, resembled a provincial shopping mall with its coffee houses, grocers and a sausage shop displaying onions sizzling in pans in the window. Who would have thought then that its ultimate destiny would be the historic and legendary home of the British press?

The romantic story, believed by some, is that the Press Association was conceived in a four-wheeled hansom cab, making painfully slow progress through a typical London pea-souper to Brixton. The density of the fog allegedly gave its four occupants – the founding fathers of PA – time to deliberate in detail the blueprint for a unique, British, co-operative organisation to serve the nation's provincial newspapers. It was mapped out and all but signed and sealed before the end of the journey.

There may well have been some truth in the story, although the names of the occupants of that cab have never been revealed. It is more likely, however, that the uncomfortable journey produced just the rudiments of an idea that had been buzzing around the minds of provincial news chiefs for months. The catalyst for them was an event on 31 July 1868, the day Queen Victoria gave her royal assent to an historic piece of socialism by Disraeli's Conservative government: the Telegraph Act, which nationalised the private telegraph companies in the United Kingdom.

The coming of the telegraph wires had been a revolution. They had been put up along more than two thousand miles of railway track and were created primarily to carry messages for the train companies. But it was soon realised that they could carry news of events as well. Before their arrival, newspapers had to wait for news notes carried by sailing ships, horse riders, donkey carts and pigeons. The trouble was, however, that the wires were in the sole control of a few private firms, brought together under the banner of the Magnetic and Electric Companies. But now came a piece of legislation that newspapers had eagerly awaited. For Disraeli's new law meant the death of the telegraph companies' own news-agency activities – a ramshackle, hit-and-miss business, whose owners simply regarded newspaper editors not so much as their clients but as their serfs. Through their 'intelligence departments', formed in 1852, these companies gathered all types of news, including parliamentary reports, political speeches, industrial data, commercial information and sport.

Provincial newspapers were particularly at the mercy of these companies for events outside their own circulation areas. But the telegraphed reports, which were highly expensive, were often full of errors because they were not double-checked. Several famously concerned Chancellor William Gladstone's Budget speech in 1860, when income tax in England leapt from 9d. to 10d. (just below to just above 4 pence) in the pound. The telegraphed mistakes reproduced in newspapers caused an uproar. Among the publications that kept suffering was *The Scotsman*. The newspaper records: 'Errors and delays were endless, and to the enterprising conductors of newspapers they became intolerable. Obstacles were raised at every step.'

The Magnetic and Electric Companies held a monopoly control of the supply of news by telegraph and they exploited that power ruthlessly. Their attitude towards newspapers was autocratic, unbending and often arrogant. If a newspaper complained too loudly or too offensively about the service, their charges were increased without warning. And, if the paper complained about the new costs, the service was cut off altogether. It was no wonder, therefore, that provincial newspaper bosses had long cherished the vision of a news agency of their own. Now came the chance to make that dream a reality.

So, just before the Telegraph Act reached the Statute Book, they joined together to form the Press Association. Its objectives then, as now, were to record with accuracy and without bias all events of sufficient news interest, free from all outside pressure, and to circulate the reports as speedily as possible.

From the very moment of its birth, the PA's motto has been 'No bias . . . No opinions . . . No views'. That guiding principle has never wavered from that day, almost a century and a half ago, to this. News, unvarnished and unspun, was and is the vital commodity.

On 6 November 1868, the Press Association was registered as a limited company, with the aim of giving the kind of reports newspapers – and other subscribers – wanted, when they wanted them and at the length they wanted them. Its first chairman was John Edward Taylor, of the *Manchester Guardian*, a man of deep vision and rare business acumen. He is the man credited more than any other as responsible for the birth of PA. He said, 'One of the first persons to whom I mentioned a proposal to form this association was Mr Frederick Clifford of the *Sheffield Telegraph*. It was on a walk through a quiet street in Westminster that he and I canvassed the possibility of amalgamating or associating the varied interests which are to be found amongst the newspaper proprietors of England and of getting them into harmonious action.'

Taylor came from a newspaper family. His father, John Edward Taylor Snr, founded the *Manchester Guardian* as a weekly newspaper in 1821 and edited it until he died in 1844. His eldest son, Russell Scott Taylor, succeeded him as editor, aged just 18, but died at 23 of typhoid. John Taylor Jnr, meanwhile, studied at Manchester New College and the University of Bonn before being called to the bar. But on the death of his brother he became even more involved in the newspaper business. Colleagues always said he had a commanding presence and formidable zeal but was capable of gentle self-mockery. He banned racing tips in the *Guardian* and his only other real interest apart from newspapers was his art collection, which included Italian masters, Turner watercolours and medieval stained glass.

Now, as Britain led the industrial world and the railways and electric telegraph system brought its people closer together, Taylor took charge of the greatest news-gathering operation of the century. Under him was a committee of management. Its members were John Jaffray, of the *Birmingham Daily Post*, Frederick Clifford, QC, of the *Sheffield Telegraph,* George Harper of the *Huddersfield Chronicle* and William Saunders of the *Western Morning News*. On Taylor's insistence, a provision was written into the Association's rules that one director should retire from the committee at each annual general meeting to ensure a constant supply of new blood. He wanted every kind of newspaper, large or small, morning, evening or weekly, to be represented at some time or another.

It would not be until February 1870 that the physical transfer of the telegraphs could take place and the real business of the Press Association could begin. In the meantime, there were extensive negotiations between the government and the private telegraph companies over compensation. Finally, the matter was settled with the shareholders receiving a staggering sum of £5.5 million – around £100 million today – much to the annoyance of newspaper proprietors. As the Post Office began to plan its new telegraph business, the Press Association appointed its first manager, John Lovell, at a salary of £450 a year. The 34-year-old son of a Guildford, Surrey, shoemaker was chosen from 450 applicants. He had virtually no formal schooling but had learned to read through his fascination with Charles Dickens. He then took up Pitman's shorthand because David Copperfield could do it, landing his first job as a district reporter on the weekly *Surrey Standard*. Lovell was described as 'an immense smoker, tea drinker and brilliant talker'. He worked slavishly to ensure that the three principles of the Press Association were maintained: 'accuracy, promptitude and absolute impartiality'. The role of manager was a tough one. The committee had been looking for a man who understood the needs of newspapers, could organise and run an editorial office in London and a nationwide network of correspondents across the country and would be at home in the commercial world.

The first annual meeting of members of the Press Association took place in the Salisbury Hotel, London, on 3 March 1869. But it was more than just an inaugural get-together. The transfer of the telegraphs from the private companies to the state had not yet been formally completed, and negotiations with the government were under way on the new telegraph charges that would affect the price of the PA service to subscribers. That was not the only thorny subject. At the meeting, different papers demanded different services. The *Leeds Mercury* did not want long parliamentary reports, for example, and many evening papers, who published at different hours in different towns with one, two or three editions, required news during some of the most barren parts of the day.

Setting the PA tariffs and tailoring the service to suit everyone, therefore, was a minefield. In addition, the quality of news supplied by the private companies was the very reason the agency was set up – so now Taylor and his team, working from an office in London's Strand, had the job of making sure they could do better, and that meant organising a network of correspondents to feed in reports from all over the British Isles. This they did by hiring journalists, clergymen, solicitors, town clerks, businessmen and schoolmasters to supply reliable information from London to Glasgow and Manchester to Cork.

Then came a masterstroke. The Press Association brokered a deal with Paul Julius de Reuter, who had set up an organisation in London in 1851 that was to grow into a world news agency. The former German bank clerk, who had three years earlier set up an organisation for sending commercial news by pigeon, signed a contract in 1869 under which Reuters supplied the PA with foreign telegrams for exclusive use in the British Isles outside London. In turn, Reuters would disseminate Press Association news overseas. That was the beginning of a relationship that strengthened over the years.

On 1 January 1870, with the foundation stones of the business laid, the Press Association moved from its temporary offices in the Strand to a new headquarters at 7 Wine Office Court, a narrow alleyway off Fleet Street, home of the famous pub Ye Olde Cheshire Cheese, old drinking haunt of Charles Dickens and Dr Samuel Johnson. It was flagged by a sign on a Fleet Street gas lamp, simply saying 'Press Association Limited', and displaying an arrow pointing towards Wine Office Court underneath.

The big day, when the state would take over the telegraphs, was now just a month away and things were moving fast. A junior clerk with shorthand knowledge was hired for eight shillings (40 pence) a week and a journalist was taken on a few days later to report events in London. Next came a team of 'spacemen' – freelance journalists used for reporting jobs when required. This was followed by the agency's first breed of subeditors – three men taken on at £4.10s (£4.50) a week to collate all the incoming copy and rework it into various lengths for different customers. Records reveal: 'They all had considerable experience in metropolitan journalism and two had the additional qualification of experience in provincial journalism.'

One of these men was Edmund Robbins, a name that would one day find a firm place in the Press Association history book. Robbins had started his newspaper career at the age of eleven on a weekly newspaper in Launceston, Cornwall, as a printer's apprentice. At eighteen, he went to London, where he worked as a compositor for three years at Central Press, a news agency set up by William Saunders. In 1868, Saunders made Robbins a junior subeditor, then permanent subeditor, then night editor, all within two years.

Finally the Press Association's charges were set – in strict proportion to the amount of news the customer ordered. The first year's annual subscriptions were to vary from 14s. 6d. (72½ pence) to £400. Then at 5 a.m. on Saturday, 5 February, the doors of the Post Office opened for their first transactions, involving private and press-rate telegrams. At that moment the Press Association, appropriately, sent the first ever press telegram.

The message had been prepared by 22-year-old Robbins, one of the three newly appointed subeditors on the staff. It appeared in the *Birmingham Daily Post* and read:

GENERAL NEWS (Press Association Telegraph).
:: Wind and weather reports from all ports.
:: Rumoured in military circles that Sir Henry Storks has tendered his resignation.
:: Admiral Sir H. Leeke is lying dangerously ill.
:: An order has been issued raising the standard of the Royal Marine Corps half an inch.

Everyone was ecstatic. The long-awaited day had turned out to be a success – but not for long. Within 24 hours the system had virtually collapsed, bringing chaos to the agency. The trouble was that the Post Office could not cope with the load imposed on it. On that first day, the number of normal telegrams soared by 20 per cent as press messages poured into the telegraph offices – and telegraph poles went down in bad weather. Many press stories never reached the newspapers who were paying for them and others arrived the day after they were handed in. Wine Office Court was bombarded with complaints. Newspapers filled up some of the space that should have been taken by Press Association news, with editorials about 'powerful atmospheric derangements' affecting the transmission of re-ports. It was to be several weeks before things settled down and everyone got into the routine with town clerks, vicars, school-teachers and firemen making daily trips to file their stories to the London headquarters. All had been told, 'Fact, not fiction!' They were to be paid lineage on the basis of how much copy was used.

Finally, the system began to work well. It was – as it is today – accurate and unopinionated, and with a staunch independence that brooked no interference.

2 The Boys' Army

ON 15 JULY 1870, Napoleon II declared war on Germany – and his proclamation sparked the first big test for the Press Association. The outbreak of the Franco-Prussian conflict that summer was the new agency's initiation into handling war news – and where the agreement with Reuters was vital. The telegraph wires were buzzing when, on 4 August, the Press Association issued reports of the Battle of Wisembourg, forty miles north of Strasbourg. Twenty-five thousand Prussian troops attacked four thousand French soldiers in the town. The Prussians took the area in six hours with the loss of 1,500 men. Over the next few months, the PA, with its vital Reuters link, was able to report the battles leading to the surrender of Paris the following year. It was a breathtaking and history-making news operation.

The decade that followed, however, saw John Lovell fighting a difficult battle against the inefficiencies of the Post Office and its constant attempts to extract more money from newspapers and news agencies. The 1868 Act had stipulated that the object was to create 'a cheaper, more widely extended and more expeditious system of telegraphy'. But costs were escalating for everybody and finally a Treasury Committee was appointed to investigate the causes. It was critical of the Post Office. The state-run organisation, stung by the report, blamed the press, claiming that the cheaper rates enjoyed by the media were uneconomical.

In 1875, the Post Office struck its first blow. Hotels and taverns were removed from the list of PA subscribers entitled to receive telegrams at press rates. Very few of these customers were prepared to pay for news to be telegraphed to them at the full public rate and PA lost more than £4,500 a year in revenue. Worse was to come. The Postmaster General, Lord John Manners, announced that press rates had to be revised – and that meant upwards. The war of words between the Press Association and the Post Office continued unabated. Finally, a compromise was reached, with several hundred pounds a year being added to the agency's transmission bill. The effect at the agency was much stricter editing on the length of its news messages.

At the end of the decade, Lovell made a note of the work involved during a typical Press Association day. He chose a Friday when Parliament was sitting. He wrote:

> On that day, as many as 436 separate messages, varying in length from a brief racing result or a single-line market report to a speech of four columns in length, and consisting of 39,000 words, passed into the hands of the Press Association staff to be dealt with. A considerable number of those messages poured in from all parts of the world through Reuter's agency. An equal number poured in from all parts of the United Kingdom from the Association's correspondents. Some were distributed from race meetings, others from the great commercial centres in different parts of the country. A large number originated in the City office in Copthall Court, Threadneedle Street, and a still larger number in the gallery of the House of Commons and its annexes. The work of the Association, however, did not end in receiving these messages. Its business was to manipulate them into classes and to multiply and distribute them to the newspapers and newsrooms of Great Britain; and when it had done its work, it had multiplied the 436 messages into 7,897 addresses, while the 39,000 words had become 262,000 . . .

Even in those relatively early days, the traffic in news was considerable.

By now, subeditor Robbins was growing in stature and was to hold various posts, among them secretary and assistant manager. One of his most irritating assignments was to persuade the Post Office to agree to the most minuscule change imaginable: a modest concession over the time it would accept messages for transmission at the cheaper night rate, for the Press Association was sending telegrams for morning papers at the night rate, which began at 6 p.m. These telegrams were being prepared throughout the afternoon, but the Central Telegraph Office would not accept them at the concessionary rate *until* that hour. Anything handed in before then would be charged at the more expensive day rate, which would push up costs by as much as one-third. Press rates were a shilling (5 pence) for 75 words during the day – and a shilling a hundred at night, when the wires were not as busy.

This ridiculous situation was repeated night after night. The messages piled up at the agency's office and then, on the dot of 6 p.m., they were delivered to the Central Telegraph Office, causing a massive logjam to the system and resulting in frustration and anger at morning newspaper offices up and down the country, as news staff waited for the crucial telegrams to arrive. The simple and totally reasonable request of the Press Association was that the Post Office should accept the telegrams before six o'clock so that they could be copied ready for transmission as soon as the deadline came. But the plea was met with total disdain. It would create 'insurmountable difficulties', the Post Office said. What it would not admit was that the hour between five and six o'clock was tea-break time for Telegraph Office staff.

Finally, the new Postmaster General, Sydney Buxton, agreed to an experiment. The wheels were grinding slowly – but at least they were grinding. Stories for the morning papers were handed in to the Telegraph Office at five o'clock onwards and prepared for dispatch at six. This minor but common-sense reform cut delivery time to the papers by between twenty minutes and half an hour. There is no record, however, of whether the telegraph workers sacrificed their tea break. How they did it remains a mystery.

During these difficult years, the agency also had to contend with a large measure of red tape from the Post Office, the kind of bureaucracy that gave birth to the British civil service being made the butt of so many derogatory jokes. It was the agency's practice to send out news reports in sections. If, for instance, a telegram was sent out about an election in Harrogate, and was followed by a second, possibly an hour later, the catchline on the top would read 'add Harrogate', so that the recipient would be aware that this was an addition to a story already sent. Nothing, it seemed, could be more simple and clear. Not to the Post Office. Those two words were paid for at the cheaper press rate until it suddenly decided that, since the word 'add' was not a piece of news, it must be paid for separately as a private message. Nothing was more ridiculous in the eyes of the agency's journalists. But the Post Office stuck to its guns.

Luckily, a few years earlier, the local post office at South Shields had tried the same trick and it had taken George B

Hodgson, the editor of the *Shields Daily Gazette*, Britain's first regional evening newspaper, three months of battling with officials to sort it out.

Taking note of the row, the Post Office finally accepted the Press Association argument, to the relief of all concerned. But it insisted on having the last word. It ruled that if a reporter used the word 'continued' that would be passed at the special press rate but if he used the word 'add' it must be paid for as a private telegram. No one actually ever discovered why 'continued' was all right and 'add' was all wrong, but there was no point in taking the matter further, as the concession had been granted.

Towards the end of the century the Wine Office Court premises were no longer big enough to house the increasing staff of the Press Association. The new chairman, Robert Eadon Leader, of the *Sheffield Independent*, referred to the conditions in which journalists and other trades had to work as 'insanitary and wanting ventilation'. It was a fetid atmosphere that 'no proprietors with any conscience or heart ought to allow to continue'. Hanging over the front windows of the Press Association building, for example, were large patent reflectors, necessary to bring daylight into the rooms. There was talk of building an extension to the offices but this was not practicable. The agency had to move. And not before time, for in 1887 part of a chimney had fallen into the office, injuring one of the workers.

The new premises, at 14 New Bridge Street, hardly a stone's throw away, were not entirely suitable, but at least there was plenty of room. It was a substantial pile, yet even in those days it was regarded as old-fashioned. Cynics were not slow to point out that the Press Association had leased it from the trustees of the Bridewell Royal Hospital, which also controlled the Bedlam Lunatic Asylum. Its great advantage, however, was that it was only two minutes' walk to the Ludgate Circus Post Office and close to most of the important newspaper offices, which by now were congregating in that part of London. But what particularly appealed to the next chairman, Francis Hewitt, of the *Leicester Daily Post*, was the prestigious nature of the new building. At the annual meeting there, on 9 May 1893, he stood in front of the large stained-glass window in the boardroom, and treated his colleagues to a grand discourse on its history.

'The place upon which we stand,' he said, 'is historic ground. Here the Norman kings held their court, and on this site were important buildings which, from the Norman era, were of service in the history of London and England. Here for several centuries was an edifice which served as a prison and poorhouse and where, for many generations, London's refractory apprentices were confined and punished after the fashion of those times.'

There were still six cells in the building to prove the accuracy of his words. But Hewitt was by no means finished: '. . . the stately gents and dames of that olden time in these very rooms read their small, dear and meagre newspapers, and gossiped over the news, a fortnight old, from Scotland and Ireland, three months old from Austria, America and Russia, and a year old from our distant colonies. If they could visit their former abode and witness a busy hive of workmen day and night all the year round, sending and receiving instantaneous news to and from all parts of the world – how surprised they would be . . .'

As he continued to wax lyrical in similar vein, through the other rooms of what he called 'this mansion', the workforce was doing precisely what he described.

Soon after the move to New Bridge Street, more new technology came to the Press Association: a single telephone. Surprisingly, however, it was seldom used for editorial purposes and it was not until the South African war in 1899 that it assumed an important role, linking London to Johannesburg. That same year Julius Reuter died.

In the basement of New Bridge Street dwelled Henry Wright, the PA accountant, a portly man with mutton-chop whiskers who was nicknamed 'Curry' Wright because he reeked of Asian spices. His coat was powdered with snuff and he was widely regarded as an eccentric. He was a deeply religious man, too, and on Sundays he went to church morning and evening, as well as taking a Bible class in the afternoon. Incongruously, during the week he exercised the kind of vocabulary of which a Billingsgate porter would have been proud. So assiduous was he in attending to the Press Association's finances that even when – as happened from time to time – the malodorous Fleet River overflowed into his basement, he merely tucked up his legs on his high stool and carried on as if nothing had happened. However, his eccentricity eventually got the better of him. And, as one of his contemporaries sadly reported, 'Religious mania got him in the end and he died in Bedlam.'

In these early days, PA employed a regular army of messengers, in the charge of the very portly and heavily mustachioed

Walter Joseph Cattermole. He had the manner of a regimental sergeant major and sought to instil a military sense of discipline and smartness into the boys. But he was a kindly man for all that. The lads wore dark-blue uniforms, with red piping around the cuffs and down the trousers. Each had a number in blue emblazoned on his red collar and the words 'Press Association' were embroidered in blue on a flat military-type cap. In true military style, senior to them were dispatch clerks, who were ranked as sergeants, corporals and lance corporals and who carried out a daily inspection of brass buttons, boots, hair, face, hands and fingernails. Most of the boys came from the poorest parts of London and, as they set off from home in their uniforms, they were often followed by the cry of 'pick-a-nanny', the Cockney corruption of 'pig-in-harness', a nineteenth-century term of abuse for men who disgraced their families by enlisting in the regular army and wearing uniforms.

The first messenger was appointed on 12 February 1870, just a week after the agency had transmitted its first message. Between then and 30 May 1881, a total of 334 boys were employed, many of them for short periods only. The boys' 'Admission and Discharge Book' of the period lists some colourful reasons why messengers were dismissed from time to time. These included smoking in the kitchen, using bad language, throwing a live dog out of the first-floor window, calling Mr Cuthbert a bloody Scotch haddock and destroying and burning seats in the kitchen. One unfortunate lad was discharged after he had been given a shilling (5 pence) to pay the cab from Westminster to the Press Association with important copy. Instead, he took the train from Westminster Bridge to Temple Station and kept the 10d. (4 pence) change, delaying the story.

A misconduct book was also maintained, listing the complaints that had been lodged against various errant boys. These included 'making unnecessary noise by running up the stairs', 'throwing shoe brushes around' and 'tossing coins for beer in the reporting room'. One boy was disciplined because it took '17 minutes before he opened the door for Mr Cuthbert'. It certainly was not an easy life for these lads, but it was at least a job and many of them worked hard to help their struggling parents. They worked an eight-hour day, six days a week, and their pay started at five shillings (25 pence) a week with 3d. (1 penny) an hour overtime and an extra shilling (5 pence) for those on the all-night shift.

The boys were supposed to get a one-shilling rise every six months for the first two years, but that was not how it worked out in practice. The rises did not come automatically – far from it. The boy had to apply for the increase, which may sound reasonable, but in fact the transaction was far from straightforward. Although his application would go in at the end of the first six months, the messenger usually had to wait from four to six weeks for it to be approved. That little delay, and the subsequent slow processing of the increase, no doubt contrived by a frugal management, meant that the lad's next rise would not be due for another six months from the original date.

The Press Association was run as a tight ship, for the management had to account to its masters, the newspapers, for every penny spent. A complaint about this practice would have led to on-the-spot dismissal. On the credit side, however, for those who lasted the course, there were good opportunities for promotion in the editorial, managerial and secretarial departments – as well as elsewhere in Fleet Street.

As the century drew to a close, the boys in their familiar blue uniforms could be seen hurrying through the streets of London to a new destination – a little office over a pub near the War Office. It was 1899 and the Press Association had moved staff into the rooms to deal with communiqués on the Boer War. But the man who was put in charge of it, George Smith, was soon to be involved in one of the most historic reports of his time – the death of Queen Victoria. And the former schoolmaster and insurance agent would also make history himself – by writing a message to the nation for a king who was busy dining.

3 Westminster Watch

HE PRESS ASSOCIATION wasted no time, after its birth in 1868, in establishing credentials at Westminster. That very first year a PA reporter was peering down at the legislators below, feverishly scribbling, in high-speed shorthand, the words uttered in the chamber.

The Press Gallery then, however, was not the comfortable place it is today, with near perfect acoustics. Charles Dickens, who arrived there a few years before the Press Association, vividly described its shortcomings:

I have worn my knees by writing on them on the old back row of the old Press Gallery of the old House of Commons. I have worn my feet standing to write in a preposterous pen in the old House of Lords where we used to huddle together like so many sheep, kept in waiting until the Woolsack might want restuffing.

The Press Association had quickly recognised that the Palace of Westminster was the best and most prolific single source of news in the country. So it selected as its first parliamentary reporter a man who had already worked there for some years, who could take notes at speed and keep a cool head, and was known for his impeccable accuracy. George Moir Bussy – 'a gentleman of lengthened experience in the gallery' – was the first chief of the PA parliamentary staff and commanded a salary of five guineas (£5.25) a week, a princely sum in those days. The agency also took over the government's printing office at Westminster to enable running reports of parliamentary debates to be set in type, printed on slips and speedily delivered to gentlemen's clubs throughout the capital. Bussy already had a deputy and, with the demise of the old *Morning Star*, a third gallery seat became available. The Press Association snapped it up and at the same time acquired the services of a third man.

By 1874, one of the original PA subeditors, Edmund Robbins, who sported a fine walrus moustache, had become the agency's first lobby correspondent. Robbins had landed the Commons job almost by chance, following the story of a ministerial crisis over Gladstone's defeat by a majority of three on the Irish University Bill. A fervent follower of politics, Robbins suggested that it would be of interest to the newsroom if he went to the House of Commons to obtain more information of what was going on in political circles, particularly during such a ministerial crisis.

Robbins was a young man who enjoyed the rough-and-tumble world of ministers and MPs and there was nothing he liked more than a good argument, particularly if he was in the right. An example of this is the Gladstone affair. In January 1874, the Liberal Prime Minister William Gladstone decided on the dissolution of Parliament and instructions were issued that his manifesto to this effect should be sent to the London newspapers only. Furious, Robbins went to the Treasury the following day, demanding to know why the Press Association had been ignored in this way. The Treasury Secretary justified the action on the ludicrous grounds that, since Gladstone was MP for Greenwich and Greenwich was a metropolitan borough, it was therefore necessary to send the information only to the metropolitan papers. There was at the time a heavily pro-metropolitan bias in Whitehall – against which the PA and the provincial press constantly had to battle. The view was that virtually anything north of Watford or west of Reading barely merited consideration in media terms.

At this time, however, perhaps the most remarkable political figure in the Press Association was Walter Hepburn, the PA's first chief reporter. He was a huge man, weighing nearly 20 stone, with an appropriately dignified manner to go with it. In those halcyon days when political correctness was a concept not yet born, he was cheerfully known by all as 'Mr Gladstone's Fat Reporter'. It was Hepburn who accompanied Gladstone on his famous Midlothian campaign in the North of England and southern Scotland during which the Grand Old Man denounced the Disraeli government with 'lofty, sonorous eloquence'. During this whistle-stop campaign, crowds gathered wherever Gladstone's train halted, to hear him deliver a speech, usually of great length with much gesticulation and declaiming. And, like all wise politicians, Gladstone did his best to make sure that a Press Association reporter was always close at hand. But he developed a special affection for Hepburn and accorded him the privilege of travelling in his own private coach.

If, by any mischance, Hepburn was not to hand at the crucial moment when an oration was about to begin, Gladstone would cry out imperiously, 'Where's my reporter?' And he would wait until Hepburn was not only in his place, but comfortably settled there in the most advantageous seat at the press table, which was always placed just below the platform.

On one celebrated occasion, a deputation met Gladstone at a railway station and presented him with an address. Gladstone was on the point of making what would have been a typically long-winded reply, when the guard, no respecter of even eminent personages, blew the whistle for the train to move off. Gladstone had to hop on again smartly as the surprised deputation, left standing helplessly on the platform, fast receded from his view. But the absence of an audience was no deterrent to such a determined speechmaker. So, as the train rattled on to the next destination, Gladstone dictated to Hepburn the speech he would have made had the guard not so rudely prevented it from happening!

Hepburn dutifully filed his copy, and the papers duly printed it the following day. The disembodied gentlemen on the railway station platform to whom it was addressed must have been surprised to read it in the morning, having been, so to speak, left speechless.

Gladstone was not only a good friend to the Press Association – through Walter Hepburn – but he also knew a few tricks of the trade, which was useful both for him and the agency, although on one occasion things went slightly awry. He had planned to make what he regarded as an important speech at a remote station from where, he realised, it would have been impossible for Hepburn to send a wire. So he dictated it to Hepburn in advance and, even though the embargo system was very much in its infancy, the PA man wired it with a 'time for release' memo on the top. However, unfortunately, the train failed to stop at the designated station, even though it was scheduled to do so, and Gladstone and his speech went whistling through. Hepburn was helpless. He had no means of communicating with the newsroom to warn them that the speech had not been delivered. The speech-that-never-was, therefore, appeared in the papers the following morning – much to Gladstone's satisfaction.

In the spring of 1880, the Press Association got one of its biggest political scoops. The Tories had been defeated and on 19

May, a few days after leaving office, Benjamin Disraeli (who had become the Earl of Beaconsfield) called a meeting of leading Tories to discuss the future of the party in opposition. News quickly leaked out that the meeting was to take place in the privacy of Disraeli's London house. Burly officers from the Commons and the Lords were brought in to keep journalists at bay.

But it was all in vain, because the next day, 20 May, most of the newspapers carried a detailed and vivid account of the meeting, including a long report of the new earl's own speech, in which he stressed the private nature of the gathering. It looked like a leak on a grand scale. The reports, put out by the Press Association, were too detailed to suggest that the story had been made up. The earl's rage knew no bounds and immediate action was taken to discredit the story. Lord Rowton, the earl's private secretary, was ordered to tell the Press Association's rival, Central News, that the report was 'absolutely fictitious'. A few days later, *The Times* published a letter from the earl himself, saying:

> The liberty of the press is one of the most precious privileges of Englishmen and, therefore, it is in their interest that it should not be abused. I have never been apt to complain of the reports of anything that I may have said in public if they only contained inaccuracies, which pressure, or even some little malice, might occasion or inspire. But when an elaborate declaration of policy is placed in my mouth, as in the report of the proceedings at Bridgewater-house in your issue on Thursday, not one single word of which was delivered by me, and which conveys, in every sense, the reverse of what I expressed, I think it a duty to request that you will make this disclaimer on my part as public as the statement which you have circulated.

Strong stuff. But equally trenchantly the Press Association stood by its report, claiming that the substance of it was obtained from an MP who attended the meeting. There appears to have been no further inquest. Whoever the reporter was seems to have convinced his masters at the PA of the veracity of his report, since, surprisingly, no reference to this incident appears in the minutes of the meetings of the PA committee of management at the time. The scoop soon became history and there was silence on all sides.

By now, the agency's manager, John Lovell, felt his job was done and it was time to hand over the mantle to a successor who would take the organisation through to the exciting new challenges of the twentieth century. Lovell resigned to take up the post of editor of the *Liverpool Mercury*, one of the top jobs in provincial journalism. Tributes to him flowed in from across Britain – for no one had done more to help the Press Association grow. In recognition of his service, the committee of management agreed to spend 'not more than 100 guineas [£105]' on a testimonial to him.

Taking Lovell's place would be Edmund Robbins, the fiery young man from the House of Commons, who had by now made quite a name for himself. There was to be a Robbins occupying the managerial chair for the next 58 years. Meanwhile, Saunders, Harper, Jaffray and Clifford had all retired from the original committee of management. Other distinguished newspapermen began to take their places, such as Peter Steward Macliver of the *Western Daily Press* in Bristol, John Willox of the *Liverpool Courier*, Frederick Spark of the *Leeds Express*, George Toulmin of the *Guardian* in Preston, John Jevons of the *Nottingham Daily Express*, Joseph Glover of the *Leamington Spa Courier* and James Lancelot Foster of the *Yorkshire Gazette*, later to be hailed as the Father of Provincial Journalism.

Gladstone, meanwhile, continued to be a big money-spinner for the Press Association. In fact, his withdrawal from public life was given as the main reason for the loss on the year's revenue reported in 1895 by the PA's chairman Alexander Jeans of the *Liverpool Daily Post*. He said: 'All those who have been connected with newspapers know that we have passed through a period of very great calm. I have had a good many years' experience myself of newspaper life, and I think that last year was probably the dullest we have had for many years. The most serious loss was, no doubt, the withdrawal of Mr Gladstone from public life. Probably two-thirds of the falling off in the revenue has been due to that cause, for not only did Mr Gladstone make a large number of speeches himself, which almost every newspaper in the country reported, but he also provoked a large number of replies, which were also reported.'

Those were the days when speeches by major political figures warranted verbatim reports by the Press Association and the copy was widely and fully used by many newspapers. Thus, speeches made outside Parliament by the likes of Gladstone were reported by the agency as 'offered specials' and news-papers paid extra for them at the rate of ten shillings (50 pence) for a column of 2,000 words. In London, special reports were sent direct from the place where the meeting was being held. The reporters carried special styli, enabling them to make as many as sixteen carbon copies. Then the army of Press Association messengers swung into action, taking some of them to the Post Office for transmission to the provinces. The rest were delivered by hand to the offices of the London papers.

The reputation of the agency's reporters for accuracy and speed was now well established. Sometimes as many as half a dozen reporters were sent on such assignments, with all the travelling costs and hotel expenses that involved. The London papers thought so highly of the Press Association's coverage of these major out-of-town political meetings that they invariably relied on the agency and did not send any of their own reporters. Even so, only a handful of statesmen were considered important enough to merit verbatim coverage by the PA. In the late nineteenth century, apart from Gladstone, the only ones in this 'class' were Lord Salisbury, Lord Rosebery, AJ Balfour, Joseph Chamberlain, Sir Henry Campbell-Bannerman, John Morley and Sir William Harcourt.

General elections in the nineteenth century were, hardly surprisingly, barely recognisable in comparison with the media-orientated elections of the present day. For instance, polling did not take place everywhere on the same day and sometimes a fortnight could elapse before the final result was declared. These days the excitement is all concentrated upon one momentous night, but in those days that excitement was sometimes spread over as long as two weeks, with individual constituency results dribbling through day by day.

Local post offices stayed open late to receive Press Association messages of results declared overnight. And, as soon as the main Fleet Street newspapers received them, they displayed the results for the benefit of the crowds gathered in front of their windows. The PA charged 1s. 6d. (7½ pence) for a twenty-word message, not only to the papers, but to shopkeepers who also exhibited them in their windows.

By 1900, the Press Association had six men in the day editorial and nine on the evening and all-night shift. In addition, there were five general reporters and a chief reporter, Walter Hepburn, apart from the specialist staff reporting Parliament and the Law Courts. Each and every one of them had to be capable of sustaining a verbatim shorthand note for long periods – those were the sorts of reports the newspapers demanded. Another attribute demanded of them – unofficially, of course – was an ability to play whist. This was because Hepburn insisted on a 'school' every afternoon in his room when things were quiet.

Press Association reporters of that era had a high reputation – both in Fleet Street and among the provincial papers. They were regarded as the ultimate professionals. Not only did they enjoy this status, but they defended it heroically. And none more so than Sam Perks, during a political meeting he was covering outside London. The speaker, a leading politician of the day, used the word 'ingenuous'. Then, in the sort of patronising mode that some politicians are still capable of, he said, 'I will repeat that word – "ingenuous" – because reporters invariably confuse it with "ingenious".' Perks, a short, stout man with an explosive temper, who was also an erudite, fluent and fine raconteur, jumped up. Trembling with fury, he accused the speaker of committing a gross insult on the members of the press and demanded a grovelling apology. The politician, shocked beyond measure to be interrupted at all, never mind in such a ferocious way, did muster a faltering apology, but by this time he had completely lost the thread of his speech and he hurriedly brought his theme to a premature and humiliating end. Needless to say, Perks was the toast of his fellow reporters that evening.

Around this time, Robbins's son Harry joined the agency, for a princely sum of £2.10s (£2.50) a week. He arrived as a junior subeditor and began on what was then called the 'victim turn', starting at midnight and working through until 8.30 in the morning.

Meanwhile, as the new century began, Robbins was in his prime as Press Association manager and his power was extraordinary. With his now white walrus moustache, he ruled with a rod of iron. Matters had to be dealt with his way – and to his convenience. Even the committee of management was under his firm control. His habits could not be broken. He always left the office at 5 p.m. – and it would need a national disaster to stop him. It is said that on one occasion, a meeting of the management committee was in full swing when, at 4.58 p.m., Robbins rose from his chair and announced, 'Gentlemen, the meeting is adjourned.' With that he promptly went home.

Robbins also hated the telephone and it was alleged that he refused to pick it up or even speak on it. But, tough as he was, he had a reputation for being a caring man. He knew about the private lives of his staff – and when one of them had a new baby in the family he would try to give him extra work to earn a few more shillings a week. In fact, he was the prime mover behind setting up the first insurance and endowment scheme for staff. He had always been shocked at the effects of Fleet Street life on journalists, seeing them die so young – some not even reaching thirty and only a small number surviving until forty. Hard work, long hours, heavy smoking and an abundance of all-night pubs and greasy eating houses were a recipe for disaster. Such was Fleet Street in those days and it was not to change much for nearly a century.

4 On a Winner

THE PRESS ASSOCIATION almost drifted into sports reporting in the nineteenth century – and its first steps into that world were faltering. In those days football made virtually no impact, and it was to be decades before the game drew mass audiences and dominated the sports sections of newspapers. But cricket was gaining in popularity among Victorians. It was also a well-organised and well-controlled sport and had a strong enough following for newspapers to want to carry dependable and, of course, readable news about it.

The initiative to cover sport did not come from the Press Association's management but from a senior subeditor on the staff, Charles F Pardon, a name that to this day is inextricably and honourably linked to sports journalism. Pardon offered to organise a service. Strangely, however, although the agency wanted to run such a wire, he was not asked to set it up from within and no one seems to be able to explain why this should have been the case. Instead, by mutual agreement, Pardon left the Press Association in 1880 – armed with a presentation silver flask – to found the firm of Pardon's, or the Cricket Reporting Agency, which was its formal title.

Gradually, and inevitably, Pardon began to expand beyond cricket. Football as well as other less prominent sports all came within his sphere. His company dealt with all the agency's sporting interests, including some racing (but not the results or betting from the course). And then, even more bizarrely, in 1883, Charles Pardon was appointed the Press Association's sporting editor, but he remained outside the company. However, the setup seemed to work successfully, and it was not until 1901 that the agency took over the last of the racing work done for it by Pardon's and appointed as sporting editor a member of its own staff. But the fruitful and friendly connection between the Press Association and Pardon's continued for many decades to come, right up, in fact, to modern times.

It was in the 1880s that horse racing entered into the scheme of things. The Press Association's original racing service was operated by CH Ashley, but that partnership was relatively short-lived. Ashley and the agency parted company at the end of 1883 because he refused to give an undertaking not to extend, for his own benefit, his own list of direct newspaper subscribers. It was then that the Press Association turned its attention to Hultons of Manchester, a burgeoning organisation, which had successfully founded the *Sporting Chronicle* and was to give birth to the legendary *Picture Post*, the jewel in the crown of this go-ahead and thrusting company.

However, relations between the agency and Hultons were frequently stormy and it was a partnership that was maintained with difficulty for many years. Gradually, Hultons became less important to the Press Association as the agency extended its outside racing staff to cover meetings itself, but the spectre of Ashley, who had earlier left the agency in acrimonious circumstances, was still uncomfortably hovering around. For a time he was a powerful and dangerous competitor because, in addition to his racing service, he also sold a comprehensive cricket service at a threateningly cheap rate, which was a thorn in the side of the Press Association.

The PA manager, Edmund Robbins, saw Ashley not only as an enemy but as someone whose very existence was injurious to newspapers as well as to the Press Association itself. That may well have been Robbins's instinctively negative attitude to all agencies that he saw as competing with his. But towards Ashley he seemed to be particularly virulent. In 1888, Robbins wrote a letter on the subject to Pardon, some of it couched in dramatic language, in which he waxed hot and strong about the evils of Ashley and the irresponsibility of those newspapers that still took his service to the exclusion of the Press Association. Pardon was a man in whom Robbins often confided on all sorts of matters.

Robbins wrote,

It should not be forgotten that the Press Association was the only organisation which could grapple with Ashley's monopoly and which, having grappled with it, had completely beaten it down. This, however, is not enough, and the *Manchester Evening News* and the *Manchester Guardian* should remember that it is only by still supporting the Association that the monster can be slain. At present he is only scotched, not killed, and if other papers followed in the wake of those at Manchester, they would find in a few years that the Press Association could not possibly spend its money in keeping up an expensive staff, and thus the old grievance would be renewed with increased intensity.

Meanwhile, sporting competition between the PA and the Exchange Telegraph (Extel) was at its most ferocious and there were daily battles as rival and highly resourceful racing reporters did everything to get the results back to their offices first. One incident involved the last race at Brighton. It was to be a match between two well-known horses, but the course was hidden from the spectators as thick mist swirled in from the sea. The authorities ruled that the race would go ahead, even in these conditions, which – apart from the plight of the jockeys involved – made it nearly impossible for racing reporters to operate.

The Press Association's Tim Harrington remained undaunted. He groped his way through the mist to a nearby gypsy encampment on the Sussex Downs. He had been there only that morning to hire a grey mare for his own private enjoyment and now he asked the gypsy owner to let him hire it again. Harrington led the mare as near to the winning post as possible, mounted her and waited for the horses to come thundering in. His ingenuity paid off. Number Five was the winner, and Harrington galloped away, sticking to the outside of the rails. His mission was to meet up with his colleague, Arthur Winn, as arranged. Winn was at the appointed spot and was shocked to see Harrington galloping out of the mist. There was no time for explanations. Harrington yelled out, 'It's Number Five that won.' That was enough for Winn, who filed the result to the Press Association, well ahead of his rivals.

One assumes that the agency must have looked benignly on Harrington's expenses claim: 'To hire of one old grey mare'!

For years, the Press Association has been at the forefront of horse racing. No one else has ever been able to come anywhere near matching the speed, accuracy and comprehensiveness of its racing operation. This was exemplified in the words of Frank Turner, a former night editor of the Press Association in the early 1900s, when he said:

It is not a boast but a statement of fact that the winner of a big horse race is known in every newspaper office in the country before it has been pulled up by his jockey. The horses' numbers have been sent in advance and the telephone lines are cleared just before starting time. An operator with headphones hears his opposite number on the course say 'Off 3.5' and calls it through a megaphone. Six telegraphists tap this out and one can almost imagine the horses galloping as the still room waits. When the winning horse's number is boomed out over the megaphone, six Morse keys tap out in unison, like violinists' bows in an orchestra, and that's that!

What is strange is the apparent reluctance with which the Press Association adopted the telephone, despite the fact that its rivals had cottoned on to the fact that it was quicker to send sports results that way than by telegram. Right up to the end of the nineteenth century, reporters always sent racing results and cricket scores back to their offices by telegram. And the Post Office helped by having travelling staffs of telegraphists at racecourses and county cricket grounds so that the traffic could be handled without any undue delays or queues. But, even though telegrams were supposed to be sent on a 'first come, first served' basis, this did not always happen, either through favouritism or, worse, bribery, or even a muddle on the part of the telegraphists.

It soon became clear, however, as the technology improved, that the telephone offered a much faster and more efficient means of collecting and disseminating information, and it had the added advantage of not involving so many intermediaries as telegrams. It remains a mystery why the Press Association was slow to perceive the value of the telephone. The agency's rival, Exchange Telegraph, had already recognised its significance and superiority over telegrams, and had started to use it, fairly regularly, about the turn of the century.

Many of the Press Association's subscribers pressed it to follow suit but it was not until July 1905, at a special general meeting of members, that they gave the green light to the use of a telephone to supply sports results and brief 'snapshots' of general news items. Once the service was belatedly started, the agency went into it with a vengeance and invested large sums of money in the project. The service was organised by Alan Greaves, a larger-than-life character, who had been running a business in Sheffield, supplying news by telephone to newspapers and bookmakers.

The agency, now fully recognising the importance of this innovation, gave Greaves a seven-year contract at the then astronomical sum of £1,000 a year. Special telephone centres were opened in Birmingham, Bristol, Leeds, Liverpool, Manchester, Newcastle, Nottingham and Sheffield, and one in London at 150 Fleet Street. Each was fully equipped with expert staff and the most up-to-date technology.

There was great excitement when the new service began, on the first Saturday in September 1905, to coincide with the start of the football season. It was a great success. But the shock came when the telephone bills began to arrive. Within a very few weeks of this 'revolution', the managers and the board were beginning to count the cost and wonder if the decision to embrace the telephone had been the right one. Robbins, who had always hated telephones, could scarcely contain himself. 'I told you so . . .' he roared. However, there was no turning back, so the management had to think of ways of ensuring that the telephone was not simply a drain on resources but a way of earning money.

It had been accepted that the only way to keep pace with Exchange Telegraph, let alone beat them, in the telephoning of racing results and betting was to 'capture' a trunk line from each racecourse. This involved booking a long series of consecutive calls and thus holding open a line to London. This caused costs to soar. Robbins decided that the only way to make the service pay was to offer it to bookmakers. It was then decided to seek the custom of what were genteelly termed 'the more respectable commission agents', as well as gentlemen's clubs. But things were to get much, much worse before they got better. The Press Association was already doing more and spending far, far more than it had intended. And Exchange Telegraph withdrew its offer to supply the agency with tape machines. But, at the same time, Extel asked the Press Association to consider the possibility of working together instead of in competition. The PA, which was becoming fearsomely independent-minded, rejected this overture, choosing a tape machine supplied through the London office of Siemens. Unfortunately, it was put into service before it had been properly tested and there were scores of teething troubles and complaints.

By 1906, there was no love lost between the Press Association and Exchange Telegraph. The competition was bitter and ferocious. And, in the heat of battle, good intentions perished and precious principles were abandoned. The rates for services were cut, which only a few months earlier had been regarded as something that would never happen. And all this time the Press Association's telephone bill was reaching astronomical heights. The telephone service was heading for a disastrous loss of £7,000 a year. The Central News, which was also distributing information by telephone in London, offered to come to some working arrangement with the Press Association. But that offer was rejected, too. It was obvious that things could not go on as they were. And the one sure way of ending the competition – and the calamitous drain on finances – was to gain control of the Exchange Telegraph.

Secret talks were held at the Howard Hotel in central London between Robbins and Wilfred King, the managing director of Extel. But King was too proud to allow the Press Association to take over his company, and instead he suggested joint working. Once again the agency rejected the offer and the war, which had cooled down while these abortive negotiations were going on, quickly hotted up again to a ferocious pitch. By April that year, the PA was renting its own telephone lines on racecourses and football and cricket grounds. But by now the fierce competition had led to eight men covering a race meeting, instead of two. The crisis was so deep and the fight so desperate that for a short time even the proudly independent Press Association agreed to co-operate in race reporting with Central News.

It was now a war of attrition between the Press Association and the Exchange Telegraph. It seemed inevitable – unless something could be salvaged – that one of them, or both, would be destroyed. The only beneficiaries in this sorry state of affairs were the Postmaster General and the National Telephone Company, who must have been metaphorically rubbing their hands with glee. It was an untenable situation and gradually it dawned on the Press Association that they must now fall in with Exchange Telegraph's earlier conclusion that the two simply had to work together. So lawyers were drafted in and an agreement was drawn up and signed in July 1906. Basically, although there were a few exceptions, the two companies were to share the costs and divide the revenue. This, however, was not achieved without pain. Economies were instantly carried out. For instance, in those towns where each company had a telephone centre, one was closed down. There was a fusion of staff leading to job losses and ill feeling. But since 'economising' was the watchword behind this entire operation, it was no surprise that so many sackings had to occur. However, the agreed new management setup looked (with the benefit of hindsight) like a recipe for disaster and friction – and it was not long before disaster struck.

Robbins and King were joint managers of the new service, with two directors from each company forming a joint committee. The contract set out that in the event of a disagreement the parties had to go to arbitration. The first disagreement was so trivial and petty that it is hard to believe grown men could have fallen out over it, let alone failed to resolve it. This concerned the circular to be sent out to prospective subscribers for football results in the 1906–7 season. The Press Association view was that there should be just one letter sent out signed by both PA and Extel. The Extel view, however, was that each agency should send its own, identical letter. It was as silly as that. And, to cap this absurdity, neither side could decide what form the arbiter should take. The Press Association said it should be a lawyer and Extel wanted a commercial man. Finally, they settled on the general manager of the Great Eastern Railway – a man, you might think, who ought to have more important things, such as timetables, on his mind.

However, before the railway boss could address his mind to the letter squabble, more PA/Extel troubles piled up on his desk as trivial as the original one. They were indicative of the general and unabated fractious nature of the new joint setup and of how incompetently the agreement between the two sides had been drawn up in the first place. The joint committee degenerated into a raucous and ill-tempered bear garden, with disputes about the most ludicrous things, even down to the phrasing of the minutes of their unproductive meetings. A bad situation simply got worse. Then one row, bigger than all the previous ones, was more than the man from Great Eastern could handle – and it went, at considerable expense, to the High Court.

It concerned the Press Association's claim – hotly disputed by Exchange Telegraph – that it had the right to telephone brief summaries, known as 'snapshots', of Reuters news direct from London to newspaper subscribers. Unfortunately for the Press Association, a King's Counsel was brought in to arbitrate and subsequently the High Court backed the Extel view. There were more, and worse, arguments to come, some of them having material consequences as well as pouring money into the pockets of the legal profession. However, on 3 July 1906, an agreement was signed by the Press Association and Exchange Telegraph whereby competition over the collection, collation and distribution of racing, cricket and football news ended and a partnership was established. The first man to be put in charge of this joint sports venture was Alan Greaves, who, as we saw earlier, had been head-hunted from his Sheffield sports agency.

Greaves was a racehorse owner, compulsive gambler and heavy drinker – scarcely the man, you might think, to be chosen for this particular post. He died in 1916 from chronic alcoholism. But he spared no expense to make the new undertaking a going concern and brought down from Sheffield several of his top men to run the service. One of his successors, Allen Taylor, who retired in 1981 as the joint service supervisor, described how things were in the old days at Bath racecourse. The Press Association telephone was in a hut nearly a mile from the stands and the agency had provided 'as standard equipment' a telescope and a flag.

'On a signal from us in the hut, the waving of the flag, our stands representative, a paunchy, florid gent named Arthur Winn, sporting a pair of white gloves, would start his ticktack performance,' he said. 'Should the afternoon be misty or should rain be sweeping across the Lansdowne Heights and obliterating our colleague, it fell to me to run along the course and collect what Winn could not signal. Often the result was being passed over the phone as the runners were going to the post for the next event. But no one complained. I talk of a more tranquil age.'

One of the great PA sports scoops of all time was the world exclusive over Roger Bannister's first ever four-minute mile. Bannister's triumph is still regarded as one of the sporting pinnacles of the entire twentieth century.

It was a blustery evening at Oxford on 6 May 1954 when a veteran PA reporter, Norman Gowers, was standing near the tape as Bannister strode into the record books. He carried his own stopwatch, which, as it turned out, recorded the time precisely, but he had to wait for the official announcement. This came within seconds, whereupon Gowers dashed to a prudently open telephone line under a rugby stand, where he sat on a wheelbarrow filing the historic news ahead of the rest of the world. But he nearly did not reach the phone at all. As he rushed to it, Gowers had to dodge out of the way of a javelin being hurled by another athlete, which threatened to decapitate him.

In those days, the sports editor was Harry Gee, who retired in 1971. During that period he performed a Herculean task in adapting the sports coverage to the ever-changing, and indeed ever more insatiable, demands of the subscribers. He pruned various services to accord with changing needs and, particularly, earlier edition times.

The biggest change during his time was the introduction of Sunday League cricket, which meant extra weekend staffing and a new shape to the PA service for Monday morning and evening papers. Gee supervised all that with distinction.

It was around that time, in February 1971, that MPs defeated in the Commons an attempt to ease Sunday laws. This at least gave the PA some respite to prepare for the vast increase in Sunday sport that everyone felt in Fleet Street was bound to come eventually. And so it did.

But, when it happened, the PA was ready for it and for the virtual wall-to-wall sports coverage that the papers were demanding. Others may argue differently, but there is certainly a case for asserting that the ever-growing sports sections of the papers, including, of course, racing, are without doubt the most avidly read of all parts of the press. This is an area where the reader claims (sometimes with justice) to be at least as much of an expert as the journalist who writes in these columns.

The decision to move the PA's entire sports operation to Leeds in 1993 coincided with an explosion in sports information in general, with association football clearly in the driving seat. The live coverage of football was becoming a wall-to-wall operation on television. And the fact that more people could see more and more sports on their TV screens meant that their appetite grew with it.

The PA had acquired a business in Manchester that supplied greyhound and horse-racing information. It was then that the idea of moving to Leeds took shape.

Leeds was a developing city that had been allowed to run down in the 1960s and 1970s and low-priced property was therefore available. The city had the advantage of great communications by rail and motorway and was thus, at least on the face of it, an ideal venue for the PA's expansion of sports coverage.

Jim Donnelley, who had been with Extel for many years, was asked to come to Leeds to set up the results operation. This proved to be an instant and big success.

So it was very quickly realised that, if the results operation could work so successfully in the North of England, it would make a lot of sense to move the entire sports desk from Fleet Street to Leeds. This also gave the sports department the welcome chance to start afresh and to discard some of the old-fashioned and tiresome practices that had managed to survive and persist over the years.

The move enabled the sports department to bring in all sorts of new systems in one fell swoop. It was an opportunity not to be missed. The PA, therefore, began to develop many new sports information services. These included contracts with Ceefax and Teletext, both of which wanted live football scores that were constantly updated, and the same for cricket. There are many people who 'watch' the progress of cricket and football matches on their Ceefax and Teletext screens!

Mark Hird, who was boss of the PA new-media operation, also in Leeds, devised and developed a new cricket scoring system, which was initially aimed at regional newspapers. The problem for regional evening newspapers was that they were invariably behind with the cricket scores. By the time the scores came through on the wire and by the time they were in the paper, possibly two hours had elapsed, during which time the whole tenor of the match could have changed radically.

Under the new, electronic system, cricket scores could find their way into the newspapers with delays of only a second or two. They were also invaluable for use on Teletext and the Internet. Indeed, as was speedily realised, the Internet became a marvellous vehicle for publishing this growing volume of live sports information, and meeting the rapidly increasing market there was for it.

The Press Association then acquired another company, Computer Newspaper Services, based in Howden. They were specialists in page-ready, camera-ready products, as well as dealing in TV listings, which was also a rapidly developing market.

Over the next few years, the PA in Leeds started to move things about. Some of the operations in Howden were transferred to Leeds, and the page-ready production business eventually reached a point where pages of sports information are delivered ready for publication to *The Times*, the *Sunday Telegraph*, the *Independent* and the *Daily Express*. Nowadays, virtually every national newspaper and most regional papers take some camera-ready finished products from the PA. In a sense, these organisations hand part of their papers over to the PA. In particular, *Sport First* relies heavily on the PA. More than half this paper is produced by the Association in Leeds.

But it was not merely the headline sport with which PA was concerned. Amateur sport is also substantially covered and space is found for all the minority sports, even including curling and shinty. Regional Teletext in Scotland started to want shinty coverage, so the PA started to catch the results as well as furnishing them with league tables.

For instance the *Daily Star* carried a feature on Mondays headed: IF IT'S ON THE PARK ON SUNDAY IT'S IN *THE STAR* ON MONDAY. This meant that, if those playing a soccer match on Hackney Marshes in east London on a Sunday morning, for instance, chose to telephone the PA in Leeds after the match, their result would appear in the *Daily Star*. That entire service was run from the PA in Leeds.

Gambling has also figured large, so to speak, in the sports coverage. Because of the PA's famous independence, many bookmakers treat it as the sports bible and include in their own rules that they will pay out on the decision of the Press Association. This is not something, alas, that the bookies pay the PA for. But it is a remarkable acknowledgment not only of the PA's accuracy, but its integrity as well.

Incidentally, the bookmakers always use the PA to provide the 'official' length of each Budget, an event on which there is widespread betting interest.

Millions of pounds each day are paid out every day on the decisions taken by PA staff on the racecourses on starting prices.

Elsewhere, the PA has developed and continues to develop the type of technology that allows it to 'manipulate' information and present it in so many different forms on the Internet, in newspapers, on TV and in other growing outlets.

What is more, the video-printer on the BBC *Grandstand* programme on Saturday afternoon, showing all the results as they come up, is totally driven by the PA. Equally, the Sky sports round-up, giving the goals as they happen, each booking and each sending-off, is also provided by the PA working flat-out in Howden.

All this is marvellous exposure for the PA, although there is a minor downside to it: whenever a mistake is made, which is rare but inevitable in such a concentrated and intense performance, it is highlighted too!

The PA now provides a truly international sports service, the main pillar of which is football. News, reports and statistics are produced from more than fifty countries outside the United Kindom.

In the UK itself, the PA has a reporter and statistician at every game in England and Scotland – many of the latter being themselves former professional footballers.

Staff attend every European golf tournament, plus many others, including those in South Africa and Australia. And in tennis the PA sports budget has taken a knocking because of the relative success of the British participants in recent years.

As with all news organisations the cost, provision and security of telephones are a major concern. And this is more true of PA Sport than for any other part of the business. There are hundreds of telephones all over the country, at racecourses, football grounds and cricket grounds, plus extra ones installed for special events.

Once, at Newmarket racecourse, the telephone bill for one month came to nearly £1,500, and there had been no racing during that period! All the calls had gone through to Egypt. It turned out that there had been a lot of building work going on at the racecourse, particularly in the area occupied by the press during race meetings. After that, there was a blitz on PA's telephone security.

In April 1990, PA paid £5.14 million for Extel Sports Services. Colin Webb, the then editor-in-chief, said there had been some complaints from subscribers about the speed of information because Extel was ahead with the information.

'We now control the service and our subscribers will benefit,' he said. Roger MacDonald, previously in charge of the service for Extel, moved over to become general manager of the PA sports division.

In fact, this was just the latest in a string of PA purchases around this time that strengthened the agency's core business and held out the opportunity for a significant expansion both in the PA's traditional media areas and in nonmedia areas as well, the kind of expansion that was to blossom in the decade that followed.

In the previous two years, PA had bought the private news wire network United News Services, the PNA, Telex Monitors, the newspaper services independent CRG and finally Extel Sports Services.

Webb commented at the time, 'The 1977 Royal Commission on the Press said that PA was a non-commercial co-operative which made us sound rather like a charity club. The drive since then has been to make PA commercially responsible to its subscribers.

'We recognise the public service journalism role which we have, which is why we take on things like the Birthday Honours List and TV and radio listings, which are simply not economically viable. However, we do have a strong commercial feel as well, and this is illustrated by the Extel purchase.'

Time was when Reuters covered the Olympic Games on behalf of the PA, although the PA sent along some of their own sports experts to supplement the Reuters coverage. Nowadays, the PA sends out its own team and covers the Olympics as a completely independent operation.

One of the biggest Olympics scoops was achieved by Nelson Fairley, son of the late PA deputy parliamentary editor, Bill Fairley. Nelson, who went on to become PA sports editor, was sitting in the Reuters office at the Montreal Olympics in 1976, when he heard a whisper that 'someone' had been disqualified. There were a number of people in the Reuters team who had never covered sport before, and the significance of that may have eluded them.

But it did not elude Fairley. He jumped up from his seat and rushed out to where he thought he might glean some information. Suddenly, he saw Jim Fox, the seasoned British pentathlon hope, whose friendship he had already cultivated. Nelson struck gold, so to speak. The culprit was a 38-year-old Russian army major, Boris Onischenko, a former Olympic silver medallist, who had been fencing with Fox.

In fencing, when a 'hit' is achieved it sets off an electric impulse, so the referees can work out easily the number of 'hits' scored. But Fox was suspicious that the electronic system was registering 'hits' for Onischenko when he, Fox, did not believe he had been touched.

Fox, even though he was a close friend of Onischenko, asked for the sword to be inspected, thinking it was probably faulty. But the inspection revealed that the Russian had placed cheat wires beneath the épée's leather grip. All he had to do was to press these wires manually for an alleged 'hit' to be recorded. Nelson's scoop, variously headlined BORIS'S SWORD TRICK and SOVIET SWORD OF DISHONOUR, was splashed throughout the British papers and beyond.

Hardly surprisingly, Onischenko was expelled from the national team and sent home in disgrace, having, in the words of Tass, the Kremlin news agency, 'aroused the just condemnation of Soviet sportsmen'.

Fox gave Nelson the entire story, including a technical explanation of how the Russian had tried to cheat his way to a gold medal.

The sports operation moved to Leeds in 1993 in London House, a new building leased to the PA. PA Sportslink, the racing subsidiary previously operating from Manchester, and the sport and racing division of Computer Newspaper Services were the first to move in.

And the arrival in Leeds of PA Racing meant that all racing activities, from race cards to results, would be concentrated and organised in the one centre.

The end of the last century and the start of the new millennium saw PA Sport undergo the most rapid and dramatic growth in its history.

It was fuelled by several factors: traditional media such as newspapers began to devote more space to sport, society at large became more tuned into sport especially football, and the new technologies that appeared at the start of the 1990s started to take a hold with new media creating a voracious appetite for sports news, reports and data.

PA Sport took its traditional values of speed, accuracy and impartiality and made them a unique selling point in a quickly expanding marketplace. PA was also able to use its expertise for information gathering, earned over the previous 100 years, to take the lead among the sporting media.

The revolution began with page-ready services, where PA proved expert at taking a wealth of information and packaging it in a form that was easily digested by newspapers. National newspapers followed regionals in taking their sport 'oven ready' and the pattern was set.

From 1997 to 2001 PA Sport changed out of all recognition. The founding fathers of Fleet Street would have been impressed as the operation began to lay claim to the title of 'Europe's leading sports information provider'.

Using the main wire as its core activity, PA Sport adapted to the new world by both packaging the information it had already gathered and constantly gathering new information.

PA was helped by its close relationships with sport governing bodies. That guaranteed PA access to information, so improving its services to its customers.

Building on its traditional values, PA took the concept of 'live' information a step further – and it was no coincidence that football was the first sport to benefit.

It was becoming obvious in the late 1990s that PA could no longer rely on its traditional methods of gathering football data. Formerly, a freelance would telephone every time a goal was scored and that goalflash would be sent out on the wire. Increasingly, however, freelances were being asked to work for other organisations as well as PA and PA Sport was no longer the first and most important call on everyone's list.

The decision was then taken to place at every ground a full-time data gatherer, working alongside PA's journalist. His role was to 'talk' the game back to an operator at PA's Northern headquarters. In the 2000–2001 season, every action of every game in the top four divisions in England – goals, red and yellow cards, throw-ins, free-kicks, offsides, goalkicks, corners, shots and saves – was recorded by PA.

At the same time, the football authorities wanted to harness their own data and exploit its market value. They wanted a system that was resilient, with a proven distribution method and one that was operated by a company that was independent. They settled on PA. And for the 2001–2002 season in England, and in the Scottish Premier League, PA became the official supplier of data for the English and Scottish Premier Leagues, the English Football League and the Football Conference.

PA secured that role because of its key attributes of fast, accurate and impartial information; its route to market; and its independent reputation. And it opened the way for other sport governing bodies to follow suit.

The other major development for PA Sport was to move beyond the boundaries of the UK. SportsTicker of America were looking for a partner to develop a European operation and, after searching the continent for someone who could fit the bill, they came to PA. Once again, they recognised the traditional values which also made a perfect fit with their principles. They went about their business in exactly the same way as PA – and so PA Sport International was born.

With the USA covered by Ticker, PA began to place correspondents and stringers across Europe – to the point where every one of the 51 countries affiliated to UEFA had at least one PA correspondent by the summer of 2001. PA then secured correspondents in other parts of the world and began covering other sports internationally, such as Test cricket, golf, motor racing and tennis. For the first time, PA had a service that covered the sporting world.

5 Beating the Odds

THE HARDSHIPS EXPERIENCED by the Press Association's racing reporters and the hazardous way in which they collected their results were legendary in the thirties and forties – but in the early 1950s it was time for change. For years one man had sat on the roof of the grandstand, from where he could see the winning post and the board showing the numbers of the runners, while another colleague stationed himself beside a field telephone with a telescope.

The observer on the roof would ticktack news of the race, using an elaborate system of signalling by arm movements to the man with the telescope, who had to read the signals with unerring accuracy and transmit the information by telephone to the Press Association–Extel Joint Service Centre for release all over Britain. The scope for error was enormous, especially in bad weather, and there was an extra hazard at Goodwood, where the telephone was two miles from the observer and an intermediate man was needed to receive and pass on his signals.

The immense problems that confronted those doing this job were described by Ebenezer Eden, a Press Association telephonist who went on to the courses with two colleagues, Len Coldwell and Arthur Winn. Ebenezer described how, at Windsor, he had to carry the wooden box containing a field telephone to a meadow that backed on to the course. There, he had to find a tree stump to attach the terminals and telephone wires to, before hooking up the instrument.

Coldwell would then adjust a telescope 'of considerable length' on a portable tripod and then they were ready for 'the off'. Their customary pitch at Windsor was on the banks of a stream – and it always seemed to rain on race days. As the stream became swollen with the downpour, Coldwell and Eden were compelled to operate while standing on chairs borrowed from a nearby cottage. And when the day was over they had to return home by train in drenched clothes, which produced the inevitable outcome of another cold.

But things were to change, thanks to an episode in the 1950s that had far-reaching consequences. At this time, many racecourse managements did not find it easy to run their businesses at a reasonable profit and maintain and improve their properties. They desperately needed more people to attend races and more bookmakers to pay for stands on the courses. This was the main reason why racecourse managements resented the operations of news agency men who could communicate the results and starting prices so swiftly to the public outside and the off-course bookmakers.

Eventually, however, after years of on/off negotiations, the racecourses allowed them and the newspapers to rent telephones on the spot. But even then the racecourse managements were in a dilemma. They naturally enjoyed the publicity given to racing, but they still resented the off-course bookmaker making a big profit out of their race programmes and paying nothing in return. This finally led to legislation being introduced ensuring that off-course bookmakers paid a levy for the benefits they gained.

However, in 1956, the Racecourse Association, representing most of the courses, proposed enormous increases in the fees the Press Association–Extel Joint Service were paying for on-course telephones. The thinking behind this was that these extra charges would be passed on to the off-course bookmakers who subscribed in huge numbers to the service.

The plan was not well received, for the Press Association and Extel objected to being used as tax collectors on behalf of the racecourse managements. As a result, the Racecourse Association reluctantly dropped the idea. The following year, however, the managements of Aintree (which was not a member of the Racecourse Association) and Manchester decided to see what they could achieve by acting independently.

They demanded a payment of £500 a day from the Joint Service and other racing agencies for the use of telephone facilities. The move was rejected out of hand, and the Joint Service successfully covered the meetings without using on-course telephones. The course managements at Aintree and Manchester reverted to their former arrangements, licking their wounds.

As time went on the Press Association played a major role in providing the newspapers with the runners and riders at all race meetings. The service of 'Probables' was as good a guide as

anyone could get, but it was not infallible. Its accuracy depended, to some degree, on the mood of owners and trainers. Some
could be reticent, others obdurate, and any of them could
change their minds at the last minute for all sorts of reasons but
chiefly if the 'going' had altered and no longer suited their horse.

The majority of punters laid their bets on the basis of the
Probables list, and there was a lot of ill feeling if a horse listed
as a Probable did not run, or vice versa. The system, in
operation for years, clearly had serious shortcomings.

So it was no great surprise when the Jockey Club and the
National Hunt Committee decided that the owner of a horse that
had been entered for a race must notify Messrs Weatherby's
(racing's adminstrative body acting for the Jockey Club) by noon
on the day before the race whether the horse would run or not.
If that arrangement were not complied with and the horse did
not subsequently run, then the owner would be required to pay
a hefty forfeit. Although this was an expensive and time-
consuming operation for Weatherby's, it was agreed that the lists
should be supplied free of charge for newspaper publication –
although there were some voices who believed that the press
should pay. The new move did not eliminate the work the Joint
Service had to perform in this particular area. Since the
declarations of runners did not include the riders, the Press
Association still had to collect the jockeys' names as before.

It was a man named Frederick Inskip Harrison, the agency's
second racing editor, who was responsible for introducing to the
public the list of 'probable runners and jockeys' at race meetings, a system that replaced one that was open to abuse and
fraud and that, from time to time, was ruthlessly exploited. It
was a reform that revolutionised the horse-racing industry – and
it was down to Press Association, pure and simple.

When Harrison took over the reins as racing editor in the
1920s, runners and riders were not normally declared until 45
minutes before the race was run. This meant that all the
off-the-course backers had to guide them were the entries,
which might number sixty or more in each race. Yet the actual
runners would probably be whittled down to a handful or so.
Since most of the bets laid would be on nonrunners, it was
difficult to sustain off-course interest in racing. To overcome
this, several big races were created on which there was ante-post
betting at determined odds. The entries for these races were
published, analysed and dissected by the newspapers and

thousands took prices about their fancies with advertising bookmakers. If you won, you were paid according to the odds you accepted. If the horse was beaten, or did not run, you lost.

This inevitably led to many dubious practices. For example, newspapers were often misled about running plans, with the result that the public put their money on horses that were never intended to take part in the race. That was the highly unsatisfactory position when Harrison joined the Press Association. A reform of the system was necessary and one was devised that, up to a point, survives today. One of Harrison's staff was a dapper little chap called Harry Humphries, whose task was to report on jockeys' mounts in the so-called big races. This gave him unrivalled contacts with the riders. Indeed, his involvement was such that he was able to put spare mounts the way of jockeys who had not got a ride. Humphries wielded such influence in this area that there were few jockeys who could afford either to offend him or, worse, to mislead him. Humphries, not to put too fine a point on it, was quite imperious with the jockeys, warning them that if they were seen talking to other reporters they might be struck off his list.

Harrison and his henchman Humphries, therefore, decided to reduce the crude lists of entries for the day-to-day races at the principal meetings to 'probable runners and jockeys'. To this end, Humphries worked on the jockeys that he knew so well, while his efforts were supplemented by the efforts of regional correspondents appointed by Harrison. Many of these correspondents were railway booking clerks, responsible for engaging the horse boxes in which some of the runners travelled to the meetings.

The Jockey Club did not like the new arrangement and raised the most bitter objections to it. But the Press Association was determined to go ahead – and go ahead it did. The lists started to be published and, although they were not perfect, they were better than anything seen earlier. But there was more trouble looming.

The *Daily Mail*, Britain's top-circulation newspaper, was, like the rest of Fleet Street, deeply impressed with what the Press Association was now putting out, and tried to 'poach' Humphries with the tempting promise of a salary 'beyond the dreams of avarice' if he would work exclusively for them. It was certainly tempting enough to cause Humphries to consider quitting his beloved agency. However, Harrison set to work on him and persuaded him to stay, with a huge salary rise. Humphries's new and inflated pay packet was reputedly even bigger than the general manager's. The spin-off from this piece of Press Association enterprise had the effect of spreading off-the-course bookmaking into every town and almost every village in the United Kingdom.

The quick results service supplied with the Exchange Telegraph Company flourished, and as a result horse-race betting, from comparatively small beginnings, became the Press Association's biggest business in terms of cash turnover. It also had the effect of diminishing the number and 'importance' of the so-called big races, which had been artificially created and from which unscrupulous people had been able to make huge sums of ill-gotten cash. It also meant that ante-post betting shrank in volume.

The National Hunt season began to boom as a result. On the social consequences, Harrison and the Press Association could justifiably claim that they had surmounted a wall and given the average punter a better and fairer deal. It took the racing authorities thirty years to recognise that Harrison was right and that they were wrong. Their opposition to this reform crumbled only when the consequences of World War Two taught them that they could not run the sport satisfactorily or at all unless they had the support of the stay-at-home backers.

It was in the early 1960s, therefore, that Harrison's successor, Leolin McClean, crowned Harrison's achievements by negotiating with the Jockey Club for exclusive newspaper rights for their 24-hour declared runners. It was something that would never have been possible but for what Harrison and Humphries had done. Incredibly, Harrison never, in his fifty years' association with racing, actually set foot on a racecourse. He could not even be persuaded to attend a thanksgiving dinner planned in his honour at Haydock Park shortly after his retirement.

Meanwhile, all was not well between the Press Association and Extel. The new agreement of 1922 that had set up the Joint Service had not, quite frankly, been thoroughly thought through, and it seemed that Extel was getting more of the pickings than it rightfully deserved. It was felt on the Press Association side that a new agreement should be drawn up at the earliest opportunity that would provide a more equal share-out. The old agreement had been extended twice, virtually unamended, and it was next due to be considered again in 1961. It was in 1958, therefore, that the Press Association gave the necessary three years' notice to bring the agreement to an end.

This led to some hard bargaining. Extel came up with a few concessions, but they amounted to nothing like the radical changes being sought by the PA. It was beginning to look as though the twain would never meet. Until, that is, the arrival on the scene of Pat Winfrey, from the East Midland Allied Press, who was a Press Association director. Winfrey was a direct, no-nonsense, 'to-hell-with-protocol' sort of man and his view about the Joint Service was straightforward.

He felt the agency had to 'think big' on this issue, and that unless Extel were prepared to be involved in the Joint Service on a fair-shares basis then the Press Association should seriously consider going it alone. His view certainly concentrated the mind. For it would have meant that the agency would be in competition with Extel in providing information to newspapers and, possibly more importantly still, to bookmakers.

Extel, although clearly unnerved by the new, aggressive attitude of the PA board, did not respond at once. But, while an ultimatum was still in place, Winfrey became chairman in June 1960 – and wrote a long memorandum to his fellow directors, some of whom were becoming increasingly nervous at the prospect of walking out of the Joint Service. Nevertheless, at the September board meeting, they decided to stand firm. Extel's delay was plainly in the belief that the Press Association would back down. But the message from the September board meeting was enough and it finally accepted the PA's demands in principle.

That, however, was only the end of the beginning. Now came the real negotiations, thrashing out the broad agreement in detail – but this turned out to be less horrific than some had feared. The new agreement came into effect on 1 January 1962 and was due to expire on 1 January 2002. The fair-shares element was to be achieved gradually over a number of years and Extel had the management of all the provincial centres.

6 The Enemy

ILLIAM SAUNDERS, of the *Western Morning News* in Plymouth, had been persuaded to stay on another year with the agency in 1871, even though he had suggested that his own news business might be in competition with it, and it would be proper for him to retire. But his experience and advice were helpful in these formative years and no one wanted to let him go.

However, this happy arrangement came to a sudden end when Saunders attempted to strike a deal with the Press Association. He wanted to buy the full general news service from it and use what he wanted for his own service to London and the provincial papers. As a quid pro quo, he offered to supply the agency with its provincial news. It was no surprise when the management committee turned down all his proposals, even though it took 'a very long and grave discussion' before they reached that conclusion. Saunders was bluntly told that the Press Association would gather its own provincial news and would sell its own services direct to London and the provincial papers, thank you very much.

So, in 1871, Central News was born, out of the already existing Central Press, and unofficial war was declared in the battle for business. Saunders quickly became a hate figure in the eyes of PA. At one stage, he was accused of having 'sucked PA's brains' during his membership of the management committee. The war was to last for some seventy years, with bitter infighting, and the first fifty years were the most bloody. All sorts of ruses and ploys were employed by both sides. Some PA chiefs suggested that tariffs should be cut so brutally that it would be totally impossible for any rival to compete. But, for all sorts of reasons, this radical idea was rejected. John Jaffray, one of the founding fathers of the PA, for instance, took the healthy view that competition acted as a stimulus and should not be eradicated. He said, 'With respect to the general principle of cutting out competition at a loss to ourselves, I think no principle could be more vicious or undesirable.

'There is no doubt that the competition of other agencies does sometimes impede the transmission of our news, but it is not an unmixed evil. If we had no competition in this as in any other business, we might get rich and fat, and not attend to our business.'

But the competition, although keeping PA on its toes, was not always above board. During the 1880s there was a suspicious series of incidents that caused the Press Association to fear there was an element of corruption, possibly bribery, at work. For PA reports did not arrive in newspaper offices until after the Central News reports, even though the Press Association telegrams had been handed in first to the local post offices.

The PA lodged a formal, angry protest, and the Post Office were forced to concede that something was wrong but, despite what looked like overwhelming evidence, refused to admit any possibility of corruption. The investigations the PA conducted came within a whisker of establishing that bribery had been committed, and this was made known to the Post Office authorities. They still rejected any such suggestion, but nevertheless the Telegraphs Department sent out a strong warning, saying that press telegrams had to be dealt with strictly in order of their receipt. Within days the preferential treatment of Central News stopped abruptly.

Meanwhile, the Press Association learned that some newspapers in the Midlands had been asked by Post Office telegraphists why they did not take Central News parliamentary reports in place of the PA service. Some years after that happened, a postmaster was severely reprimanded by his superiors for 'milking' messages from PA correspondents.

But the wrongdoing may not all have been on one side. On one occasion the Post Office produced a letter by the PA's manager, John Lovell, to a Post Office clerk offering 5 per cent commission on any subscriptions he might obtain for news services. The circumstances in which this offer was made are shrouded in mystery but it is no surprise that the letter was absolutely disowned by the committee of management.

It was not long, however, before a cut-price war was raging, in spite of John Jaffray's best endeavours. In 1887, Central News slashed its charge for special-reporting items such as major political speeches from 15s. (75 pence) to 10s. (50 pence) a column. This compelled the Press Association to follow suit at a grand cost of £3,000 a year. This was done reluctantly and not without irritation.

In 1888, the manager, Edmund Robbins, wrote to the sports editor, Charles Pardon, who was visiting the North of England and Scotland on PA's behalf:

The *Edinburgh Evening News* detailed order arrived this morning. During this session we have sent them our ordinary parliamentary report at 15s. a week, supplemented at their own request with a special report of Scots questions, and also having the report carried on to a later hour than the ordinary evening paper service.

Do I understand from you that Mr Wilson, of the *Edinburgh Evening News*, expects to receive at a cheaper rate than that charged by the PA, the ordinary supply from Central News? We charge 15s. a week for an average of 1,000 words a day and I can assure you there is scarcely a penny profit after paying reporting and transmission expenses.

Your description of the Central News Parliamentary Service is a very just one. It is always straining after effect and is always crying 'Wolf, wolf' when, as a matter of fact, the reportable scenes in the House of Commons are few and far between.

In a further message to Pardon, Robbins said:

I hope and believe that you will be enabled to get back the *Manchester Guardian* for law cases. It cannot be denied for one moment that the Press Association's staff in the Law Courts is greatly superior to that of the Central News, and a great paper like the *Manchester Guardian* ought not to put the pounds, shillings and pence question first when it is well served by its own Association.

We have stood the test of time and no fault can be found with our work, yet papers rush off to any outsider who promises what he cannot perform.

What the Press Association was having to endure was competition from people who would be called 'cowboys' in modern parlance. They were offering an inferior service at a totally uneconomical price.

There was, however, a tentative suggestion in 1889 that PA should get together with Central News to eliminate 'wasteful competition'. Both agencies, for example, were sending out the same Court Circular, weather reports and texts of the Queen's speech. But these advances were rejected. Many members were appalled that the PA, a co-operative organisation representing much of the British press, should form some kind of liaison with what was rather sniffily described as 'an ordinary trading concern'.

The idea was, therefore, hastily dropped and the war proceeded unabated. But the Press Association did partially restore its charges for special reporting, going halfway back to the former charge: 12s. 6d. (62.5p). But now the battles were global. Central News started, during the 1870s, to send its own correspondents overseas and was thus, unlike PA, offering a direct service of world news. This, however, had an indirect effect on the Press Association, since Central News was battling with Reuters to corner the British market and PA relied on Reuters for foreign news to supply to its subscribers. This situation was not helped by the perception, in some quarters, that the Reuters service was stodgy in parts and its news presentation was unappealing.

In 1889, the PA bluntly told Reuters that some provincial newspapers began to suspect that Reuters was no more than a conduit for official messages. That was about the worst thing anyone could say to a news organisation. But Reuters did not want to lose its reputation as an impeccably accurate and reliable news disseminator, even though some British newspapers were growing impatient when they saw the livelier, more colourful and sometimes faster copy issued by Central News. It was altogether more refreshing to read than the sometimes turgid, but always absolutely accurate, Reuters offering.

All this led to rows between Reuters and Central News, especially after some PA subscribers complained that the Reuters service during the Sino-Japanese war of 1894–5 was far inferior to that provided by Central News.

The PA then agreed to pay its share for an extension of the service, while at the same time Reuters protested that Central News was padding and expanding its reports far beyond the limits justified by what was actually happening in the war. There was naturally, therefore, great satisfaction in the Reuters/PA camp when *The Times* printed a highly critical article in 1895 accusing Central News of embellishment in its reports. But this acted as no deterrent to the Saunders agency and both Reuters and PA were pretty powerless to do much about it. In fact, the Central News 'cowboy' operation overseas got worse.

Ten years on, during the Russo-Japanese war, Central News succumbed to reports supplied by an imaginative Italian journalist who, on seeing the meagre, dull and uninformative telegrams being issued from the Far East, realised he could make a good deal of money by writing 'reports' off the top of his head. They were far more readable than anything that was coming out of the war zone, but they bore little relation to the truth.

There was more trouble and ill feeling in October 1907, when the Central News broke an embargo announcing the forthcoming issue by the Foreign Office of the text of an Anglo-Russian treaty. The Press Association was indignant, but the frowns were replaced by smiles when Reuters beat the Foreign Office to the tape, by cabling the full text of the treaty from St Petersburg.

Those were the days when it was important to print the full text of official documents, as well as verbatim reports of long and often tedious political speeches, which in those times, unlike today, were avidly read.

Even so, whatever insults were hurled at Central News, and however dubious some of its stories were, its very existence was salutary, both to Reuters and PA. Their competitor had compelled them to spend money and innovate. Without the 'nuisance' of Central News, the other two organisations would probably have jogged along without any spur to provide a lively and speedy news service from abroad.

But the customers were still not satisfied. The provincial press wanted more and more. They demanded stories that were human, humane, colourful – and more sensational. It was a demand that Reuters was happy to meet, but it certainly could not be expected to do so without extra resources.

At the time, Press Association subscribers were receiving, through the Reuters contract, a foreign service for £300 a year, which even in those days was cheap. Meanwhile, the London papers were paying Reuters direct £1,500 a year for precisely the same service. So Reuters and the PA came up with a deal. In 1890, therefore, the Press Association started a special supplementary foreign service, later to be called Foreign Special.

Reuters hired new men who were au fait with 'new journalism' – in other words, they knew what newspaper readers actually wanted to read and what newspapers really wanted to print. Oddly, the reports they sent in from all corners of the world were much longer, in most cases, than the formal communiqués issued by the old-style foreign correspondents. But they were brighter, more stimulating and more sensational than anything else on offer. These men were like a fire brigade. They would quickly arrive at any hotspot in the world and hoover up any news around. This all cost money, way above the moderate subscriptions that the provincial papers in particular were paying. So, under the new deal, the Press Association paid half of what Reuters were outlaying for this special service.

Harry Gwynne, who was later to become editor of the *Morning Post*, was the star reporter of the day. At joint expense, the PA and Reuters sent this high-flying young man to the world's trouble spots. He was with Kitchener, then with the Turkish army in the war against the Greeks, and he was the doyen of correspondents covering the Boer War. Subscribers to PA received his Foreign Special reports for 20s. (£1) a column of 2,000 words. This was a bargain in 1890, considering the telegram charges. These were: a fairly reasonable sum of 2d. (less than 1 penny) a word from Europe and only 5d. (about 2 pence) a word from North America. But elsewhere the charges were restrictive. From India it was 1s. 4d. (over 6 pence); from South Africa 2s. 3d. (about 11 pence); from Australia anything up to 13s. 4d. (about 67 pence); from China 7s. 1d. (about 35 pence); and from South America anything up to 8s. 10d. (44 pence). Other places were even more expensive. But this represented only a fraction of the cost incurred. The pay and sometimes heavy expenses of the correspondents had also to be met.

What made it more difficult for Reuters is that it was expected to cover the entire globe, whereas Central News allowed itself to be far more selective. It simply cherry-picked those areas in the world it knew would be a major source of news at the time, and thus profitable. Reuters, then, had to operate under something of a handicap, because Central News was often able to outspend it in those areas where big international stories were breaking because it did not have global financial commitments.

In spite of this major disadvantage, Reuters was able to boast of a string of scoops which left rivals trailing. These included reports from the Commune in Paris; the Carlists in Spain; expeditions against the Ashantis, and against the natives of Sierra Leone, the Somalis, the Afridis, the Mohmands; of Arabi Pasha's revolt; the Mahdi; Kitchener's Sudan expedition; the victory at Omdurman; the Abraham Lincoln assassination; the

French humiliation over Fashoda; of Rhodes and the Transvaal, of insurrection in Mexico, revolution in China, trouble in Venezuela, revolts in Mexico and war in the Balkans.

Reuters also managed to remain streets ahead of everyone else in its coverage of war. Its biggest coup was to report the relief of Mafeking before even the War Office knew about it. And it also provided unique coverage of the Franco-Prussian conflict, the Sino-Japanese conflict, the Spanish-American conflict, the Russo-Japanese conflict, the Turco-Italian conflict and the Balkans conflict. A very impressive record. Some of these momentous events were reported in the normal Reuters service, without any extra charge to Press Association subscribers. But costs were beginning to mount alarmingly.

The Foreign Special Service was first established with an estimated cost of cabling at £1,200 a year. It was a wild underestimate. Twelve years later, the cost for cabling one news story – Joseph Chamberlain's South African tour – was much greater than that. So more and more Reuters and PA were to share the cost of stories from major trouble spots. The result was a peerless service, which, for many years, no competitor could emulate, although that situation changed when Associated Press, the American agency, appeared on the scene.

One particular accolade came in 1903 from William Brimelow of the *Bolton Evening News* of a report he had received through the Press Association of the Durbar in Delhi. He wrote, 'I never felt prouder of our evening newspaper than when we had over a column of well-written descriptive matter of those wonderful scenes at Delhi, which had occurred early on the same day.'

The Press Association was eventually to buy out Central News in 1940.

7 Libelled Lady

EDMUND ROBBINS WAS IN A QUANDARY. For the first time in his career he was not sure what to do – it was one for the committee of management. The Press Association had reported that a titled lady had admitted in court that she had been intimate with her husband 'more than once before marriage'. The trouble was she had admitted no such thing. Such a report gave rise to very serious issues of honour – and the social disgrace of indulging in carnal affairs before the knot was tied.

It was 1886 and the case of Lady Aylmer involved proceedings in which she sued her husband, an Irish baronet, for divorce chiefly on the grounds of his misconduct with a flower girl. She was awarded a decree nisi with costs. It seemed a straightforward case. Unfortunately, however, the Press Association reporter, John Saunders, was not in court at the time and had copied a paragraph from the report of another journalist. Unhappily for him and all concerned, he misread it and filed the wrong sentence about Lady Aylmer's 'admitting' to having had premarital sex with her husband. The line was printed in 55 newspapers.

Three weeks later Robbins became aware of the libel. It came to light when the *Dublin Evening Telegraph* was threatened with an action initiated by Lady Aylmer. Robbins was worried: what about the other 54 newspapers? Should the agency send them a correction and an apology? Or would the publication of an apology draw attention to something that had escaped notice for so long and thus aggravate the original libel?

His dilemma was finally resolved by the committee of management, which sensibly decided that a circular should be sent to all the newspapers that had published the libel, advising them to print an apology without delay. Things went from bad to worse, however. Even though they all printed an apology, writs for libel were still issued against them, and Lady Aylmer's solicitor, a man named Manning, who appeared to like a fight, would not brook any suggestion of a compromise settlement out of court. This legal eagle was clearly the stumbling block. The Press Association was not directly involved, for Lady Aylmer had been advised to sue the papers that had published the report and not the agency that had supplied it.

But Robbins and the management committee felt obliged to do what they could to mitigate the damage done by the reporter's 'indefensible blunder'. So a plan was devised to try to deal directly, and secretly, with Lady Aylmer, thus bypassing the stubborn Manning. The newsroom tracked down her address and the Press Association secretary, Henry Whorlow, a man of military bearing, took a cab to Clapham. But, when the door of 62 New Park Road was answered, Whorlow discovered to his consternation that he had arrived at the home of Manning, the very person he had been trying to avoid at all costs. Fortunately for him, Manning was out, and so was Lady Aylmer, who was lodging there.

But her mother was in. So Whorlow decided to take a chance and do business with her. He promised her that the newspapers that were being sued were willing to give Lady Aylmer a grand total of £500 to settle the action. She promised to report all this to her daughter and also agreed to fall in with Whorlow's somewhat awkwardly framed further request that not a word of this should get to the ears of Manning. His overtures had an almost immediate effect. The following morning Whorlow received a short note in his office. It came from another solicitor named Wynne, of Chancery Lane, and it stated that Lady Aylmer was his client and was prepared to see Whorlow.

He needed no second bidding. Whorlow strode up Fleet Street to Chancery Lane, well pleased that things appeared to be moving so swiftly and even more pleased that the demon Manning was totally unaware of what had gone on behind his back. Whorlow had a long discussion with Lady Aylmer and soon realised that, although Wynne was a lawyer, he was acting not as a solicitor but as a friend. The relatively happy outcome was that Lady Aylmer agreed to Whorlow's terms and settled for £500, plus 50 guineas (£52.50) to cover Manning's costs. Whorlow could scarcely argue with that – nor did he. The maximum contribution that any individual paper had to pay was £20, which even in those days was a relatively cheap escape.

Now Whorlow was showered with accolades from the Press Association chairman, Robert Leader, who said that both he and

Robbins were entitled to 'the warm thanks of all of us, though I know you will feel the relief equally as well as any of us'. Sadly, as the champagne flowed, another dilemma rose from the ashes. The question of what to do with the errant reporter, Saunders. He was naturally mortified by the whole affair and had written to the committee expressing his deep regret. Robbins had already removed him from his duties at the Law Courts and placed him in a junior position in the newsroom. Now, five months later, the committee had to decide his fate.

Leader said the first inclination was to sack him forthwith, and a motion was put to the committee that a man who was capable of an error of this kind was unfit to be on the staff of the Press Association. However, Saunders's considerable length of service was taken into account, as were his wife and large family. It was finally decided that the action Robbins had taken as an interim measure, to give him a subordinate position on the staff in the head office, should be adhered to. But his salary was cut from £3. 5s. (£3.25) a week to £2.10s. (£2.50). Just a few months after his severe reprimand and demotion, Saunders, who was deeply personally affected by these events, collapsed and died. It was openly said at the time that his death was hastened by this 'unfortunate business'.

However, despite Whorlow's undercover and heroic efforts, the affair was still not quite closed. For some reason, Lady Aylmer, although willing to do a deal with 54 of the 55 papers, would not in any circumstances let the *Dublin Evening Telegraph* off the hook. It was not altogether clear why she was determined to take this hard line in one individual case when their 'sin' did not seem to be any worse than that of the others. But she certainly felt that the owner of the paper, E Dwyer Gray, an MP for a Dublin constituency, had aggravated the original libel by the way he dealt with her complaints.

Whorlow virtually went down on his knees to try to dissuade her, but it was to no avail. Nothing would divert her and so the *Dublin Evening Telegraph* was left to face the music on its own. And despite everything, including evidence that the Dublin paper published an unqualified apology as soon as the libel came to its notice, the jury in the Nisi Prius Court in Dublin awarded Lady Aylmer £250 damages and costs, which was at least a lot less than the £5,000 she had sought.

Dwyer Gray, who claimed to have lost between £500 and £600, was particular upset because he had been singled out as the scapegoat. Attempts were made by some papers, notably the *Worcester Evening Post and Echo* and the *Liverpool Daily Post*, to compensate him. It was even proposed that the Press Association should pay him £250. But Gray was not looking for charity and the agency took the view that it did not and could not admit any obligation to meet his expenses. All this was carried out in the most friendly manner, but some time later the Dublin lawyers acting for Gray asked the Press Association for compensation. The agency, however, denied liability and resolved to defend any action all the way. Even though both sides started to square up for battle, there was no hostility and everything was conducted 'in a perfectly friendly spirit'.

The case was to settle once and for all the Press Association's liability in matters of this kind. But it did not reach court. Just before the case was due to be heard in Dublin, Gray suddenly died, aged only 42. The Press Association was still left with costs of £270, however. The case raised issues of lasting significance both to the Press Association and to all newspapers. The position, after Gray's untimely death, was set out by William Lewis, of the *Bristol Mercury*, who had now become chairman of the agency:

> We have felt all along that Mr Gray's position was one of great hardship, and his rebellion against it was only natural. But we could not allow our sympathy to warp our judgement, and admit a contention contrary to the fundamental principle upon which all our business is conducted, and upon which alone it is possible for the Press Association to continue to exist.
>
> We act as agents to our customers, and are in fact in the same position to them as their own reporters. We use all the care in our power, but they must publish the news they receive from us on their own responsibility. Upon any other basis it would be impossible to carry on.

He insisted that in the same way as no newspaper proprietor could make a reporter pay the damage arising from any error or lapse of judgment on his part, so the Press Association could not possibly take the legal responsibility of all their customers. To take that responsibility on behalf of 500 or 600 papers all over the country, he said, would require a reserve fund not of £9,000 but of £900,000.

And to this day the Press Association is protected, in its conditions for the supply of news, against claims from subscribers for compensation for any unfortunate consequences that may follow publication of an agency story.

The Press Association, however, faced another libel action in 1891. It was successful from the agency's point of view but, possibly even more importantly, it raised the question of reporting proceedings in open court and fixed the right to do so. The agency had distributed a report of an ex-parte application made to, and granted by, a Canterbury bench of magistrates for the issue of a summons for alleged perjury against a solicitor named Edmund Kimber. No members of the public were in court, but the hearing was certainly not in camera. The three justices had been called together by their clerk to hear the application, which took place in the customary room, and the magistrates made no order to exclude the public. Nor was any objection taken to the presence during the proceedings of the Press Association's correspondent, who sat taking comprehensive notes throughout. After the story had been distributed by the agency, Kimber sued the Press Association for libel on the grounds that this report of ex-parte proceedings, namely a hearing in which only one side of the argument is heard, was not covered by privilege, which extends to fair, accurate and contemporaneous reports of judicial proceedings.

The action was heard in July 1892 and judgment was given in favour of the Press Association with costs. Kimber appealed, but the Court of Appeal confirmed the judgment in favour of the agency, again with costs. In his judgment, the Master of the Rolls, Lord Esher, said, 'Public policy requires that some hardship should be suffered by individuals rather than that judicial proceedings should be held in secret.' He stressed that a court was an open court, and must remain so, unless the justices exercised their discretion by ordering that it be closed to the public.

But Kimber had not yet finished. He told the Press Association that he would not take the case to the House of Lords if, in return, the Association waived his payment of costs awarded by the Court of Appeal. This overture was, hardly surprisingly, greeted with outrage. Edmund Robbins, thundered, 'A more impudent proposal has never been made.' It soon became clear that Kimber's proposal, if not quite blackmail, was certainly some kind of bluff. Because he did not take the appeal to the House of Lords anyway, and he did have to pay the costs.

Around this time there was another legal row brewing for Robbins. The Press Association had put out an incorrect statement to the effect that a pending lawsuit, the celebrated Tranby Croft baccarat case, had been settled out of court. This was a mistake on the part of another Press Association reporter at the Law Courts. The story was centred on a baccarat game played at Tranby Croft, near Hull, the home of Arthur Wilson, a shipbuilder, on the eve of the St Leger. The players included the Prince of Wales, who was to become Edward VII, and Sir William Gordon-Cumming – who was discovered cheating. Edward was told and was furious. He demanded a signed statement from Gordon-Cumming to the effect that, in exchange for the silence of all present, he would never play the game again. This he acceded to, for his honour and reputation were at stake.

However, the incident seeped out into public knowledge the following year and Gordon-Cumming, in a bid to clear his name, took out a civil action against Edward and his friends. He lost his case and was forced to resign his army commission. He was socially ruined from that day on.

Robbins, meanwhile, was ordered by the courts to name the reporter who had made the mistake of reporting an out-of-court settlement, but he declined to do so, nobly taking upon himself the responsibility for having circulated the mistaken report. However, as soon as the error was discovered, another message was circulated making the vital correction. All this was disclosed when Robbins was charged with contempt in the High Court. But the judge was deeply impressed with the promptness with which the Press Association had acted to correct the mistake. Robbins, who could so easily have been sent to prison for an indeterminate period, breathed a hearty sigh of relief when the judge did no more than order him to pay the costs of the hearing.

One of the ironies, some would say shortcomings, of the laws of libel is that newspapers and the Press Association sometimes found it was cheaper to settle out of court, rather than fight an action, even when they had a good defence.

8 Graveyard Coup

T HE STORY, INVOLVING dirty tricks among the aristocracy,
centred on a coffin in Highgate Cemetery, north London.
Was there a body in it or was it simply filled with lead?
The reporter involved on the case was James McCallum, who
was chief of the parliamentary staff. He was on general
reporting duties during the House of Commons Christmas
recess and now found himself one of two British journalists –
the other from Central News – chosen to witness the exhumation of a body (or lump of lead) from the cemetery.

The coffin was supposed to contain the body of a man called
Thomas Charles Druce. Druce had allegedly been buried 43
years earlier. But the Duke of Portland, for some reason never
properly explained, had apparently chosen to masquerade from
time to time as a Mr Druce who owned a thriving furniture shop
in London's Baker Street, a stone's throw from the legendary
rooms of Sherlock Holmes. However, the duke, it seems, tired
of this little game and brought it to a conclusion by eliminating
Druce and pretending to have him buried. The popular theory
was that the funeral rites were performed over a coffin full of
lead.

Years later, the exhumation was considered necessary to
prove the succession to the Dukedom of Portland, which was
then being claimed by one of Druce's sons. The Home Office
consented that the two reporters could attend the exhumation,
but under strict conditions. They were warned not to try to beat
each other with the news and had to agree to accept official
censorship of their reports. But an elaborate plan had been set
up in advance, designed to beat Central News and to thwart the
Home Office without breaching the agreement. It meant that
within seconds of the exhumation, carried out in a wooden shed
surrounding the tomb and the vault of the Druce family, the
world knew there was a body inside the coffin and not just
chunks of lead. The *Star* newspaper of that day gave a graphic
account of the Press Association triumph.

The headlines read, THE BODY OF DRUCE ... SECRET OF THE HIGH-
GATE TOMB REVEALED THIS AFTERNOON ... LEADED COFFIN THEORY COL-
LAPSES.

And the report said:

An aged, bearded man: Thomas Charles Druce found in the
grave where he was laid 43 years ago. The Druce coffin
contains a body. This is the message conveyed first by the Press
Association. It settles definitely once and for all the allegation
that the coffin in the Highgate vault was filled with lead.

The announcement came over the tape at 12.30. A few
minutes later the official statement was issued ... 'At 12.30,'
says our reporter, 'the gates of the wooden shed opened, and
everyone held his breath in the sharp morning air. Thence
came the representatives – one each – of the Press Association and the Central News. They were arm-in-arm!

Those who had expected an undignified sprint between the
rival agency men were disappointed. It appeared that the
cemetery authorities, in their desire to avoid anything not in
accordance with the strictest decorum, had given the press-
men within their gates implicit instructions, hence these
unusual amenities. But a change came over the peaceful scene
when the gates were reached. There are some steps, and for a
moment the Men Who Knew the secret disappeared from view.

When they emerged into view again one man was blowing
his nose vigorously on a bright red handkerchief. Simultaneously, as if by magic, a long line of men who stretched right
along the road, and who had been suspiciously inactive, were
quickened into alertness. Directly the bright red bandanna
made a spot of colour in the air the first man waved a flag ...

The next man waved a flag ... the third man waved a flag
... and so all along the line – a vista of flags. At the end of
the line was a special telephone ... Another line of communication was as follows:

At the top of a long road leading from the cemetery,
standing on a wall about a quarter of a mile from the
cemetery, was a pressman with a pair of glasses. Half-a-mile
away, on the roof of a building in High Street, Highgate, was
a second man with a telescope. He took a message and sent
it direct by a telephone which had been engaged all day. The
most stringent precautions were taken to prevent uncensored
news coming out of the cemetery.

After their first appearance the privileged agency reporters had to walk into the superintendent's office at the gate. Ten minutes later both came out, each in the charge of two policemen, and handed the official report through the railings to their colleagues outside.

But it was, of course, all too late. By this time the news was already on the Press Association wires and, indeed, had been for some time. Officialdom – and the opposition – had been well and truly thwarted. The trick had been the nose-blowing. If a body was inside the coffin, McCallum would blow his nose with a red handkerchief. If the coffin was filled with lead, then McCallum would have signalled with a gaudy green handkerchief. The plot was hatched by McCallum and a colleague, Andrew Gray, who had wisely made a reconnaissance of Highgate Cemetery a few days before the event took place.

The general view was that McCallum should have been given a substantial rise after his coup. But there is no evidence that this ever happened. Sometimes the authorities had to be dealt with firmly – and with a measure of cunning as well – if a Press Association reporter met obstruction when he was trying to file a story during these years.

By now the telephone was playing a bigger role in the gathering of news for the Press Association, especially when it set up the London News Service. Thousands of cards were handed out to pubs, offices, cafés and cab ranks. They read, 'We want news, phone the Press Association – Central 7440. Remuneration given! Open day and night!'

The news did come in – by telephone and runners who were paid half a crown, or 2s. 6d. (12½ pence), for information on fires and accidents, although many half-crowns were paid for false alarms. The London News Service was set up because of competition from a new outfit, the London News Agency, which was supplying newspapers in the capital and the London offices of provincial papers with longer reports on events in the city. The new Press Association service had offices in Red Lion Court, off Fleet Street, and more messengers boys were recruited to ride smart red bicycles – ten of which were stolen in the first week. The London News Service had its own reporters and subeditors – but they were paid less than those of the General Service and their status was lower.

Meanwhile, although the news was starting to flow in by telephone, the telegraph was still the main way of disseminating news. As in the case of Jack Howe.

On a cold Christmas Eve in 1910, Howe, a PA reporter, was sent to cover a railway disaster at Aisgill Moor in which twelve people were killed. On Christmas Day morning, having got the story in his notebook, Howe took a cab to the nearest post office. It was closed, but he hammered on the door until a reluctant postmistress opened it. Howe then pushed his way in, handing her a telegram, 3,000 words long. She refused to accept it, saying it was Christmas Day and that they were having a party. Undeterred, Howe asked if she would accept a much shorter telegram. She agreed – but her jaw dropped as she read it. The message was addressed to the Postmaster General of the day – a Cabinet Minister – and it read, 'Postmistress here refuses to accept PA story of Aisgill Moor disaster. Please direct her to despatch message.'

The good lady was shocked and readily agreed to accept the full story. Naturally, the task took them several hours to complete. But by the end of it the two of them, who had made such an unpromising start together, were the best of friends – to such an extent that Howe was invited to stay on to join the family festivities. And the Postmaster General was none the wiser.

By now, Edmund Robbins's son Harry had toiled for ten years on the editorial staff and it appeared time for him to move over to the managerial side of the agency. His appointment, over the more experienced Percy A Shaw, to be deputy manager did not take place without muttering and criticism. Shaw even risked his job by writing a letter to the *Westminster Gazette* protesting, without mentioning names, about the unfair practice in some companies of giving an important executive appointment to a man whose chief qualification was that he happened to be the son of the boss.

It was a very rash thing to have done and there were people who were astonished that Shaw was not dismissed there and then. As it was, the letter seriously displeased both Edmund and Harry and, hardly surprisingly, neither of them ever forgot it. The whole affair created friction between Shaw, who eventually became company secretary, and Harry, as they worked closely together. However, they managed to get along in reasonable harmony for years, although there were occasions when Harry had to remind Shaw who was the senior of the two.

9 War on the Censor

ORLD WAR ONE provided the government with a major press problem. This was the first time Great Britain had clashed with a European power since the Crimean War, which had ended sixty years earlier. At that time there were comparatively few newspapers in Britain and, with communications in their infancy and the distance so great, there was absolutely no danger that papers would publish information from military headquarters that would be of strategic use to the enemy. By the time any 'sensitive' material was published in Britain it had long ceased to be sensitive at the front.

But things were different in 1914. The authorities were faced with the real problem of censorship. For, with the fast-growing development of communications, distances between the front line and Fleet Street no longer provided a 'natural' censor. The government had to think fast. Newspaper readers could now hear about events on the same day as they happened and that was a phenomenon that had not occurred to the authorities.

No one disputed the need for censorship to protect the military security of the Allies, least of all the newspapers themselves. So unaware were the authorities of the sometimes massive and incalculable dangers involved in the free and unchecked flow of information that there were some near-disasters. Meredith T Whittaker, of the *Scarborough Evening News*, reported to a Press Association board meeting that 'it occurred occasionally in the early part of the war that the enemy ascertained from articles published in the newspapers our positions at the Western Front, so that they were in a position to accurately fire upon them'.

This was an intolerable situation, as Fleet Street readily recognised, and it demonstrated a measure of incompetence and blundering among the government's military brasshats, putting at risk thousands of British lives. Needless to say, censorship was not so much tightened up as introduced. But, as in all these things, it became intolerably severe and degenerated ultimately into censorship with a vicelike grip.

A week before the war broke out, government officials gave every indication that their plans for censorship were well advanced. It may well have been a bluff, because, in the event, they rolled lamentably and painfully slowly into action. It was on 27 July 1914, a week before hostilities officially began, that Sir George Riddell, of the *News of the World*, representing the London newspapers, and Harry Robbins of the Press Association were summoned to the War Office to meet two top civil servants, Sir Graham Greene, from the Admiralty, and Sir Reginald Brade, of the War Office. Sir Graham, speaking in sonorous tones, told them, 'I have a very serious communication to make to you gentlemen. It is highly probable that in the next few days the country will be involved in a war with Germany. The government is very anxious to make arrangements with the press to secure that no news shall leak out as to the movement of battleships and troops.' Robbins later circulated to the newspapers an account of the government's position.

Not long after war had been formally declared, Riddell returned to the War Office, this time with Edmund Robbins, for further talks with Sir Reginald. They were not impressed with what they heard. All the indications were that the government really did not have a clue how to handle this very important aspect of fighting a war. And that, whatever happened, neither finesse nor reasonableness would be involved on the part of the authorities. Censorship, once the government realised what was at stake, would be crude and severe. Robbins summed up their feelings as they left. He turned to Riddell and said, 'You know, old chap, I think we are in for a devil of a mess.'

What must have been going through Robbins's mind was the ruthless censorship of the Boer War. It got so bad then that, in July 1900, Herbert de Reuter wrote to Robbins to tell him:

The censor's action is nothing short of a scandal. The censor, undoubtedly acting under orders, suppresses everything which is not favourable. The way in which the British public are being continuously misled and the honesty of the correspondents frustrated is a disgrace to the authorities.

The Press Association's inclination at that time was to make a firm and formal protest to the Minister of War. But Reuter, despite the furious tone of his letter, astonishingly advised caution. His view, regarded as timid, was that to make a protest would make the censorship even worse. But that would have been hard to achieve.

Two years later in 1902 there had been even more savage criticism of censorship, this time from the Press Association chairman, Thomas Bullock, of the *Staffordshire Sentinel*. Bullock raged: 'It was so drastic, that if anyone had told us three years ago that Englishmen would be subjected to such treatment we should have said it was impossible.'

What enraged newspapers more than anything was that the government used the South African war not only to suppress 'legitimate' information because it was not favourable, but also to interfere with news that had nothing to do with the conflict. For instance, Bullock gave an example of a telegram that came under the scrutiny of the censors and concerned the activities of Princess Radziwill, a treacherous woman who was trying, in vain, to connive a permanent place for herself in Cecil Rhodes's bachelor life. She was eventually imprisoned for forging promissory notes in his name. But, as fascinating as all this was, there seemed to be no rhyme or reason to incorporate these activities into censorship that was supposed to relate to the war.

These events, Bullock insisted, with every justification in the world, had not the slightest connection with the hostilities. And things even reached the ludicrous situation where telegrams from London to the correspondents in South Africa were stopped.

It was the memory of all this that Robbins had in mind when he passed his remark as he left the War Office on that fateful day in 1914. Already a Parliamentary Bill had been drafted designed to control news in emergency situations but, thanks to pressure from the Press Association among others, this Bill was not proceeded with. Instead a committee was set up, which was the forerunner of the D (Defence) Notice Committee, under which newspapers were asked not to refer to certain matters, or to consult the War Office before doing so. It was a system that was greeted with some suspicion by the news agencies in particular. Edmund Robbins became its secretary.

The 1914–18 war had been in progress for some eight months before the government was persuaded that it would be safe, let alone advisable, to allow a journalist anywhere near the fighting. Grudgingly, and in the face of much pressure from Fleet Street, it allowed a single war correspondent, representing the Press Association and Reuters, 'to tour the British lines' on the Western Front. Later, another was permitted to cover the attack on the Dardanelles from on board a British battle-ship.

The first few months of the war had proved difficult and irksome for the Press Association. It was a matter of picking up whatever crumbs of news were available, from anywhere except where it was actually happening. Largely, the Press Association and Reuters had to arrange for a regular service of telegrams from Paris, Vienna, Rome, Petrograd, Athens, Cape Town and various places in India and Japan.

In addition, they had to rely heavily on reports in foreign newspapers. It was inadequate, cumbersome, unreliable and above all very costly. For example, a description of the naval battle fought off the coast of Chile was telegraphed from Santiago at what was regarded as the exorbitant rate of 1s. 4d. (about 6½ pence) a word (the equivalent at the start of the twenty-first century of today's £3.22). Even this had to pass through the merciless censor, who cost the Press Association, and other agencies, enormous sums of money for cables that they would not allow to be used. After eighteen months, it was calculated that more than £1,000 worth of cables had been barred by the censor. That would be the equivalent of £46,000 today.

What made a bad situation even worse was the fact that the only eyewitness stories that became available were those written by so-called 'able but anonymous officers'. These reports were issued by the authorities and bylined simply 'Eye Witness'. Whatever else they may have had to commend them, these reports were certainly not objective. It was thus a long, lumbering journey that the government had to pursue before it belatedly dawned on it that there was a need, on behalf of the many thousands of people with sons at the front, for accurate and as far as possible undoctored news. It was not just a case of satisfying the Press Association, but of enabling the people on the home front to be as aware as possible of what was going on, as was their right. Slowly, very slowly, the situation changed, thanks in particular to Edmund Robbins, as well as Admiral Sir Douglas Brownrigg, the popular and understanding chief naval censor, who appreciated the situation far better than most of his colleagues.

* * *

By 1916, the Press Association, through its arrangements with Reuters, had war correspondents at British headquarters in France and the Canal Zone, in the Balkans and in East Africa. The men, appointed by the Press Association and Reuters, endured heavy physical strain and were often put in peril. Their importance is measured by the fact that, for most of the British press, they were the sole links with the actual fighting.

The Press Association also continued its arrangement with *The Times* and arranged to receive telegrams from the correspondents of the *Morning Post* and the *Daily Telegraph* in particular theatres of war. Two of the most distinguished of these PA correspondents were Herbert Russell, who was with the British Army, and Lester Lawrence, who was with the French. Both of them broke down after the end of the war because of what they had experienced. But their skills and importance were recognised: Russell received a knighthood, and Lawrence was honoured by the French government.

What these two men in particular had achieved was to correct the misconception in the military mind about reporters on the front line. There was never any question of rumour and invention being reported as fact. The integrity and courage of these early-day, pioneering war correspondents deeply impressed the military authorities.

The Press Association was also far more cautious and 'correct' in that it voluntarily submitted to the Official Press Bureau (the censor) any item of news it had acquired that related directly or indirectly to the war. In some of these cases, the item had already appeared in newspapers. But the agency wanted to be absolutely sure that none of its subscribers would fall foul of the censor by printing material, however tenuously it may have been related to the war, that had not been officially approved. And, although the agency sometimes felt it was being penalised for 'playing the game', it was in the long run a sensible and prudent policy to have adopted. It confirmed and consolidated the PA's already established reputation for fairness, straightforwardness and integrity.

Even so, there was an occasion when the Press Association fell foul of the censors. It happened when a Reuters message was put out without being submitted to the Press Bureau because the Press Association wrongly assumed that Reuters had already submitted it. The report claimed that an armistice had been signed. But, only seventeen minutes later, an urgent message was issued by the agency, instructing papers to 'kill' the story, which was false. The agency came close to facing 'drastic action' for having committed, in the view of the Director of Public Prosecutions, an offence under the Defence of the Realm Act, affectionately known as 'DORA'.

The Attorney General of the day was sorely tempted to take action but there were strong mitigating circumstances, which ultimately caused him to change his mind: the Press Association had taken immediate steps to stop the story and the armistice was in fact signed only 84 hours later. The story, therefore, as one relieved agency man said at the time, 'wasn't all that wrong'.

One cheeky band of young men were not concerned about censorship at all during this time, however – the Press Association messengers. Throughout World War One, they were supposed to collect the casualty lists from the War Office and bring them back to the Press Association by fast hansom cab. However, since the cab fare was one shilling (5 pence) and the return omnibus fare 2d. (1 penny), the messengers used to take bus to Charing Cross and then 'run like a blinking rabbit' to the War Office and back again to Charing Cross, thus making a considerable profit on the errand.

With the war years behind it, the Press Association looked forward to a bright future, extending the breadth and depth of its coverage. And by now the agency was becoming known as a vehicle to announce momentous events – and even inventions.

One bright afternoon in 1923, a man in his early thirties arrived at the reception desk in Byron House in Fleet Street and told the attendant he wanted to talk to a reporter about his work on transmitting moving pictures by wireless. His visit was treated with scepticism because some years earlier he had called in at the Press Association to announce that he had invented a new type of everlasting shoe polish, and socks that, he claimed, stayed warm in the winter and cool in the summer. So Mr Logie Baird was considered to be something of a crank and a nuisance by the news desk.

But, courteous as always, the news editor sent a reporter, Bill Fox, down to see him in the first-floor visiting room. Baird was wearing grey flannel trousers and a well-worn sports coat. The top of his head was a mass of fair, lion-mane hair in an impossible tangle. He looked like the Nutty Professor. Fox had gone down to see him with the clear instruction from the news editor ringing in his ears: 'Listen to him say all he wants to say, and then get rid of him! Whatever else you do, do not, repeat do not, make any promises!'

Baird told the young reporter, 'I have come to tell you that I have achieved television.' He seemed to deliberately avoid using the word 'invented'. Fox, at first hugely sceptical, warmed to the visitor. The reporter was himself interested in communications, having just built his own wireless set. They both found they had something in common.

'As I talked to him, I found out what he meant, that it was possible to convert any scene you saw into electrical impulses and to send them by wireless to a given receiver, which would reproduce them,' Fox recorded. But, when Fox did 'get rid' of Mr Baird and returned to the newsroom, he did not receive much interest from his colleagues. 'We know what you mean. You mean that amateurs have been experimenting with cinematograph film,' one said.

Fox was highly indignant at this response. It was precisely, he insisted, what he did not mean. And he told the subeditors as much in robust language. 'In fact, I was quite rude to them,' he recalled later. However, he failed to convince them and the Press Association finally put out a story about 'experimental cinematograph', which was exactly what it was not. Fox knew in his heart that the story was wrong – and kicked up a fierce row.

Even so, the toned-down story did have its effect. It was widely used in both the national and provincial press and attracted sufficient financial support to enable Baird to leave his home in Hastings and move to London, where he was to carry out some of his most celebrated and momentous experiments.

Baird remained impressed with the power of the Press Association to attract attention to his work, even though the story was wrongly watered down. After that, he was continuously on the telephone asking for Fox, to the irritation of the rest of the news desk. Fox finally left the agency in 1928 – at a time when Baird was working on colour. He went to work for the inventor, helping publicise and demonstrate television.

The original company, Baird Television Ltd, which Baird founded in 1928, went into receivership in 1939, and when he died at Bexhill in 1946, aged 58, Baird left just £7,370. Fox died in 1988, aged 98.

10 Men of Action

A S BRITAIN SWUNG THROUGH the Roaring Twenties, the Press Association had on its board men who were anxious that the agency should take on a modern look.

Among them was Colonel Sir Joseph Reed, of the *Newcastle Daily Chronicle*, who was a hard taskmaster and a man who sometimes skipped the niceties of protocol in his resolve to get things done and done quickly. Other significant figures were Arthur Pickering, of the *North Eastern Daily Gazette*, Middlesbrough, and the chairman of the Press Association in the mid-1920s, Sir Charles Hyde, of the *Birmingham Post*, whose contempt for the mass-circulation press and the Fleet Street newspaper barons was well known. These men plus, later on, Sir James Owen, of the *Exeter Express and Echo*, played a leading part in ensuring that the Press Association not only kept up with the times, but kept ahead as well. Reed, a tough, square-jawed industrialist, and Sir George Toulmin, who had a long personal experience of the Press Association, were responsible for pushing the agency into a new headquarters.

The New Bridge Street offices were regarded as inadequate, and the search was on for something more modern and more suitable, but every building they looked at was deficient in some way or other. For a while they contemplated erecting a new headquarters in New Bridge Street, but they calculated that it would cost £100,000 and they would be faced with the additional problem of where to go while the building was taking place.

There was much pontificating but very little happening. Both Reed and Toulmin, who were men of action, tired of the delay. Then Reed discovered that the leasehold of Byron House in Fleet Street, which had a frontage running from Bride Avenue to Salisbury Court, could be bought for £20,000. Without further ado, they snapped it up. Then they informed their colleagues on the management committee and told them they could have it at the same price. The Press Association directors took up the offer, and so the agency moved in.

Byron House was decorated with tiles inscribed 'Crede Byron'. It was not a beautiful building, with its fussy façade, bits of mock Gothic and cluster of chimneys, and it took more than a year before all the departments had moved across from the old premises, which bore the unflattering sobriquet of 'the Black Hole of Calcutta'.

The process, however, was more expensive than the Press Association had envisaged. Whatever survey was carried out on the premises could not have been particularly thorough, for the construction of the building had not been of the highest order, and much costly repair had to be undertaken. Even so, it was a judicious purchase and Reed and Toulmin, with justifiable immodesty, congratulated themselves on having executed a good stroke of business.

The following year, 1922, the Press Association bought the freehold of Byron House for £75,000 and also the leasehold and freehold of an adjoining building in Salisbury Court. And within twelve months the agency, which had operated for its first half-century in rented property, was now the owner of over £100,000 worth of real estate (with a mortgage of £55,000 – to be paid off in 1925).

One of the curiosities of the Press Association newsroom in London during these formative years was the creation of an area in Byron House, known scornfully as the 'hen roost'. It was a place set aside for women reporters who, the management feared, might be corrupted by the male-dominated atmosphere of the newsroom and 'the odd swear word', which might sully their shell-like ears. Mercifully, it was a short-lived experiment.

The story was later related by Betty Naylor, who joined the Press Association as the only woman reporter in 1923 and worked quite happily in the same room as the men, until, after a year or two, two other women reporters joined her. Then it was announced that women reporters were to be banished to a little room of their own on a lower floor.

'I hated the new arrangement,' Betty said. 'It was fitted with all the necessary equipment for making tea, even down to pretty cups and saucers, pot, kettle and tea towels. The official line was that we were supposed to remain there "out of harm's way".'

Fortunately, the hen roost did not last long. 'Gradually we edged our way back to the main room, finding it necessary to spend longer and longer there each time we climbed the stairs with copy or to consult reference books,' said Betty. 'After a few weeks, the "roost" became permanently deserted and no further attempts were made to ban women reporters from their rightful place.'

Equality was restored and honour satisfied. Later, the Press Association was to become the first Fleet Street organisation to employ women subeditors.

One of the first great achievements after the move to Byron House was its adaptation to the Press Association's particular requirements. This was largely the work of George Hodgson from South Shields, who had long been campaigning vociferously for a private wire system.

Reed was highly complimentary of Hodgson, whom he admired immensely. 'If he had not become a successful journalist, he would have made a first-class architect,' Reed said. But Hodgson's contribution to adapting Byron House was only a fraction of his work towards expanding the Press Association and its operations.

When Harry Robbins became manager in 1917, Hodgson, a former evening paper editor, was appointed assistant manager. Two years later he and Robbins became joint general managers. This was a partnership about which there was considerable foreboding. There were those who feared that it could end in tears with a clash of two very different personalities.

Happily, the prophets of doom were proved wrong. The partnership, in fact, worked extremely well. Robbins, short and thin, and Hodgson, large and stout, complemented each other perfectly, both in personal appearance and style. In later years, they were likened to Laurel and Hardy – in appearance only, not behaviour. Robbins, however, was always careful to ensure that his seniority was recognised, something Hodgson did not resent in the slightest.

During this important period for the Press Association, Hodgson achieved his dream: the creation of a private wire system, worked out with the help of a technical 'genius' called Jock Newlands, who was the first chief of the agency's telegraph department.

Once the initial decision had been taken, years of hard and often frustrating work followed. When it was finally completed, there were 3,000 miles of wire, radiating from Byron House, linking the Press Association with practically every morning and evening paper in the land. It was a triumph for Hodgson, and

Robbins was unstinting in his praise, never once seeking to take any part of the credit for himself.

Hodgson's journalistic background, his drive and enthusiasm ensured that the Press Association was well ahead of the field. He was one of the pioneers without whose persistence, skill and vision the agency could well have lagged behind its would-be rivals. This was the period when the Press Association started to throb with new life and vigour. The committee of management had been increased from five to seven and the agency's reporters were at the forefront of journalism.

At a murder trial at Carmarthen Assizes, two of them accomplished the considerable feat of sending by telephone in one day no fewer than 18,000 words – about eighteen columns of broadsheet newspaper text. They dictated straight from their shorthand notes to London and had completed their task minutes after the court rose for the day. These were the days when newspapers wanted virtually verbatim reports of sensational trials and important political speeches.

It was around this time that the Press Association pulled off one of its biggest scoops – concerning the division in the Dail Eireann over the Irish Treaty. The vote, in January 1922, was crucial because it meant the Dail would either accept or reject the Treaty, which the Republican Michael Collins had signed in London. Acceptance of the Treaty would make Ireland a Free State and end – it was confidently hoped – the bigger conflict between Great Britain and the Irish Republicans.

Richard Eccleston was the agency's man in Dublin and the competition he faced from rivals over the coverage of this event was awesome. In addition to more than 400 journalists from all corners of the globe, there were specialist writers from the London newspapers as well as staff from the other British news agencies. His first problem was that many of his rivals had been dispensing money like confetti, buying up or tying up virtually all the known means of communication from Dublin to the outside world. For example, the private wires to London of the three Dublin daily newspapers were all barred to Eccleston and it was to be another year before the Press Association's own private wire system was extended to them. Therefore, if Eccleston was to rely on the existing, orthodox telephone or telegraph networks to London, he would automatically be beaten by his competitors.

His bold solution was to use the British government's private line between Dublin Castle and the Irish Office in London. Basil

Clarke, who was resident at the castle at the time, acting for the Irish Office as liaison officer with the press, was not at all sympathetic to the request. But he finally succumbed to the blandishments of Eccleston's own special brand of sweet talking. One hurdle was cleared – but there were more formidable ones ahead.

Clarke then had to persuade the men from the ministry in London that the government required to hear the news as quickly as possible, and what better and quicker way could there be than by relying on the Press Association to do it for them? Even though there was some head-shaking by the silver beards in Whitehall, the move was approved. Eccleston was then left to arrange the other vital links in the chain – such as having a man inside the Chamber of the Dail, waiting to hear the result of the division. The plan was that he would rush it to Eccleston, who had acquired a telephone inside the Dail. Eccleston would then pass on the news to another colleague, standing by at Dublin Castle with the telephone link to the Irish Office in London – where yet another Press Association man would be holding a line open to the newsroom in Fleet Street. Every link in the chain had to function properly.

At the appointed hour, everything was in place. But the debate dragged on and it was a relatively late hour when Michael Collins demanded an end to the talking. The house was prepared for the most crucial division in its history. Eccleston made his way to the telephone he had 'requisitioned' and thankfully found no difficulty in making contact with his colleague at Dublin Castle. Then the waiting game began.

The two of them had to start talking, and continue talking, about anything – their wives, football, the weather – as they waited for the result to come through. They feared that if they fell into silence the operator would simply assume that the call was over and cut them off. The minutes ticked by as Eccleston talked on, but strained his ears for the sound of footsteps, which would indicate that the news was on the way. At one point, the Irish girl at the telephone exchange interrupted the conversation to ask, 'Haven't you finished on this line yet?'

'Not quite,' said Eccleston, as calmly as he could. 'Just give me time to talk about all my troubles.'

The girl laughed and replied, 'Sure, you men are worse than any women. You just can't stop talking.' To their relief she left them alone to carry on with their bogus chitchat.

Still the minutes ticked by and there were no footsteps along the corridor outside. Then came the sound of someone leaping down the stairs from the chamber at about three at a time. The puffing man arrived at the phone booth and gasped out the result to Eccleston, who spun round to pass the news on, only to hear the dulcet tones of the Irish telephone girl piping in.

'You'll have to finish with this line now,' she said, in a strong, authoritative voice.

'Just one more second,' a frantic Eccleston pleaded. The girl reluctantly agreed and Eccleston boomed down the line, 'Treaty accepted!' before banging down the phone.

And so, within three minutes of the announcement inside the Dail, the result of the division was being flashed around the world by the Press Association and Reuters. Eccleston and his merry band, stretching across the Irish Sea, had beaten the pants off their 400 competitors.

Soon after these events, a reporter, Donald Spendlove, was the first member of 'the general public' to speak by telephone from London to New York. Spendlove, speaking from an experimental telephone exchange in Queen Victoria Street, not far from the Press Association office, chatted over a crackly line with the *New York Herald*. Even so, despite the atmospherics, he reported that 'the hearing was excellent'.

Another 'first' was achieved by another reporter, Charles Cutler, who was the first pressman ever to receive an instruction from his office by wireless telephone while in a plane. He was flying over Epsom, Surrey, viewing a police manhunt below, when the Press Association news desk ordered him to pursue another story. The news editor had telephoned Croydon aerodrome, where the message was relayed over the link to the plane.

Meanwhile, copytaking at this time was a laborious affair. Subeditors took a shorthand note from the reporters and re-dictated it to typists who cut waxes for subsequent duplication. These copies were then sent to the Dispatch Department and parcelled up for transit to the newspapers by train.

Five years after his son Harry was appointed Press Association manager, Edmund Robbins died. And in March 1926 Hodgson died too, suddenly in early middle age after a brief illness. His death was a blow. He and the young Robbins had yet more plans to improve and brighten the editorial department.

On his death, an urgent meeting of the management committee was called, at which attendance was confined to directors,
which meant, to his dismay, that even Harry Robbins was
excluded. It was at this crucial meeting that radical decisions
were taken, including the appointment of an editor-in-chief.
This had the effect of removing from the general manager the
ultimate control of the editorial department, which had been the
responsibility of that office from the first day of operations in
1870. Even though the general manager still required to be
consulted about matters affecting staff or involving new spending, it was a considerable blow to Robbins, who saw it as a
demotion. But, as future years were to prove, this was a right
decision and one that laid the foundations for the development
of the Press Association for the rest of the century and beyond.

11 The Editors and Others

THE FIRST EDITOR-IN-CHIEF of the Press Association was Arthur L Cranfield, who joined in November 1926 and resigned after only thirteen months. But he was a man who, despite the relative brevity of his tenure of office, did make a long-lasting impact, which was both distinctive and powerful.

Cranfield, known as 'Cran' to the rest of Fleet Street, had behind him a solid and successful career, first in provincial journalism in Warwick, Sheffield and Birmingham, and then in London. During the four years before he joined the Press Association, he was chief subeditor of the *London Evening News*. He was a bustling man of great energy and enthusiasm, qualities that infected the staff. And he effectively took the agency's editorial services by the scruff of the neck and revolutionised them. The old, heavily stylised Press Association reporting was abandoned and reporters, to their great glee, were instructed not so much to be formal recorders of events but to ensure that the most important and arresting facts were at the top of their stories.

This meant that newspapers that were on the verge of going to press could manage to get at least the guts of a story in their editions at the last minute, or even a paragraph in the stop press. The old-style Press Association reporting did not lend itself to such tough deadlines. Cranfield, who had unprece-dented editorial powers, strictly adhered to the immovable rules of the agency – speed, accuracy, impartiality – but he inter-preted them in a wholly contemporary way. Reporters were required to introduce more background details to stories and embellish them with brief biographical sketches of the people to whom these stories related. This was the forerunner to the 'profiles' of today's journalism. Comparable events were in-cluded and far more descriptive material was not only allowed but encouraged.

Under Cranfield's stewardship, the agency's stories needed far less work on them by subeditors on the newspapers than before.

He had recruited new young men who were attuned, by outlook and temperament, to the demands of modern journalism. In particular, he hired men from provincial papers who knew precisely what the customers wanted from the Press Association and – just as important – when. Cranfield also introduced 'snaps' and 'rushes' – a quick sentence rushed out containing the salient fact and nothing else, a few moments ahead of the full version of the story. Later the 'flash' was introduced, to be used only on hugely momentous items such as the declaration of war, the death of royalty or the resignation of a prime minister.

Summaries of the contents of weighty government documents – written in an attractive, readable style – were prepared and issued in advance, bearing the date and time the material could be published. This and many other Cranfield innovations were of immense advantage to the newspapers, and it was the dawning of a new respect for the agency. In turn the reporters and subeditors felt a new pride in their work and some of the best young journalistic talent was being attracted to the Press Association's ranks.

Cranfield was like a blast of fresh air on the editorial floor. But a man with such vitality, such energy and such a bustling approach to the job was bound to make enemies. Given the history of the Press Association up to that point, Harry Robbins might well have been expected to get this post and the decision to appoint Cranfield was obviously a serious blow to his status. His disappointment was hardly surprising, as the general manager of the agency had been in ultimate control of the editorial department since its birth in 1870. But Cranfield's work brought such quick results that, within six months of his arrival, the consultative board recorded its view that there had been 'a very considerable improvement in the news services'.

Robbins could hardly be expected to join in the general excitement and eventually the redefinition of the general manager's responsibilities and those of the other executives, including the editor-in-chief, led to problems and jealousies. In the end, Cranfield left. The Press Association directors put it on record that they were sorry he had left them after such a short stay, and they reiterated the view that the decision to employ him in this new and powerful capacity had been a wise one.

Arthur Cranfield's new way of working at the agency had led to calls for more research material. Up until now, the editorial staff of the Press Association had to rely largely on *Whitaker's*

Almanac, Who's Who, Dods Parliamentary Companion and a review copy of *Debrett's Peerage* for their researches. But they also had another source of reference – an individual known as 'Prosser' Chanter, who had a phenomenal memory for all sorts of facts, trivial and momentous. Chanter was a walking encyclopedia, in constant demand by reporters working on backgrounds to stories.

There was also another useful Press Association staffer known as 'Baron' Stembridge, who reputedly knew more about the peerage than any other living person. Debrett to him was a beloved friend. Stembridge could quote vast passages of Debrett, verbatim. He was also smartly attired, as befitted a man with such an obsession. He always had a copy of Debrett within reach and was never happier than when he was explaining to a reporter the mysteries and complexities of the British aristocracy system. But, as the Press Association grew, and became even more diverse, reporters needed more than Chanter and Stembridge for their backgrounds.

And so the Press Association library was formed in 1928. The first librarian was Tom Smith with Ben Howell as his deputy. A third man, Harry Williams, was also brought in. They started diligently to build up a cuttings library with just one wooden cabinet at their disposal. But that was soon bursting at the seams and was replaced with steel cabinets. Within a few years there were more than a million cuttings filed away. The team started in two small cubicles used by the newsroom and reporting staffs as their 'quiet rooms'. Soon, however, this new department had outgrown its accommodation. More and more space was required and gradually it infiltrated the stores area and then the switchboard operators had to move as the library's tentacles spread. Today more than 13 million cuttings are filed away, plus an ever-expanding electronic 'store' of information.

In spite of all the enthusiasm that accompanied the move into Byron House soon after World War One, it soon became apparent that the building was not up to the job. Various inadequacies were evident. The messengers began to notice cracks in the walls of their room and at first began to put sticky tape over them. But before long, as the fissures grew bigger, it was clear that the old building was crumbling. It was then discovered that the foundations had to be strengthened at a very heavy cost. It seemed as though the Press Association had hardly moved in before there was talk of moving out. More

The siege in Sidney Street, 1911

A camel mows the lawn, 1911

Above Serious faces as lunch-time crowds reflect on the news of the death of King George VI in Ludgate Circus, 1952

Left Fleet Street and the Strand blacked out – the first picture the PA transmitted, 1945

Above The funeral of Sir Winston Churchill, 1965

Top left John Haigh, charged with the murder of 69-year-old widow Olivia Durand-Deacon, arriving at Horsham Magistrates Court, 1949. Haigh was known as the 'acid bath murderer' after his chosen method of disposing of his victims' bodies

Left England's and Preston North End's Tom Finney in a shower of spray at Stamford Bridge, London, 1956

Above The Aberfan disaster, 1966

Below Demonstrators in Grosvenor Square during the march on the American Embassy in 1968 following the 'Solidarity with Vietnam' rally

Lord George Brown in the gutter, March 1976

Defence Secretary, Fred Mulley, asleep next to the Queen at an RAF fly-past, 1978

ambitious proposals were being bandied about to put up an edifice worthy to be the home not only of the agency, the official representatives of the provincial press in London, but of Reuters, with its 'imperial and international importance and its world connections and ramifications'. They were grand words indeed, but they also demonstrated that the Press Association had set its sights too low in choosing Byron House, which, apart from other shortcomings, was structurally imperfect and presented a threat of more and more expense in the future – money that could be far more usefully spent elsewhere.

The man chosen to succeed Cranfield was Henry Martin, a stern disciplinarian who took an aggressive pride in the Press Association and who demonstrated that he was not afraid to take on even prime ministers, should the occasion arise. Martin was only 38 when he became editor-in-chief, but he already had more than twenty years in journalism behind him, most of them in Fleet Street, including eleven years with the old London News Agency. But his reputation as a hard taskmaster was tempered by a kindly disposition, as one reporter, who suffered under his lash, recorded. Geoffrey Morley, in his early days at the Press Association, committed 'a frightful bloomer' and got the full treatment from Martin. 'It was pretty terrifying while it lasted and naturally I thought it was the end of the world,' Morley admitted.

But Martin suddenly decided that it was time to restore the reporter's shattered morale, and he recounted a serious mistake he had made as a young man. Martin had apparently been sent to cover a Lloyd George speech and put over a sentence that included the phrase 'knighthoods for fortunes', which, given the Welsh wizard's unorthodox approach to the honours system, seemed a likely enough expression. But Martin had seriously misheard him. What Lloyd George had actually said was 'ninepence for fourpence' – a joke about not getting value for money. A furious row followed and Martin had been carpeted. Morley said, 'This cheered me no end. It was a remarkably kind action, to confess such a thing to a young reporter. I never forgot it. Henry Martin was a stickler for perfection and gave an impression of ruthlessness in its pursuit, but he was also a very sensitive human being with a very warm heart.'

Right from the beginning of his tenure of office, Martin impressed upon all government departments that they should use the agency before any other organisation as their outlet for news. And he made sure that provincial editors up and down the country knew him personally. He called himself an 'apostle' of the provincial press, and throughout his career he kept a watchful eye on contemporary developments in news gathering and handling, often innovating them himself and always keeping abreast of the game or ahead of it. Sometimes, however, he found himself on a collision course with Fleet Street with his occasional moralist utterances about journalism. For he was an antiquarian, who was passionate about music and literature, plus having a more than passing interest in philosophy and religion.

Martin's own personal and sometimes stuffy creed got an unexpected public airing when he, along with the chairman and general manager, submitted written evidence for the 1947 Royal Commission to answer oral questions. When Martin was asked whether there was any real clash between his own personal sense of what was important and that of individual newspaper editors, he replied, 'Two or three years ago, the Archbishop of York sent me a speech he was to make on Saturday afternoon on sex and the abuse of sex by young people, and drawing on the Christian moral. I decided that I could not issue fewer than eight hundred words of that speech. I issued it all over the country, and should say that every evening newspaper that Saturday afternoon published those eight hundred words as we sent it, so that anyone of intelligence and of a religious turn of mind could see exactly what the Archbishop of York was trying to inculcate . . . the Christian idea of sex and marriage.

'The London newspapers cut that considerably and one Sunday newspaper just picked out the reference to sex, without printing anything of the moral attached to it, and that, I think, may be typical of the difference between the London newspapers and the provincial ones.'

But Martin, who appeared to be setting foot on dangerous ground by criticising a section of the Press Association's own clientele, did not stop there. He also told the Commission, 'I am afraid I have refused to modify my ideas. I have a sense of responsibility (and I think it is a very strong stewardship) towards the reading public, and whatever newspapers may or may not publish, particularly in London, does not influence me in the least.

'I know that for instance, in the last two or three years, there has been a greater stream of co-ordinated religious news passed through the Press Association than ever before and it is welcomed by the bulk of the provincial newspapers, who are closely in touch with the public.' Then Martin really started to trail his coat: 'I would also say that, on cultural matters generally, the Press Association is years ahead of the newspapers ... excepting perhaps *The Times* and the *Manchester Guardian*. I send out news on archaeology, on music and on a range of subjects in which I happen to be interested, and because I am interested in them I think there must be a large section of the population interested in them.' To cap it all, Martin controversially compared the provincial editor with the Fleet Street editor. He said that the provincial editor was in much closer touch with his readers, but in London 'there is a remoteness between the editor and his reader'.

Needless to say, his words did not pass unchallenged. Arthur Christiansen, the legendary editor of the *Daily Express*, took up the cudgels with letters of protest to both the chairman of the Press Association and the chairman of the Royal Commission. Christian railed against 'Mr Martin's outrageous comments on the standards of education and cultural values among journalists on the *Daily Express*'. The *Express*, he said, far from employing reporters and subeditors with 'practically no cultural standards', took the utmost care to see that its employees were not only thoroughly trained in the craft of journalism but were men of wide culture and learning. Martin's trenchant comments and the no less robust response from Christiansen clearly embarrassed the Press Association board. Eventually, after much scratching of heads and drafting and redrafting, a reply of sorts was sent to Christiansen. It read as though it had been painfully penned.

Under the signature of Walter Hawkins, of the *Bristol Evening Post*, who was chairman of the Press Association at this time, it said:

> The Board fully accepts responsibility for the factual evidence given to the Royal Commission on the press about the Association's services and organisation, but the Association does not deal in opinions, and it was clear from the phrasing of some of the questions put to Mr Henry Martin by the members of the Royal Commission that it was his personal opinion which was sought, which he gave, and to which you have taken exception.
>
> While you may not agree with the opinions he expressed, your letter shows that you would be among the first to defend his right freely to speak his views ...

Martin's enthusiasm over causes he embraced sometimes betrayed itself on the agency wire. In the early 1930s his mind was deeply engaged by the Oxford Movement. Over several months, a dispassionate observer of the Press Association output might have noticed excessive attention being paid to the organisation. But, although such things caused the odd eyebrow to be raised from time to time, the PA board recognised the value of the man. For he had been in the post just a few years when the board decided to 'grapple him to our souls with hooks of steel' – by offering him a long-term contract. Martin was never remote from his job as editor-in-chief, in spite of his many outside interests.

Charles Jervis, a compact youthful-looking white-haired man, became editor-in-chief of the Press Association in 1954. He summed up his attitude to the PA in his speech when he retired eleven years later. 'My one object,' he said, 'was to humanise the organisation, to recognise that every man is a human being with feelings – and I have done all I could to make a man feel he is something worth while.'

But Jervis was a man who was said to enjoy his weekends and was not often seen on the premises after normal office hours, an attitude that does not sit happily with the PA's ceaseless operation, although during World War Two he was credited with spending most of his waking hours – and some more – on the PA premises.

Jervis was well based in provincial journalism before he joined the Press Association in 1937. He had moved from the *Liverpool Express* to the *Westmorland Gazette* and then to the *Croydon Times* in his journey to Fleet Street.

He had a very early association with Arthur Christiansen, the *Daily Express* editor with whom Henry Martin had seriously clashed. In an article in the *World's Press News* in September 1963, Christiansen recalled his early memories of Southport:

Every year I had to cover its famous flower show for the *Liverpool Evening Express*. In my last year on the paper, 1924, I took along a young messenger named Jervis to telephone my copy. He told me he had applied for a reporter's job in the Lake District but hadn't got the rail fare for the crucial personal interview. I loaned it to him and he got the job.

Jervis's motto was little different from those of the men who preceded and succeeded him as editor-in-chief. He was concerned with collecting facts, checking facts, but not speculating on the facts.

He was editor at a time when much of Fleet Street was under attack for alleged intrusion in a variety of fields. But Jervis took the view that the PA did not have to follow every Fleet Street method in pursuit of a story.

Charles Jervis was succeeded in 1965 by John ('Jack') Williamson, another man with a Lancashire background with long service on the PA. His period in the editor's chair was not of the most spectacular – but this was not necessarily his fault. He was appointed managing editor rather than editor-in-chief and he seemed to fall under the sway of Ernest Harvey, who was assistant general manager and company secretary.

Harvey, an accountant, 'interfered' in the editorial affairs of the PA in a way that depressed many of the working journalists. The absence of the words 'in chief' from Williamson's title made it that much easier for Harvey to dominate the scene on the editorial floor on election nights and on other momentous occasions.

Williamson entered journalism in his native Lancashire before moving to a London suburban paper, the *East Ham Echo*. He joined the PA in 1938, just a year after Jervis.

During the war, his unrivalled shorthand note stood him in good stead when he was one of the team in the Judge Advocate General's Department, entrusted with the task of taking verbatim notes of court-martial cases and war-crimes trials.

On his return to 85 Fleet Street after the war he eventually became deputy chief subeditor with special responsibilities for the control of the news service to provincial evening papers. And after the death of Donald Spendlove, Williamson succeeded him as chief news editor, a post he held until his appointment, in October 1965, as managing editor.

He was an easy-mannered, unpretentious man who seemed to lack the drive and energy that one associates with chief news editors. But he was fascinated by the history of PA and held in awe the men from the Victorian era who helped to found it.

His own attitude towards the PA was characterised by the view he took of the reporting of the notorious Moors Murders case in 1966. Much of the evidence in that case was sadistic and horrifying and Williamson's view was that the PA should not make a judgment on what to issue and what to leave out.

He said, 'It is not our job to act as censors. We had to send it all out because it is our job to provide a service for the papers and it is for them to decide what they want to use of it.' But, oddly, he qualified that by adding, 'Of course, we would not publish anything obscene.'

Williamson was replaced by David Chipp, and the title editor-in-chief was reinstated. He was to sharpen up the agency in a way none of his predecessors had done before. What had become looked on as an organisation merely to record history was transformed into a news-gathering centre that wrote bright, readable, hard-hitting stories – never straying from the code of strict accuracy, fairness, speed of delivery and nonalignment to any cause.

Chipp had the distinction of editing two major news agencies – both Reuters and the Press Association – but the description he was most proud of was the occupation he entered in his passport: 'Reporter'. He was Reuters' first resident correspondent in Peking after the Communist takeover and became the editor of Reuters in London in 1968. A year later he was recruited by Lord Barnetson, then a director of both agencies, as editor-in-chief of the Press Association, a post he held until his retirement in 1986.

Chipp was approached by Lord Barnetson on the stairs at 85 Fleet Street and offered the job. It was as simple as that. His appointment followed a period of uncertain leadership in the Press Association. There was, at that time, an atmosphere of depression which had spread to the journalists.

Jack Williamson, whom he succeeded, had been regarded as being subservient to the assistant general manager, Ernest Harvey, an accountant with an extremely arrogant and egocentric attitude. Now Chipp's arrival brought about a sudden and welcome change in the atmosphere. His enthusiasm for the job and his warm – but not uncritical – manner soon endeared him to the staff. He summed up his philosophy at his first Press Association editorial conference. 'Journalism should be fun and, if we do not find it so, we might as well be bank clerks,' he said. In the job he was extrovert, exuberant, gregarious and occasionally explosive. And, although he was unmarried, he always maintained that families came first and had a warm understanding of personal problems.

One of Chipp's first acts was to introduce bylines for the Press Association's journalists, whose forerunners had toiled away for a hundred years filling the newspapers without any public recognition for their work. When Chipp joined the Press Association from Reuters on 1 March 1969, the company was in a depressed state. What was desperately needed was someone who could drive through change and revitalise an organisation considered to be rather dull and 'establishment'. One of the first things he did was to change the times of the editorial conferences, which, he announced, were at 'absolutely the wrong parts of the day' for evening papers. He then indulged in what he called 'shameless self-advertisements' – ensuring that he got the Press Association's name, and his, noticed by making statements and stands on various issues. In particular, he pitched into a London Guildhall event on Europe. Reporters had been told that they would not be invited to the dinner but could come in from the cellars afterwards to report the speeches. Chipp put out a statement saying that the Press Association would not be covering the evening after being treated that way, particularly as some guests would be writing on the issues. The boycott was joined by Associated Press, the *Daily Telegraph*, the *Sun* and the *Daily Mail*. It was a sharp reminder to the 'Guildhall set' that Fleet Street did not intend being treated like second-class citizens.

When he arrived at the agency, Chipp found a great deal of deadwood among the journalistic staff. He could easily have got rid of half of them without any harm to the Press Association. But in those days such a move was not a practical proposition, nor was there the option of early retirement. His task, therefore, was to move people who were square pegs in round holes to other jobs and to try to encourage other people to go. It was not an easy task. Added to this was formidable opposition from the unions of the day – the National Union of Journalists, the National Society of Print Operatives and Associates and the National Graphical Association.

Chipp had inherited a large staff. And in some areas, such as Parliament, the Law Courts, racing and special reporting, the subscribers demanded it, even though it meant the agency suffered a loss. Sport, at that time, employed some of the best and most highly regarded journalists in Britain. But sometimes their ideas were not up to date. For example, the sports editor of the day did not think it valid to take results from radio or television. And these were also the days when anything south of Dover was regarded as off-limits for the Press Association and strictly Reuters territory. Although the PA had often provided cricket correspondents to Reuters for overseas tours and occasionally athletic reporters for such events as the Olympic Games, it was becoming clear that Reuters no longer had the staff or the policy to meet the Press Association's requirements for the British media at overseas sports events.

Chipp persuaded the general manager and the board that the agency must cover many overseas events themselves, marking the beginning of a change in the whole PA–Reuters relationship. This culminated in the appointment of a correspondent in Brussels in 1978. Duncan Jeffery became the first overseas staff correspondent ever appointed by the Press Association. Similarly, some four years later, Chipp had no hesitation in insisting that a PA man sail with the Falklands task force, something that displeased Reuters considerably – largely because Reuters had quite wrongly, at first, been denied accreditation. But there was, of course, a history, that the Press Association had provided war correspondents for a PA–Reuters service during World War One.

During the early years of Chipp's editorship, a Luddite atmosphere prevented the production of a service that was tailored to the needs of the subscribers. The nationals, the mornings and a couple of the larger evening papers wanted 'all that you can throw at us'. However, the evening papers generally wanted much less, and the smaller of them required a highly selective service. But the cost of separating such services, in money and manpower, was prohibitive. And the unions would not allow anything to happen without more cash for their members. Chipp became a much-quoted spokesman and champion of the freedom to report at this time. He made news himself in 1979, when the agency's print union telegraphists, who transmitted the Press Association's output, supported a strike by regional journalists, decreeing they would handle copy only if it had been personally edited by Chipp himself. So, for nearly seven arduous weeks, Chipp sat at a desk in the centre of the editorial floor, subediting the entire 24-hour PA service: general news, parliamentary, sport, racing information, financial news, stock prices and picture captions. He worked seven days a week, snatching just a few hours' sleep each night at his flat just off Fleet Street. He was responsible for ensuring that regional morning and evening papers were able to run credible editions during this long-running and acrimonious dispute.

Chipp was always fiercely loyal to his staff. Once, the left-wing firebrand Labour MP Dennis Skinner publicly accused the Press Association of right-wing bias and of seeking to undermine the Labour government and trade unions. Skinner had collared a PA reporter on the pavement outside Labour's headquarters in Walworth Road, southeast London, after a meeting of the party's ruling national executive. He said he 'wanted to go on the record' with his views about the Press Association.

'It is a right-wing organ within the right-wing media in Britain,' he thundered. 'It tends to gather facts constantly against workers and trade unionists who are fighting to improve their low pay and conditions. It rarely manages to gain the views of the management who, in all industrial disputes, are at least half the cause of the trouble and in my estimation 80 or 90 per cent the cause of the trouble. And on questions relating to Labour governments the Press Association goes out of its way to undermine them and the trade union movement generally, and yet there is little or nothing about the operation of the Tory government.'

Chipp issued the attack as a story, adding his own telling comment at the bottom: 'We have issued this drivel from Skinner because otherwise he would accuse us of censorship. His accusation is an insult to every journalist working for the Press Association.' This was not the only brush with Skinner. In January 1977 Skinner told Chipp at a meeting in the lobby of the House of Commons that the whole Press Association service was unbalanced 'as of course it must be bearing in mind the background from which you come' – a remark that Geelong- and Cambridge-educated Chipp dismissed with contempt.

Chipp also had trouble with another Labour MP, Joe Ashton, who wrote a letter to the *Miner* (the journal of the National Union of Mineworkers, with whom the Press Association had excellent relations) accusing the agency of sending out 'a garbled, distorted item so as to deliberately create trouble in my constituency'. Chipp, along with senior management personnel from the PA, had already, some weeks earlier, seen Ashton to dispose of a previous allegation of distortion and other reporting matters. But this letter was another matter altogether.

Lawyers were consulted and agreed with Chipp that suggestions that the Press Association had published a story with the intention of creating trouble for Ashton were highly damaging.

The editor of *The Miner* agreed with the PA that the accusation was without the slightest foundation. He was alarmed at what he had published and saw Ashton. Ashton in turn consulted a lawyer MP to draft a retraction, which subsequently appeared in the publication. But amid all that unpleasantness there was something for Chipp to smile about. He received a letter from Anne Armstrong, the outgoing United States Ambassador, which in his own words gave him 'more pleasure' than any other he had received. She wrote:

> On the eve of my departure from Great Britain, I wanted to tell you how impressed I have been by the efficiency and professionalism of the Press Association. It has certainly made my work in this country go smoothly, and I would like to express the appreciation of my colleagues for the first-class performance of your organisation.

Right from the start of his 'reign', Chipp built up an editorial team that was close to him professionally and personally. He virtually went to war with the Ministry of Defence over the number of journalists they would allow to sail with the task force to the Falklands after the Argentine invasion. It was a war in which he triumphed, even before the task force majestically set sail on its historic and victorious mission. And it was a war that he continued to wage on the Ministry of Defence throughout the conflict and after it as well. As a result he acquired the affectionate title 'Admiral Chipp'.

Chipp was much in demand as a speaker and writer on media affairs. And he delighted in ruffling feathers. He harboured a deep dislike for the Westminster lobby system, which he described as 'a gift for lazy journalists'. Even so, the Press Association's political reporters continued to operate the system, despite his detestation of it. Before his arrival, the agency was rarely the recipient of leaked documents from government or other sources. But the way Chipp changed its image led to the agency's receiving several major leaks, including Cabinet papers and defence documents. After the most careful consideration, Chipp approved the stories that emanated from these leaks and, inevitably, faced severe criticism for doing so. But he responded with his usual equanimity, insisting: 'The Press Association has done something for real communication.'

In 1980, Chipp resigned from the D-notice committee, describing it as 'irrelevant' to modern needs and practices. His resignation came at a time when it was just beginning a review of the system after the Commons Defence Committee had said it was failing to fulfil the role for which it was created. Chipp's response was, 'As I think it should be totally abolished, it would be quite wrong for me to remain as a member and take part in the revision.' The D-notice committee, he felt, was a relic of the time when Fleet Street had a very cosy relationship with Whitehall.

He told a Commonwealth Press Union conference in Melbourne in 1981, 'I don't think I am suffering from the general paranoia of a reporter in thinking that restraint on our freedom to report is the great danger we as journalists face worldwide, and certainly in Britain. The attack is insidious and slow and is often justified by what are superficially very worthy motives. Our vigilance must be continuous, our suspicion constant and our opposition to incursions resolute.'

But it was difficult to beat the system. A striking example of this has been the gradual but unmistakable erosion in the freedom to report what happens in the courts of law. There are now serious restraints on reporting of rape cases, divorce proceedings and of course preliminary hearings of criminal cases in magistrates' courts, all of which rely on public money to function. Yet it is open for any member of the population to go along to these courts and to hear – and discuss outside – events that are not allowed to be printed in the newspapers or broadcast on radio or television.

One of the low moments of Chipp's leadership came in June 1977, when a strike by four unions over payment for Jubilee Day working led to the first extended break in service in the agency's history. There was a limited hand service to London offices, but no wire service for 24 hours. At the time he said, 'I am humiliated and depressed, and the damage is incalculable.'

Chipp was born in London's Kew Gardens, where his father was assistant director. He went to school at Geelong in Australia and returned to England by cargo ship to join the Middlesex Regiment in the closing stages of the war. He joined Reuters as a graduate entrant, after reading history at King's College, Cambridge. It was the east coast floods in 1952 that gave Chipp, who was then subbing on Reuters' sports desk, his first really big break. He was visiting friends in Cambridge when the story broke and rang his office to say, 'I'm here!' He speedily drove to the scene, Hunstanton, on the Norfolk coast, and his story of

Americans caught up in the disaster was accorded huge play in the US newspapers. This delighted his chiefs and he was promised the first overseas vacancy that arose. The following year, he was posted to Asia and he opened the first Reuters bureau in Rangoon since before the war.

Chipp covered the fighting in Burma and Indo-China. Then, in 1956, he became the first resident Reuters correspondent in Peking after the Communist takeover. He got an amazing and exclusive interview with the last Emperor of China, who was then in prison and had not been heard of since before the war. Chipp formed an enduring friendship with Chou En Lai, Mao's second-in-command. He also struck up friendships with dissident Chinese academics who disappeared during the Gang of Four purges and who emerged many years later to contact him.

But Chipp also wrongly felt guilty for having been part of the team that appointed Anthony Grey as the Reuters correspondent in Peking. It was Grey who was held incommunicado under house arrest by the Chinese authorities for two years in the late 1960s.

Colin Webb took over the editorship of the PA in 1986 at the age of 46. He had a varied and successful journalistic background, which included a brief spell, of about eighteen months, as a general reporter on the PA in the 1960s.

He had trained on the *Evening News* in Portsmouth and then, after his reporting spell at the PA, he joined *The Times* as part of their news team of 'firefighters', dashing off at a moment's notice to wherever in the world a big story was breaking.

Webb became news editor of *The Times* and then for eight years edited the *Cambridge Evening News*. The late Charlie Douglas-Home, who was editor of *The Times*, rang him 'out of the blue' and said he was looking for a deputy. Would Mr Webb oblige? Well, he did, and remained there as one of the most influential editorial figures on *The Times* until the PA offer came along.

When he arrived he was met with not so much a culture shock as a technology shock. As has been explained elsewhere, partly through trade union intransigence and the management's apparent unwillingness to impose its will on them, the PA was not, at that time, exactly in the forefront of electronic achievement. He said that after his twenty-plus years' absence from the PA he found there 'the last dregs of the old technology'.

He went on: 'We didn't even have a fax machine in the building. Copy was still being carried forward by a conveyor belt. It was all typewriters. We had about three walkie-talkie phones – the big sit-up-and-beg ones that you had to charge on a car battery charger about every half an hour.

'I remember saying, "Good heavens, we must get a fax machine." And the management said they were not sure why we should have a fax machine. The management said to me are you sure you don't want a fax machine just because everybody else has one? I thought, that is exactly the point. Everyone does have one. You would probably have made the same point about the telephone fifty years before.

'So the PA was at that time with the final dregs of the old technology. With the conveyor belt, copy being carried forward, with typewriters, whatever. I don't think many reporters had tape recorders. We had about three. I had just come from Wapping where we were at the front end of new technology change.'

It was the night of the Zeebrugge disaster when Webb became aware, more than at any other times, of the shortcomings of what to him was old technology.

Webb did much to alter that, leading the PA to what, in the current cliché, is termed the cutting edge of technology. But his editorship was marred by the fact that he presided over a period when, because of economic conditions over which neither he nor the PA had any control, there were bound to be job losses on the editorial staff.

And he was also there when the first murmurings of what was to be the ill-fated would-be competitor, UK News, were heard. These were difficult and frustrating times, but throughout it all, Webb maintained what he regarded as the basic ABC of the Press Association: Authority, Balance, Clarity – and he might have added Accuracy, too.

One of his successful innovations was the 'crème de la crème' news service in 1990: PA Select. This meant that, for the first time in its history, PA was taking on the copy-tasting and subbing role of regional newspapers, by providing a brief and lively summary of the main stories of the day.

For many provincial editors this was a godsend. One of them, Mike Woods, editor of the *Dorset Evening Echo*, commented at the time, 'This means that I don't need to have someone scrolling for four hours through the full service.'

The general idea of PA Select was to offer an average of 20,000 words a day in 100 items, including perhaps 40 home and foreign stories and a dozen or so sports stories.

Webb also introduced political opinion polls for the first time in PA's history. But they were by no means routine. Whereas the bulk of polls commissioned and carried by newspapers involved a sample of around 1,000 people, the PA polls ran to 10,000 people. And as well as setting out the national picture of voting intentions, they could also be broken down into twelve regional areas, giving a clear indication of the voting intentions in each of them. These polls were widely used in all their forms by both the regional and national press. And in each case they proved to be uncannily accurate when compared with the 'actualité'.

Webb was also responsible for commissioning surveys other than specifically political polls about voter intentions. One, for instance, in October 1987, showed that alcohol had become Britain's third greatest killer after heart disease and cancer. The survey, an innovation for the Press Association, was carried out in thirteen different regions of the country.

These surveys were prominently used in both the national and especially the provincial press, for whom the regional breakdowns were particularly valuable. In recent years the PA's expanded network of regional reporters has allowed such surveys to be even more detailed.

It was the sudden and sad death of Phil Stevens, who had been the PA's chief subeditor for something like thirty years, that gave Webb his opportunity to reshape the editorial structure in a comprehensive way. One of the main beneficiaries of this was the features department, which, Webb thought, had taken a back seat for far too long. A considerable amount of investment was put into that and the department was given a much higher profile. Specialist writers, for instance, were encouraged to write opinionated columns about their own particular subjects. It was a new venture for PA and it was a success.

Webb also had a tendency to move staff to jobs where they would, at first blush, have seemed unlikely candidates. For instance, Harry Aspey, who had spent all his years on PA subbing or as weekend editor, was appointed picture editor, and Don Bratley was made sports editor despite having never shown any great interest in sport.

But Webb's plan to turn Ray Smith, then chief news editor, into the picture editor in a swap with Aspey never came to fruition. Smith made clear his dislike of this decision, and promptly resigned, in defiance of the personal advice given to him by Reg Evans, the then associate editor, and other friends, to accept the post and stay on.

Webb's editorship will be remembered in particular for the fact that he brought about those technology changes whose arrival at PA had been so unfortunately delayed, and also for the fact that he had to battle through a period of recession and the first stirrings of attempts, by UK News, to put the Press Association out of business altogether.

Paul Potts, one of Fleet Street's brightest and most energetic executives, and a man with a distinguished journalistic record, became editor of the Press Association in May 1995 and editor-in-chief some fifteen months later. At the turn of the Millennium he became chief executive as well as editor-in-chief.

His arrival at the PA at the age of 45 coincided with the bitter war that was breaking out with UK News and the threatened shedding from PA of many of her most valued and valuable subscribers, including some national papers.

Potts can justifiably claim much of the credit for having seduced back into the PA fold those who had temporarily wandered elsewhere and for bringing to an end the most serious threat faced by the Press Association since its creation in 1868.

He thus arrived at PA at a time when the agency, if not exactly in the doldrums, was not in its most upbeat mood. There had been three major tranches of redundancies, and the threat posed by UK News was looming menacingly.

Potts also arrived shortly before the PA left Fleet Street and moved into their new hi-tech offices near Victoria.

He came to PA after being deputy editor of the *Daily Express*. He started in journalism at the age of 17 after what he regarded as a tough schooling at Worksop College and a short spell of door-to-door selling. He then worked for United Provincial Newspapers from 1967 to 1978 on the *Star* in Sheffield and then the *Yorkshire Post*, as a general reporter, municipal correspondent and lobby correspondent.

He moved to the *Daily Telegraph* and *Mail on Sunday*, and spent four years on the *News of the World* as political editor. Potts joined the *Daily Express* in 1986, initially as political editor.

As commentators pointed out at the time of his appointment to the PA, Potts was going to have his work cut out, holding on to subscriptions from the big regional evening newspapers while seeking new outlets in the electronic media.

In short, he came to a PA that was under some sort of siege. For a variety of reasons its supremacy was being challenged. Some provincial newspaper editors were downright rude about the service, and there was an almost tangible despondency in the PA newsroom.

Potts set about this problem with energy and verve. UK News was snapping at the heels, but Potts simply referred to it as 'the rival agency', not wishing to dignify it with its name. He had no intention of seeing PA's supremacy in the field dwindle, let alone disappear. Within months, the situation was reversed. UK News was effectively on its knees and those papers that had left the flock were returning to it.

But, while all this drama was being enacted, Potts was beefing up the news desk. He brought in Mike Parry, a former *Express* colleague, as news editor, and the newsroom suddenly seemed vibrant once again. Parry had a reputation in Fleet Street of total commitment to and enthusiasm for hard news. This he demonstrated to everyone's benefit during his relatively brief period with the PA.

Some people who had long service on the PA left – and dozens more people were taken on in the provinces. The PA's network of staff outside London had increased to hitherto unknown proportions. Local news for Teletext and Ceefax was high on their agenda.

This was particularly true of Scotland where a new bureau was set up, composed of eight new and former Scottish staff. There is – as in Wales for the Assembly there – a separate political unit to cover the new Scottish Parliament.

In London, the new office was spectacular compared with 85 Fleet Street. It was said, for instance, that each desk in the newsroom could send out PA's entire 400,000 word daily output in less than five seconds. It became known – before the millennium – as Newsroom 2000.

But Potts was careful not to regard hi-tech as the be-all-and-end-all of the Press Association. He warned just before the PA moved house: 'There's going to be no magic as the journalists walk through the new building to change them into supermen.

'They will just bring all the skills they have into a modern environment. Technology is only a delivery system. We shouldn't get dazzled by it.'

In February 2000, Robert Simpson, the PA's chief executive, left the agency to run, from London, the Leeds-based Ananova company with its fully animated virtual news presenter of that name. At that point Potts was appointed chief executive of PA, retaining the title editor-in-chief. Jonathan Grun, a long-serving PA man, was appointed editor.

Grun, who joined the PA as a general reporter in 1979, had risen steadily through the organisation.

Throughout his years on the PA, Grun has been a fast and reliable operator and – which is vital in a busy and occasionally frenetic news agency newsroom – possesses a cool head and has demonstrated an unerring ability to take quick decisions in moments of crisis.

Despite his modest bearing he was marked out early as a future high flyer. He held a number of posts including news editor, night editor, day editor, deputy editor and finally editor.

Reg Evans, who was the Press Association's associate editor for eighteen years, was, as such, the key figure on the agency in that he was in charge of day-to-day news. The brief that David Chipp gave him on his appointment in 1973 specifically excluded his having to deal with administrative work, a situation that pleased Evans immensely.

His first job, after leaving school, was tearing news agency copy from the teleprinter and getting sandwiches for subeditors at the old *Daily Graphic*. This was followed by a job on a local paper in northeast London, followed by his two years of national service. Evans was one of the last army newspapermen, running a tiny daily paper for British and American troops in Trieste, then a free territory between Italy and Yugoslavia.

And then, at the age of 23, he joined Extel, PA's rival home agency, as a reporter. His early years on the PA were spent at the Law Courts as part of the joint PA–Extel law service, of which he became editor. And for years he covered nearly all the big civil trials. Along the way he picked up the massive reservoir of legal knowledge that was to prove so vital later on. Evans was running the law service when David Chipp arrived at the PA in 1969. He 'tried Evans out' as general election news editor in 1970 and after that Evans was appointed PA's first weekend editor. His remit was to highlight a part of the week that Chipp felt was not getting the treatment that PA's subscribers deserved.

The latter half of the week was spent by Evans and his colleagues working up and developing ideas for weekend stories. And, during his years in that job, the PA weekend file improved unrecognisably.

Evans transformed the weekends for PA. Before his time, if there were no big weekend newsbreaks, the file was often pitifully thin. So Evans spent the week thinking up and encouraging reporters – specialists as well as general reporters – to produce 'soft', oddball, quirky stories. This everyone contributed to with relish.

The outcome was an attractive file, Saturday and Sunday, which occupied much space in the Monday papers, both national and provincial. Evans was weekend editor for nearly three years. Often big stories that happened during the week were resurrected as 'weekender' talking points. Sometimes PA weekend stories also added words and expressions to the English language such as the notorious 'mile-high club', an accolade that has stuck to this day to those who have succeeded in engaging sexually in an aircraft.

There was also the case of the vivid word 'gazumping', which was introduced formally to the English language by courtesy of an Evans-inspired weekend story. John Shaw, one of PA's outstanding 'digging' reporters, was the man responsible. He was engaged in a story about house purchase when the word 'gazumping' crossed his path. It was a 'low-life' term used in the 1930s in the old second-hand car trade.

This is how Shaw's story began: 'A new and sinister word has entered the cut-throat business of buying and selling houses: gazumping.' It was that word that transformed a fairly humdrum story into a page lead in most of the national newspapers the following day.

As Evans observed later with some justifiable satisfaction: 'It is nice to contribute to the English language, even in a small way.'

Evans's weekend stint came to an end with the impending retirement of Leslie Inglis, who had been deputy editor-in-chief to three editors, Jervis, Williamson and Chipp. The senior editorial team was then reorganised by Chipp, giving him effectively two deputies: Brian Robins was made executive editor with responsibilities for administration and the planning and control of election operations – a matter of great importance for PA.

Evans was made associate editor which meant being responsible to the editor-in-chief for the day-to-day running of the PA service, news, sport and pictures – and strictly no administrative work!

He was positively lyrical about it: 'It was a job I did with enormous enjoyment from 1972/3 until I retired in 1991. It was always enormous fun to walk down Ludgate Hill early every morning and wonder what will be the stories that will excite us today. There was always a terrific buzz as one stepped inside 85 Fleet Street and up to the editorial floor.'

In fact, throughout this period – 'the most interesting and satisfying' part of his career – Evans was at the centre of every major story that broke.

Ray Smith, probably the only Fleet Street journalist to have undergone a heart transplant, was a brilliant and effective yet taciturn chief news editor. He had the operation at Papworth Hospital, Cambridgeshire, when heart transplants were virtually in their infancy, on 28 August 1983. He was the 54th heart transplant patient at this hospital. The situation had become so desperate that afterwards one of the Papworth surgeons told him, 'We've snatched you back from the brink of the grave.'

Later, Smith, who was 44 at the time of the operation, was to say, 'As far as I am concerned, my life began at 10.40 that night when I left the operating theatre with a good, strong heart and feeling really well for the first time in years.'

And any doubts that he might have difficulty in coping with such a stressful job after he was able to return to work were swiftly dispelled. He was quickly back in the fray and the tumult of a Fleet Street newsroom as if nothing had happened.

But he also admitted, 'I fortunately soon passed through the stage of feeling indestructible, which stemmed from the thought that I had kicked sand in the face of the Grim Reaper. At the time, I needed one of those characters who stood beside the Roman generals during a triumph, whispering, "Remember, you are mortal" as the crowds went wild.'

Smith said, too, that he was brought down to earth a little later with a slight rejection problem, which caused him to be kept in hospital for a course of treatment. Some twenty years have now elapsed since those critical days, and Smith remains as fit as ever. He joined the Press Association in 1966 after six years with *The News*, Portsmouth, two of them in charge of the Newport, Isle of Wight, office. At the age of 35, he was appointed PA's deputy news editor and was to become chief news editor when he was 41.

His service as chief news editor brought a new zest to the newsroom. He was immensely popular with the reporters and maintained a cool and measured demeanour when surrounded by tumult whenever a big story broke. He was probably the most untypical news editor in Fleet Street. He masterminded every story that came his way with complete cool – and a brevity of words.

Unhappily, after such distinguished service – ten years in that job and twenty-five years on the Press Association – his employment was to end on a controversial note.

He refused the editor-in-chief Colin Webb's decision that he should swap jobs with the then picture editor, Harry Aspey. Smith applied for voluntary redundancy and left. But the circumstances of his departure angered reporters in all departments of the Press Association. A letter was sent on their behalf to Webb saying:

We are frustrated at the prospect of the loss of a chief news editor who has long had as much confidence among his staff as is humanly possible.

Ray Smith often surprises new reporters at PA as someone who does not fit the popular conception of a news desk chief. But they quickly learn his quiet approach belies an ability to take instant decisions which virtually always turn out to be correct. His air of quiet confidence that what we are doing is right is infectious, and his enviable record is one we find it hard to believe PA can lose at any time, but particularly at a time when confidence is sorely needed.

The former editor-in-chief, David Chipp, was among those who tried to persuade Smith to change his mind and accept Webb's decision. But it was to no avail. Smith was determined that, if he could not remain on the news desk, there was nothing else he wanted to do at PA.

So he departed, in his early fifties, when there should have been many more years of top-flight journalism in him.

Hugh Stalker, who died in May 1988 aged 92, was for 33 years night news editor of the PA. He was described as the last of the Victorians on the newsroom staff. His memory was indelibly preserved for generations of reporters in nine words: 'Here's a wee jobbie, laddie, on your way home.'

He was a stickler for formal attire. In his brief time as a reporter before he went on the desk, Stalker, resplendent in black jacket and waistcoat, striped trousers and bowler hat, was sent to make enquiries about a murder.

First he went to Scotland Yard but the duty inspector refused to help him. Then he went to the local police station. 'I've just come from Scotland Yard,' he said, accurately if misleadingly. 'Can you tell me something about this murder?' The station sergeant passed over the occurrence book to his imposing visitor. Hugh noted what he wanted and politely made his farewell.

On another occasion when PA was having problems over covering a train crash in the north Midlands, Stalker asked the switchboard to locate the local correspondent, Mr Bishop of Lichfield. When the call came through, Stalker proceeded to berate the culprit in spicy language. After a few moments' embarrassed silence, Stalker was grovelling, saying, 'I *do* beg your pardon, my Lord Bishop . . .' when he realised the understandable mistake by the switchboard.

Stalker was an imposing figure at six foot two, with a back as straight as a ramrod, as you would expect from a former Scots Guardsman. But, although he was always regarded as a great news editor, he did have his shortcomings. Sometimes the addresses to which he sent reporters were not quite so precise as they might have been.

Once he sent a reporter, one Noel Richley, later to become chief news editor, on a murder enquiry in 'north London'. Richley searched around in vain for the street he was supposed to visit. He reluctantly telephoned Stalker to tell him he could not find the street in question. 'Where are you, laddie? Homerton?' enquired Stalker. 'When I said Homerton I meant Lewisham, sorry.'

Poor Richley could hardly have been further away – within the boundaries of London – from his true destination.

George Cromarty Bloom, who became general manager of the Press Association in 1960, had begun his news agency career some thirty years earlier as a junior in the Reuters office in Shanghai. After tours of duty in Shanghai, the Philippines and North China, he returned to head office in

Shanghai as commercial services manager for the Far East. On 8 December 1941, the day the world reeled to the news from Pearl Harbor, Bloom fell into the hands of the Japanese. At that time he was temporarily in charge of Reuters' Far Eastern operations. After ten months as a prisoner, he was exchanged with a group of Allied prisoners.

Much of the rest of his time with Reuters was spent in Central and South America concerned with the general as well as the commercial news services.

He was a trim, athletic, friendly man who moved over to the Press Association from Reuters, where he was assistant general manager. At that time he was largely ignorant of its affairs and the ways and the needs of the provincial press. But it did not take him long to recognise the peculiar family feeling that, only the cynics would deny, has always been present at the Press Association.

Bloom also quickly gained respect for the historical roots of the men sitting around the boardroom table at 85 Fleet Street, most of them now representing newspaper groups, nearly all of them professional managers like himself, but still reaching back to those provincial traditions and values upon which the PA itself had been built.

Bloom's arrival came at a time when the PA had to start thinking really seriously about adapting and equipping itself for the electronic revolution that was just about to be launched. They had not only to equal but to outdo the pace of change. He had come to the PA with an unrivalled knowledge of the techniques and activities of the world's news agencies and he possessed the boldness and enterprise to prepare the agency for the rapidly changing future.

Management consultants were brought in to try to make everything more efficient and economic, although one professional recommendation that the PA should send its stories out by post was not greeted with acclamation. But overall he succeeded in rationalising the operation, even to the extent of bringing Associated Press into the comprehensive service. He merged the Parliamentary Service with the Central News Service, which operated next door in the Commons. That was largely achieved by knocking down a wall and making the two rooms into one.

And in 1967, thanks to Bloom, a start was made, after years of research and preparation, with tele-typesetting (TTS). This meant that certain kinds of news, transmitted from the PA in Fleet Street in the form of punched tape, were translated by automatic process, in provincial newspaper offices, into columns of type ready for direct insertion into the page. At first TTS was confined to the transmission of the daily race card – a form of news deliberately chosen for its complexity. One provincial editor calculated that it had saved him two and a half hours in the setting of each card. The system, which began relatively slowly, gradually built up until it became the norm. It was also under the leadership of George Bloom that plans were laid for the modernisation of the whole of the PA's networks, including transistorised equipment and new fast printers.

Bloom was the man who set the PA on the road to cyberspace.

Ernest J Harvey, who was assistant general manager to Bloom and secretary of the PA, was one of the most controversial figures on the staff. He was a combative and ambitious character who developed a reputation for interfering far too much – and overtly – in the editorial activities of the agency.

Harvey joined Reuters at the age of 21 as an assistant accountant in their audit and accounts department after two junior posts in the City of London. And then, in 1939, the PA advertised for a company secretary. Harvey, then aged only 26 and in competition with about 100 applicants, secured the job.

He took over the post – despite blandishments by Reuters for him to stay there – on 1 January 1940. But he joined the Army in 1942 and after eighteen months was commissioned in the Intelligence Corps, serving as an intelligence officer, ultimately as a captain, in India, Burma and Singapore. In Burma he said his task was to crack Japanese codes.

Modesty and humility were not his most obvious qualities. For instance, he used to delight in telling his colleagues that he beat all records in completing his test at the War Office selection board in 1942. So outstanding was his performance, he used to recount, that the officer in charge enquired whether he had been through the assessment before.

On his return from war service in 1946, Harvey was reappointed secretary and chief accountant. But his years with the Press Association were certainly far from serene, and he was far from being a popular figure. But his self-acclaimed genius for arithmetic was hugely beneficial to the PA. He used this rare talent, he would say, to revolutionise the compiling and reporting of general election results in Britain in the 1950s and 1960s.

During the 1950 general election, in fact, he used new methods to ensure that updates on the state of the parties were both faster and more accurate than ever. This was an exceptionally close election. Clement Attlee's Labour administration had been in power since its landslide victory of 1945. But in 1950 Labour finished with a majority of just five. Partly through Harvey's efforts, the PA succeeded in giving a minute-by-minute service for newspapers to use in successive editions on the night of the election.

The operation, for which Harvey took the credit, was acclaimed for the 'machine-like precision' of its calculations. The PA went on to maintain its pre-eminence at the general election of 1951, beating its competitor Extel both in speed and volume of information. By the general election of 1964, Harvey helped to introduce an NCR315 computer, into which was fed a mass of information about candidates, the parties, previous results, majorities and so on. Although nowadays the electronic storage of such information is commonplace, in those days it was revolutionary. It was the first time the country could learn of swings and forecasts at the simple touch of a button. Unfortunately, the NCR315 was too large to be housed in the PA's then headquarters at 85 Fleet Street. It had to be installed a mile away and the results telephoned to the computer team there. Calculations of swings were then telephoned back to the office, a process that caused small but crucial delays of up to a minute and a half.

For the 1966 general election, a teleprinter link was installed, which cut the delay to half a minute. By now – and again some thanks are due to Ernest Harvey – the PA could run a forecast of the ultimate result. But the pace of all this proved too hot for Extel, and they decided to bow out of the race and leave the field of election coverage to PA.

Harvey retired from the PA on 30 June 1968, centenary year, for 'family reasons'. But the view was widespread among the journalistic staff at the time that he was pushed out of the PA, rather than that he jumped.

It was well known that he used to 'fight' with the then general manager, G Cromarty Bloom, whose job he almost certainly coveted. Harvey's friends used to warn him against these battles, saying that he would always finish up losing.

And that is what almost certainly happened. The key is in the civil but icily cold words of Cromarty Bloom when Harvey did go. This is what he said: 'He had been thinking about it since last year, and, having got through the major part of the centenary celebrations, he sought the board's permission to leave.'

One would have expected a form of words just a little more flattering from a general manager to his deputy on departure. In fact, the two men were at daggers drawn. After leaving the PA, Harvey went to Conservative Central Office as their chief accountant. He was awarded the OBE in 1981 for political services.

Harvey died in May 1998, aged 85.

Bernard Henry 'Pinky' Scarlett MBE was PA's crime reporter for almost forty years until his retirement in 1984. Tall, neat and soft-spoken, Scarlett was the confidant of police officers of all ranks and throughout the United Kingdom. He covered all the major crime stories from the 1940s onwards until his retirement.

Once, when a so-called top-secret document emerged from Scotland Yard claiming that several prominent figures, including Cabinet ministers, were in league with the corrupt architect John Poulson, Scarlett adjudged it a fake even before the Yard's own experts were certain of its authenticity or not.

Scarlett joined the Press Association as a telephonist in 1935. After wartime service with the London Scottish Regiment he returned to the PA and spent the whole of his subsequent career as a crime correspondent working out of Scotland Yard. In 1945, he became a founder member of the Association of Crime Reporters, which was formed to break down the anti-press sentiments prevalent among many police officers at that time.

He died in 1995 aged 76.

Harry Butler, who was in turn night news editor and regional news editor of the Press Association, was, in addition to being a good newspaperman, one of the leading exponents of his day of shorthand. He was often a hard taskmaster but his news judgments were virtually always impeccable. And he was a great believer in the view that it was those journalists who stuck doggedly and punctiliously to recognised journalistic practices who got the scoops. Once, when a reporter served up an item that had seen better days, Butler rebuked him: 'News, like fish, must be fresh.'

And one reporter, telephoning from a riot-torn Belfast, boasted to Butler that he had nearly got shot. Butler made him write the story – which was very vivid – and then severely dressed him down. 'Dead reporters are no good to me,' he told him. 'Just keep out of the way of the bullets in future.'

Butler, who died in 1993 aged eighty, started to learn shorthand at the age of twelve and achieved a phenomenal speed of some 220 words a minute – more even than most *Hansard* reporters can claim to write.

After working as a reporter in Peterborough and Kettering, Butler joined the PA in 1947, after serving in the war, as a reporter specialising in verbatim shorthand writing, in addition to covering a wide variety of general news.

He was the author of *The Story of British Shorthand* (1951) and was shorthand consultant to the National Council for the Training of Journalists. He also helped to develop the Teeline system of shorthand, which towards the end of the twentieth century came to be used by reporters more than any other system.

After retiring from PA in 1978, Butler started a new career as a teacher in the postgraduate journalism course at the City University, London, where he launched many ambitious youngsters on successful journalistic careers.

Phil Stevens, who was day editor at the time of his sudden death in 1987 at the age of 61, was a staunch operator on the PA for nearly forty years. For much of the time he was in charge of the subeditors, a familiar figure, rarely seen without a pipe.

He was a man with a most meticulous mind. In his letter of acceptance on joining PA in 1948, he wrote, 'I will do my very best to uphold at all times the high standards expected of a member of the Press Association staff.' Which is precisely what he did. Stevens, an agency man from tip to toe, was one of the unsung heroes of PA, a man with a passion for straightforward reporting, without unnecessary frills.

David Chipp summed him up at a thanksgiving service in his honour at St Bride's Church in Fleet Street: 'Phil Stevens's craft was writing and the sentence was its product; created by the tools he had mastered long ago – words.

'What in many of us would be described as fussy and outdated pedantry was seen in him as a wholly admirable discipline. His philosophy echoed Dean Swift's advice to a young clergyman: "Proper words in proper places makes the true definition of style." '

Stevens was appointed chief sub in 1961 and day editor in 1973. Before joining the PA he had worked on the *Barnet Press* before serving as a sublieutenant in the Royal Navy from 1943 to 1946, and taking part in the D-Day landings.

The legendary Arthur Harold Booth, who spent 37 years on the Press Association as one of its most prolific and reliable reporters, retired in 1965 as chief reporter.

He operated in the days when senior general reporters like himself, rather than the parliamentary staff, covered the party political conferences and also followed the principal political figures during general election campaigns.

Booth, often a taciturn but nevertheless genial figure, had an awesome shorthand note, a graphic eye and a sense of observation that enabled him to supply the PA with top-class stories, often from an unusual or unexpected angle.

Booth started his journalistic career with the *Rotherham Advertiser* in 1924, before moving across to the *Birmingham Independent*, where he remained until 1927, when he succumbed to the lure of Fleet Street and joined the PA.

Few reporters have covered such a range of big stories. One of his last achievements was his exclusive interview with Aneurin Bevan: Booth was the last reporter to speak to the founder of the National Health Service, who died only a few weeks later. The interview received splash treatment in newspapers throughout the country.

Booth was also the author of a number of books, including *British Hustings*, his first, in 1954, which racily described his encounters with leading political figures during the many general elections he covered.

He also wrote books on Sir Winston Churchill, World War One, the French Revolution, great religions of the world, Queen Victoria and the American Civil War.

Ian Yates was chief executive of the Press Association for fifteen years until he retired at the age of sixty in October 1990. He was the epitome of courtesy, a quiet, modest and kindly but resilient man, whose term of office coincided with some of the most bitter industrial troubles that have faced the PA.

113

And although he was realistic enough to recognise that in those days it would have been folly for him to declare all-out war on the trade unions, who were at their strongest and most irresponsible at that time in Fleet Street, he was certainly no pushover.

Yates joined the Press Association as general manager and chief executive late in 1975. He had been managing director of Bradford and District Newspapers (Westminster Press Limited), publishers of the *Bradford Telegraph and Argus* and the *Keighley News*. He was also a director of the Planning Division of Westminster Press.

Up to that point, he had spent the whole of his career with Westminster Press, starting at the *Westmorland Gazette*, Kendal, in 1953. After training at Kendal and Bradford, he became assistant to the managing director of King & Hutchings, Uxbridge, returning to Bradford in 1960 as assistant manager with special responsibility for production. He became general manager in 1963 and managing director six years later.

More than once he issued stark warnings about the damage that industrial action was doing to PA's reputation, and the threat that this posed for the very future of the agency.

Mostly, but certainly not always, the PA was being drawn into disputes to which it was not a party. Yates drove the point home particularly when a National Graphical Association dispute gravely disrupted the PA's coverage of the Budget in 1980.

He was driven to telling them, 'If the PA is to be drawn into the disputes of its subscribers, and its credibility and reliability increasingly damaged, it will not survive.'

Yates also had skirmishes with the National Union of Journalists, although the PA chapel of the NUJ was, in general terms, by no means as solid as were their 'brothers and sisters' in the NGA. But there were militants, too, among the journalists, and it was with these that Yates had to contend.

But Yates's gentlemanliness, and his resolve not to get ruffled, always shone through even the most bitter exchanges he had with trade union negotiators. Once, in response to NUJ demands, Yates, setting out the management's position, told them, 'Finally – and I assure you that I do not say this in a spirit of contention or hostility – it is only right that I should make clear the finality of the offer and the consequent conclusion of negotiations.'

This courteous approach – untypical of union negotiations at that time, or indeed at any time – was not just honeyed words from Yates. He genuinely meant what he said. He was a nonconfrontational man and did not relish getting engaged in acrimonious disputes.

It cannot be said, however, that his relatively gentle approach to these matters rubbed off very much on those with whom he had to deal.

In retrospect, it was a pity that Yates's stewardship of the PA should have appeared, to the outside world at least, to have been dominated by the handling of industrial disputes.

For he was a first-class administrator, with an immense fund of knowledge about the ways of the media world, and he steered the PA, with great skill, through some of its most difficult times.

Don Bristow, who retired as assistant general manager of the Press Association in 1985, was an influential figure during his seventeen years with the company.

He came to the PA in 1968 with a wealth of journalistic and especially agency experience behind him, which was to make him a valuable acquisition. One of his principal roles was that of handling industrial relations, which at that time was one of the most critical, and probably frustrating, occupations that had to be performed. Such was the industrial 'climate' at the time that it meant that good journalistic and managerial brains like Bristow's often had to be employed in this area more than they would have wished.

However, Bristow's chief role in Press Association was concerned with planning and development. Before joining the PA he had been editor of the Exchange Telegraph Company, where, before that, he had been in turn reporter, chief reporter and assistant editor.

Bristow's journalistic career began before the war on the *Surrey Times* at Guildford. During the war he served with Royal Air Force Bomber Command, and was one of a crew of three of a Blenheim bomber who were taken prisoner by the Germans in 1941.

Bristow was a man with an impish sense of humour. Indeed, he used to recall, with much joviality, his 21st birthday in a German prisoner-of-war camp, which was celebrated with one great luxury: half a cauliflower – 'a rare relief from the low and dreary diet of caraway seed in everything. My taste-bud memories tell me that the half-cauliflower shared in a celebratory mood was as mouth-watering as any birthday cake.'

12 Top Secret

SECRET DEALS BETWEEN the government and Reuters just before the outbreak of World War Two led to turmoil in the higher echelons of the Press Association. In November 1937, Reuters' chairman, Sir Roderick Jones, discussed secret subsidy proposals to transmit his news service with the Prime Minister, Neville Chamberlain, an event that, if it had come to light, would have created a massive row in the media.

Jones appealed directly to Chamberlain, who granted him an interview at which the Reuters man stressed the threat to British news services worldwide from subsidised foreign competitors. Jones pointed out that, although most foreign newspapers still wanted to take Reuters because of its reputation for accuracy and independence, they were tempted to take news from Paris or Berlin – because it was free. But that news was often anti-British.

Eight months later Jones was able to finalise his clandestine arrangements, which involved the use of cut-rate government transmission facilities. However, although his further negotiations had been carried out with the Treasury, the Foreign Office strongly disapproved and was highly critical of Reuters' general performance in some areas. So much so that it was actively working for Jones's removal. The ostrich-like Jones, meanwhile, refused to regard the granting of low wireless transmission rates from the government as the equivalent of a subsidy.

On 22 September 1938, as Hitler invaded Sudetenland, the government began its subsidy of Reuters' wireless transmission from Leafield and Rugby and in the year 1939 to 1940 the Ministry of Information calculated that the company had received £64,000 for 'propaganda purposes' from the Treasury. At a formal meeting of the Reuters board in February 1941, Jones's secret arrangements with the government became apparent. He was repeatedly questioned about a letter that had come to light. It came from Lord Perth, the director-general designate of the

Ministry of Information, and he had received it eighteen months earlier. It was to become known as the Perth Letter and set out various understandings with the MOI about the financing and expansion of overseas news services.

Jones insisted that the letter had no existence as a valid and effective document since it was merely a draft, which had never been signed or acknowledged by him. But the board remained sceptical and unsatisfied. The meeting reached a dramatic point where Jones felt impelled to challenge the members: 'Is there any colleague of mine on this board who believes that I have withheld information or documents from him?' he asked. To everyone's astonishment, someone piped up: 'I do.' It was the voice of William Haley, who was later to become director-general of the BBC and then editor of *The Times*. Grim-looking Jones rose from his seat, collected his papers and left the room amid what was described as 'a terrible silence'.

The damage had been done, and there was only one course to take: his removal. There was talk of outright dismissal, but ultimately it was agreed, on the instigation of Alex McLean Ewing, a past and future chairman of the Press Association, that Jones should be given the option to resign. Soon after these events, the Press Association chairman, James Henderson, went with Ewing to see Jones, and the terms of the resignation were agreed. There was to be no explanation of the decision, which was to be announced as retirement. Jones would receive his full monetary entitlements up to the end of that year, and would be paid a pension of £5,000 per annum for the remainder of his life. The agreement that there would be no public explanation for the departure of Jones angered some newspapers, who wanted to know how Reuters would now be run. Sir Samuel Storey (later to become Lord Buckton and a Deputy Speaker in the Commons) was immediately appointed chairman. These new moves preceded a traumatic period involving heated discussions and an element of skulduggery over the new ownership structure of Reuters. World War Two was going on, but behind the closed doors of Fleet Street another battle was raging and the Press Association was pivotal to it all.

Ewing, and some of his fellow-directors, felt it was time to suggest to the London newspapers that they should take some sort of stake in Reuters. Some years earlier, in 1925, the Newspaper Proprietors' Association had missed the opportunity – largely because of their own internal squabbling – to buy into the world news agency. Many newspapers at this time, however, were justifiably, suspicious about the relationship between Reuters and the government. There were three possible schemes: the NPA might appoint one or more directors to the board of Reuters, even though they had no shareholding in the company; the NPA might become part-owners in Reuters; Reuters might be turned into some form of national trust.

After a series of high-powered and largely clandestine discussions, the Fleet Street press barons made a formal approach to the Press Association and suggested they would like to join it as joint and equal owners of Reuters. Meanwhile, at the height of all these negotiations, a 1,250-kilogram land mine was caught suspended in the trolley-bus wires outside the front door of the Reuters and Press Association headquarters at 85 Fleet Street. The building was evacuated for three and a half hours, and fortunately the mine came down upside down, which meant it could be rendered harmless.

But the old animosities and suspicions between the London and provincial press owners were proving less easy to defuse. The provincial press were worried lest the sale of half the Reuters shares to the NPA would change the balance of power between the two, and feared that the NPA would dominate Reuters. But the NPA made clear that the joint working would not depreciate the position of the provincial press and that the London newspapers were making their request 'in a spirit of collaboration'.

The NPA also made the following statement in their memorandum, giving an airing to their suspicions about the relationship between Reuters and the government:

If common agreement cannot be found we would have to ask Reuters to disclose to us what steps are being taken to organise the collection of news in the present German-controlled countries and elsewhere. Agencies that are now mere puppets of their governments must be suspect for many years and we should have to know the sources of foreign news so that we could determine whether we should remain as subscribers or organise our own news collecting and distributing agency, or make other arrangements. We doubt if the provincial newspapers have the experience necessary to satisfy us who have our own representatives in all parts of the world.

But there was also bickering among the London papers. Lord Beaverbrook, owner of the *Daily Express*, performed a spectacular U-turn. He started off as a firm supporter of the scheme only to become a fervent opponent when he saw his arch-rival Lord Rothermere, proprietor of the *Daily Mail*, taking what he considered to be too prominent a role in the negotiations. The haggling continued, and one unfortunate consequence was that the short-lived chairmanship of Samuel Storey came to an end. He had always been opposed to the idea of the NPA taking half the Reuters shares and had argued his case trenchantly on the Press Association board.

Storey's suspicion of the deal was profound. He believed there had been trickery involved in the proposal, and even went to the lengths of composing a piece of limerick-style doggerel on the subject, based on the sad story of the young lady from Riga who went for a ride on a tiger. It went:

Three men from the Reuters–PA Boards
Went out for a ride with two press lords;
They came back from the ride,
Reuters–PA inside,
And a smile on the face of the press lords.

Storey even went to the lengths of sponsoring a debate on the subject in the House of Commons on 22 October 1941. On 17 October, just a few days before that debate, some 66 members of the Press Association had filed into the conference room overlooking the burned-out shell of St Bride's Church for what was to be a tense meeting. Ewing, as chairman of the agency, argued in favour of the sale of half the Reuters shares on the grounds that it would make for a stronger British news agency. It would also, he pointed out, prove of financial advantage to the PA. But he faced ferocious opposition to his idea, led by Samuel Storey, who with others launched into what some saw as an intemperate diatribe against the London press lords, accusing them of tactics ranging from 'plain unfriendly' to 'domineering' and 'contemptuous' of the Press Association itself. Storey was no less opposed to the idea of a Trust 'with high-sounding phrases'. And representatives from the provincial papers feared that this would mean the domination of Reuters by London to the detriment and disadvantage of papers outside the capital.

Meanwhile, Prime Minister Winston Churchill, who was frustrated by the inadequate performance of the Ministry of

Information, had appointed his own man, Brendan Bracken, a one-time successful journalist, as the new minister at this crucial wartime department. So, in the Commons, Storey appealed to Bracken to intervene, and to do so quickly. For he feared the NPA might come to dominate Reuters and what was required was 'a genuine trust'. He said it was true that the proposed sale was coupled with a proposal for the creation of a Reuters Trust, but this Trust, he claimed, would have no real power. 'The trustees will not even hold the shares in Reuters Limited or the income arising from the shares. They will appoint the directors, but they can only appoint those persons who have been nominated to them by the shareholders.'

Storey went on: 'It is certainly not in the national interest that a section of the newspaper industry, particularly one composed of so few individuals, should be in a position to exert a dominating influence over a national institution performing so vital a service as Reuters performs, and enjoying such facilities as Reuters enjoys.'

Bracken took the view that Reuters could not carry on as it was going. It had lost much ground to Associated Press, the United States agency, 'in a most remarkable way'. The minister lamented the fact that no one had spoken up for the 'the bold, bad barons of Fleet Street', but he had no reason to believe they would act unscrupulously if they became equal-partner owners of Reuters. However, he pooh-poohed any suggestion that the government should nationalise Reuters.

'It is quite open to the government to bring in a Bill to nationalise Reuters, but would that be helpful from the point of view of Reuters? Certainly not. If a news agency were regarded throughout the world as being the property of the British government, its news value would be very small,' he warned. 'Here is an opportunity, it is said, for the government to start their own news agency. Well, believe me, from what I have seen in my limited experience of my present ministry, I think the financial misfortunes of such a news agency would be beyond all description. Here is the House of Commons with a large Conservative majority suggesting, as far as I understand it, that we should start our own news agency if Reuters does not come to heel. I think that is a very futile argument. We are approaching a problem by way of getting all parties concerned into some form of agreement, but the thing that worries me, and must worry the Chancellor of the Exchequer far more, is: Who is going to finance this business?'

Bracken added for good measure, 'It is extremely unfair to the Newspaper Proprietors' Association to regard them as a lot of greedy bandits who are anxious to doctor the news for the benefit of their readers. They are no such thing. And, if they were, why did not the Press Association, who have sold these shares to these supposed scoundrels of Fleet Street, take that into account before this great protest began?'

Bracken was then closely questioned by MPs from all sides of the House about the extent to which the deal had gone through, but he would give no undertakings to report to the Commons before the final effect was given to any scheme that ultimately emerged. But he did say that the government had kept a 'fatherly eye on something they do not own' and would continue to do so. None of Brendan Bracken's documents were ever released by the Public Record Office and Bracken himself gave instructions that all his personal papers were to be burned within 24 hours of his death – factors that have tended to leave some of the issues in the dark.

Some questions have to remain unanswered. For instance, what was the scale of the government intervention, if any, in the negotiations for the sale to the London papers? Was the Press Association forced to sell because of the fear of competition from the NPA? Or was Brendan Bracken out for the main chance, in a bid to strengthen Reuters at a time when they were – as admitted on all sides – falling behind the American agency, Associated Press?

On the day immediately following the Commons debate, Bracken and the Chancellor of the Exchequer, Sir Kingsley Wood, met a deputation from the Press Association and Lords Rothermere, Kemsley and Astor from the NPA. The Chancellor made clear once again that the government did not want to run Reuters, but did want to see an independent chairman of the Reuters board, or at least of the trustees, someone from outside journalism, to be nominated by the Lord Chief Justice, Lord Goddard.

Storey, whose fears about the London press barons were genuine enough but proved to be unfounded in the light of subsequent events, was bounced out of the chairmanship of Reuters less than a week after the debate. His quarrels with Haley and Ewing, all honourable men, were never reconciled. The tragedy was that this affair had transformed one-time good friends into people who no longer spoke to each other.

On 29 October, the 'marriage' of the Press Association and the London papers as equal partners in Reuters was formally settled and announced. Storey's fears were groundless. There was never any attempt by the national press proprietors to exploit their strength within Reuters for their own advantage and they all, particularly in later years, played major roles as directors.

13 The Admirable Admiral

ON A CHILLY EVENING in April 1939, the Press Association's court correspondent, Louis Wulff, was one of a large party of journalists invited on board the aircraft carrier *Ark Royal* for an evening's entertainment to publicise the work of the Royal Navy Film Corporation. After a few initial pink gins, the guests joined officers and men in an improvised cinema in a hangar. Among them were Lieutenant-Commander Lord Louis Mountbatten and Lord Stanhope, First Lord of the Admiralty.

Lord Stanhope, regarded as one of the least stimulating speakers in the government, was due to make what most people expected to be no more than an informal welcome and some reporters had hardly bothered to take out their pencils. But after the expected, tedious address, during which it was quite apparent to the audience that no preparation or thought to content or delivery had been given, the First Lord added in his drab tone: 'Unfortunately, there are others who are not with us tonight, because shortly before I left the Admiralty, it became necessary to give orders to man the anti-aircraft guns of the Fleet.'

Those reporters who had been reduced to a comatose state by Lord Stanhope's dreary oratory quickly roused themselves. Such a statement, at the very time when the nerves of Europe were stretched almost to breaking point, was clearly dramatic. Whether Lord Stanhope appreciated the significance of what he had said and the explosive effect it would have on the newspapers as the war clouds gathered over the Channel has always remained open to question. The expected quiet and agreeable evening over a few drinks for Wulff and his counterparts suddenly turned into a major news event. As the PA man went hunting for the ship's telephone, Lord Mountbatten joined the reporters sitting at the back of the hangar and said, 'The First Lord has asked me to say that he has no objection whatever to his remarks being published.'

But, by the time the other journalists went to contact their news desks, Wulff had filed his report and had received a call back from the night news editor wanting to know whether he was absolutely sure of his facts and – just as important – whether Lord Stanhope was aware that what he said was being published. It was only after all those on board the *Ark Royal* had watched a George Formby comedy film that Wulff was able to speak to Lord Stanhope personally. As the final credits to the movie rolled, Stanhope said he stood by his words, explaining that he wanted to show to the world the Royal Navy was always ready, always on the alert. Wulff took a shorthand note of Stanhope's additional comments, read them back to the minister just in case there was any misunderstanding, and duly filed the extra material to the night desk.

But, as he was in the process of doing this, the news desk cut in. A D-notice had been issued from Downing Street on the instructions of Neville Chamberlain, the Prime Minister, asking newspapers not to publish the line from Stanhope's speech 'on the grounds of national security'. By then, of course, it was too late. Some papers had already used the passage in their early editions and Reuters had sent the words to all corners of the globe. As the Press Association editor, Henry Martin, explained to the Admiralty that night, it was impossible by then to recall it or cancel it.

The following day in the House of Commons, Chamberlain was called upon to explain why the D-notice had been issued. He told MPs, 'It was because I thought the words as reported would give a wrong impression and I thought it was desirable to make that request to the press.' This sounded very much like an implied criticism of the Press Association, and Martin was not slow in showing his displeasure at the Prime Minister's words. Martin then issued a long and detailed account by Wulff of precisely what happened aboard the *Ark Royal*. It was carried by many newspapers, including *The Times*. It meant that the Prime Minister performed a hasty backtrack in the Commons, explaining to unhappy MPs about the wisdom of using a D-notice on this occasion. He told them that when he used the expression 'as reported' he meant 'as reported' to him at a Foreign Office dinner. It did not sound a very convincing explanation. Chamberlain went on: 'I did not mean as reported by the reporter. It was the last thing that would occur to me to challenge the accuracy of the report. I know how extremely competent these gentlemen are who report these things.'

Observers believed that these were weasel words and double-talk of the worst kind, just to enable a Prime Minister to wriggle out of an awkward situation that he had created for himself. But these were the words that Henry Martin wanted to hear. It meant he had won his point over Neville Chamberlain.

Five months later war was declared on Germany and the Press Association was to emerge from the six-year conflict with considerable credit. But not before numerous private battles between Whitehall and Fleet Street. For at this time contacts between government and the press, nowadays almost an industry of its own, were regarded in Whitehall as very much at the bottom end of their priorities. Some ministries regarded newspapers as an irritant to be fobbed off.

There was no television. The transmission of moving pictures and speech, which had started just before the war, was abandoned for the duration of the hostilities. And the civil servants who preceded today's spin doctors had not even begun to think about the possibilities of trying to court the media and establishing a friendly rapport that would have been to everybody's advantage. What the press had to endure at the outbreak of war was described in 1940 by the Press Association chairman, Herbert Staines. He said:

> In the negotiations with the officials of the shadow Ministry of Information, there was disclosed a tendency, born of a complete lack of knowledge of press methods, to cabin and confine press facilities; and the agencies found it necessary to carve a polite but insistent way through a jungle of red tape as well as to dispel an atmosphere that the press must be content with small concessions. If, from the first, a wider view of the world-wide responsibilities of the press had been adopted; if it had been appreciated that the facilities asked for were essential in the national interests; the storm that later blew up over the newly born Ministry might have been considerably moderated.

Whitehall had obviously not learned from the lessons of World War One, and it looked, once again, as though the press were going to be beating vainly at a brick wall. Fortunately for Fleet Street, the editor-in-chief, Henry Martin, was just the man to ensure that the press were given whatever facilities could be offered, compatible with the need for security and other wartime restrictions. Martin's mission was to ensure that the Ministry of Information and all other relevant departments were kept up to the mark. The Press Association led the way, banging loud and hard and insistently at the door of Whitehall.

The Press Association wanted the government to pose the question: 'Is there any reason why we should not allow this news to be published?' rather than 'Why should we allow this news to be published?' Finally, relations between the censors and the agency became particularly cordial and sympathetic. For they discovered that, although Martin was a formidable warrior when it came to the rights of the press, he was also an understanding and reasonable person with whom to do business. But Martin became suspicious and apprehensive about what was going on. The ministry had been set up to supply Fleet Street with official and semi-official news. But now it was spreading its wings too widely and getting far too ambitious. It was beginning to assume the mantle of a news agency itself. The service began to contain items of a more general kind.

The ever-alert Henry Martin smelled a rat. There was blatant interference with news agency enterprise. For visitors from abroad were being intercepted by government agents so that they could not be interviewed by the press. Instead they were being kept back for a press conference, under the auspices of the Ministry of Information, the following day. The matter came to a head shortly before Christmas in 1941, when Henry Martin attended a Newspaper Society lunch where the Minister of Information, Brendan Bracken, was the guest. Martin bluntly asked him whether it was his policy to allow the news division, either then or after the war, to become a subsidised news agency in competition with the recognised independent agencies. Bracken, affecting ignorance and surprise at this allegation, said that there was no such intention and agreed that a subsidised agency must be suspect. Bracken obviously had a stern word with his staff when he returned to his ministry the following day, because the problem never arose again.

But the authorities imagined, in their innocence, that it was the function of the news agency to pass on, undiluted, all the 'copy' it received from Whitehall. And they appeared shocked when they discovered that the Press Association had a positive responsibility to select, edit, gut and translate the sometimes incomprehensible, sometimes pompous and wordy officialese into plain English. Gradually, however, Whitehall got round to Fleet Street's way of thinking.

As the months went on the Press Association fed a regular supply of war stories to the provincial papers, so that all of them were able to carry first-hand accounts of the fighting. These were reports that matched, in vividness and fact, the coverage that the national newspapers were receiving from their staff correspondents in all the theatres of war.

Meanwhile, the Press Association court correspondent put on a uniform to follow King George VI wherever he chose to go, whether to inspect troops in training in barracks around the United Kingdom, or to visit the Normandy beachhead. The agency's parliamentary team was also an integral part of its war effort. When Churchill delivered a major speech in the Commons, the Press Association's subscribers received a verbatim report of it – often as much as 8,000 words. And it would be preceded by as many as forty 'snaps', covering the highlights of the speech, transmitted within minutes of their delivery. The Churchill speeches were so magnificent and inspiring in their own right that there was no need for the Press Association Commons team to add colour of any kind. They spoke graphically for themselves.

Throughout the war's most difficult and dangerous periods on the home front, newspaper chiefs remained confident that the agency would continue to get the message through, even when conditions were well nigh impossible. This confidence was exemplified by Walter Hawkins of the *Bristol Evening Post*. He said: 'When our buildings and plant were threatened by enemy raids, the one thing we did not worry about was the Press Association service, because we knew it would get through somehow, and it did.' But there was one occasion at 85 Fleet Street when the curtain almost came down. It was during the great incendiary-bomb raid of 29 December 1940. That night, Fleet Street's own church, St Bride's, was gutted by fire – and the tower of the church was a mere eleven feet from the east wall of the PA building. Fortunately, the wind blew away the flames and sparks, enabling the newsroom to carry on. But all the PA's provincial telegraph channels were out of action for a short time. However, the Manchester newspapers and *The Times*, whose own circuits out of London were still working, came to the rescue. And so the agency's 'traffic' to the Manchester centre was passed from there round all the other centres and circuits.

Emergency plans had been worked out to meet any kind of contingency or adversity. The basement at 85 Fleet Street was fully equipped for editorial work over both the provincial telegraph system and the London teleprinter system. An emergency canteen was set up, along with sleeping quarters, so that work could have been carried on there indefinitely if the upper floors had been rendered useless. Quite often, during the night, the Press Association staff did have to take to the basement, particularly during the Blitz – and again during the V-1 and V-2 doodlebug attacks. One night Frank Turner, the deputy night editor, received a warning from the Press Association man at Dover that 'London is going to have a packet tonight judging by the way they are coming over here'. It was a warning that the Dover correspondent was to repeat frequently in the months that followed.

There was also a second line of defence should the situation at 85 Fleet Street become totally impossible. A deal was struck with Kemsley Newspapers to equip a big room in Kemsley House in Gray's Inn Road – about a mile away from the Press Association headquarters – from where the agency could operate in the event of an emergency. A similar emergency plan was worked out with the Exchange Telegraph. A third plan involved transferring to Manchester to work from the offices of the *Manchester Guardian* and the *Manchester Evening News*.

A more intricate plan was hatched, however, during the darkest days after the fall of France, when it was feared Britain would be invaded. The problem then would be how to deal with a situation in which some parts of the country might be cut off from all the conventional forms of communication. The Press Association decided that it would then send out news messages by wireless, and transmitters were installed for this purpose at 85 Fleet Street. In turn, the provincial papers equipped themselves with the special receiving sets needed. The Ministry of Information helpfully allocated a wavelength, and a number of successful trials took place. Happily, the radio news wire was never needed.

The war brought with it chronic shortages of everything. But the government, regarding the Press Association as a vital national service, smiled on 85 Fleet Street and the agency did not go short of much, particularly mechanical spare parts. In spite of all the momentous events of the war, life went on at the PA. On the day Winston Churchill was announcing to the Commons news of the D-Day invasion, the agency was also reporting another important parliamentary story: that government office cleaners should be referred to as such, and not as charladies.

Meanwhile the wires were buzzing with news that Persian Gulf had won the Coronation Cup at Newmarket, beating High Chancellor by three-quarters of a length. Life went on for the messengers, too – for one job that was allocated to them at this time was to walk up to the post office near St Paul's Cathedral and pick up the midnight mail. The boy then trudged back to the office in Fleet Street with his mailbag over his shoulder. Invariably, however, two policemen were waiting in the shadow of the buildings on Ludgate Hill. One would be a seasoned officer and the other new to the job. When the luckless boy loomed into view, the experienced officer instructed his colleague to question him and take him back to the PA building to confirm his story. The messengers must have begun to think they were being persecuted by the police but in fact it was all part of a Metropolitan Police training scheme.

Just after the end of the war, on the night of 22 November 1948, the court correspondent, Louis Wulff, walked into the newsroom at midnight and took the deputy editor into a room. After locking the door he told him what he had learned from his contacts at the Palace. But his story would have to be strictly embargoed until a few minutes after 1 a.m. In secrecy, a story was punched up in a secluded part of the telegraph department, and Wulff also dictated eight 'rushes'. He had learned of the postponement of King George VI's tour of Australia because of a serious operation, probably for cancer. Another journalist, sworn to secrecy, wrote up the details of the tour, biographies of the doctors named in the official statement that was in Wulff's hands and other background material. The story also recalled how the coronation of King Edward VII had been postponed at the last minute because he had to undergo an operation for appendicitis. By 1.10 a.m. the story was written and punched ready to be fed into the PA transmitters. At precisely 1.15 a.m. the words poured out on countless receivers from one end of the country to the other, and, via Reuters, throughout the world. It took two minutes for all the rushes to be transmitted. And within 28 minutes the newspapers had received 2,700 words. There was a lot of late replating of front pages in Fleet Street and up and down the land that night.

But the speed of the Press Association's service and equipment was not always appreciated. It was when Clement Attlee arrived in Downing Street, as head of the first postwar Labour government. And not only did he have a distinctly odd attitude to anything that was vaguely new-fangled, but he also had an attitude problem about the Press Association. Attlee was not a Luddite, far from it, but he possessed a healthy suspicion of mechanical instruments that he could not control or did not fully understand.

His staff pleaded with him to allow a Press Association machine to be installed in the building, but he was adamant in his refusal. Then one of the junior members of his staff hit on a bright idea, which he passed on to his superiors. The following day, a nervous official confronted Attlee in his private office and blurted out, 'Prime Minister, I am terribly sorry to raise this issue again with you, but if you have the Press Association machine installed here, you will not only be kept up to date with everything that goes on worldwide, but, sir, you will also get all the up-to-date cricket scores before they appear in the newspapers.'

The following day the machine was installed.

14 Photographic Memory

THE SEED OF THE JOINT photo venture with Reuters was planted during the D-Day landings when the official war photographers – many of them former newspapermen – had great success with their pictures, circulated through the Ministry of Information, for publication in British newspapers. But, at the beginning of 1944, the War Cabinet became concerned about the availability after the conflict of news pictures that expressed the British point of view, for there were no news-photo organisations big enough to represent the British press or stand up to the American Associated Press. Both the Press Association and Reuters were also thinking along these lines. So it was inevitable that something was going to happen.

The man who created the photo service was William Truby, who was still serving in the Royal Air Force as officer in charge of PR press photography at Air Staff Headquarters when he was headhunted by PA and Reuters. He had been recommended by Robert T ('Blos') Lewis, of the *Daily Mail*, who at that time was a director of the Press Association and an experienced and enthusiastic photographer. He had met Truby when they were both working on the *Daily Chronicle* in the mid 1920s. The deal to bring Truby to Fleet Street was clinched over a lunch of filleted sole (4s. 6d., or 22 ½ pence) at the Press Club. Truby was an important catch. He was one of the most experienced picture executives in prewar Fleet Street, leaving the *Daily Chronicle* to become photo editor of the *Sunday News*, a tabloid picture paper, in 1927. Three years later he became deputy picture editor of the *Daily Herald*, and two years before the war he joined the London Press Exchange as technical adviser and photographic manager.

As a member of the Auxiliary Air Force he was called up before the outbreak of war, and in 1941 posted to the Directorate of Public Relations at the Air Ministry as a squadron leader in charge of the photographic section. Needless to say, he was a huge success in that post. Efforts were made to get him demobbed early to take up this new, pioneering job. But it was not to be and the Press Association had to wait until one fine morning in May 1945 for Truby, still in uniform, to report for duty at 85 Fleet Street. Truby had to start virtually from scratch, soon realising that everything he needed was rationed, in short supply or just unobtainable without special permits.

The target date for starting the service was November 1945, so Truby had just seven months to prepare. He cobbled together the nucleus of a staff and assembled whatever equipment he could, since there was nothing new available. Then he set up business on the ground-floor frontage of 85 Fleet Street and in the former operations room in the basement used by the Press Association and Reuters during air raids. It was here that he devised his first production unit for the speedy processing of pictures.

Truby's problem was how to compete with ten long-established but much smaller picture agencies, none of whom would welcome an independent stranger in their midst. Truby, as he himself put it, saw many battles ahead and did not underestimate the problems.

Finding staff was difficult, because many of the most experienced cameramen were still in the forces. But by chance he discovered Leslie Burch, whom he appointed picture editor. Few people could have known more than this man about the work of a picture agency. He had been trained as a newsreel cameraman before becoming chief staff photographer of both the *Sunday Pictorial* and the London News Agency. And he had covered three royal tours of the Empire as official photographer for the British press. Gradually the staff built up. Sometimes undercover, not to say underhand methods had to be adopted to get the high-quality photographers that both Truby and Burch craved. This was done partly by frequent visits to Fleet Street taverns in the hope of enticing cameramen to join the new PA–Reuters setup.

The original staff totalled sixteen. There were seven photographers at the outset who, like the processing and editorial staff, were hand-picked for the job, specialists in their own line. It was also conditional on them that they should bring their own apparatus, since there was no, or precious little, equipment on the market in the immediate postwar period.

There were many trials and not a few tears as the new department swung into action. Daily print distribution to so many provincial newspapers had never been attempted before. And this fledgling organisation was to find itself having to compete against long-established photo agencies and the London papers themselves, all of whom possessed seasoned picture desks of their own. The initial aim was to supply the provincial newspapers with up to thirty pictures a week, which would either be delivered to their London offices or dispatched by train parcels to head offices. This new deal was included in the provincial papers' Comprehensive Service.

In the beginning the post was used for overnight dispatch (if it was mailed by 5.15 p.m. the Post Office guaranteed delivery by first post the following morning to the main cities and towns, except in Ireland). And, schedules permitting, urgent news pictures were sent by fast train. Although telephoto transmission of pictures had been in use from the early 1920s between the London offices of the national papers and their provincial printing centres, the PA had to wait some years until a provincial network was completed. Meanwhile, more staff were hired, including motorcyclists and young messenger boys, a picture librarian and salesmen.

The great launch was on 26 November 1945, only six months from the birth of the new baby. It was not, however, a big day for national news – but a local gas strike produced the first memorable publications: including the front page of the *London Evening News*, showing Fleet Street and the Strand blacked out, along with a tea-for-two scene in a Lyons tea shop. The idea for the Strand picture came from Burch himself. He said, 'The strike had been on for several days, and I couldn't see why the Fleet Street papers had failed to shoot a marvellous picture on their own doorstep!' The picture was taken by Roy Illingworth at Temple Bar and it strikingly contrasted the gloom of Fleet Street, effectively a blackout as a result of the strike, with the blaze of light in the City of Westminster a few yards away.

It was a humble but nevertheless exciting start and the number of reproductions in the provincial press went up by leaps and bounds. The national newspapers were supplied on the usual basis of payment, according to the size of the reproduction. At the end of the first year's operations, Truby was able to report that there had been 12,000 publications of PA–Reuters pictures in the provincial press, 5,400 in the London papers and magazines, and more than 16,000 overseas. The figures were quite an achievement, especially when space for pictures in newspapers was at a premium with managements still subject to the most stringent postwar paper rationing.

Ten years later these figures had grown tenfold – and continued to increase. But what was frustrating was the absence of a wire system for pictures for the provincial papers. The efforts of the picture staff to achieve speed seemed to be thwarted by their technical inability for some time to reach the provinces by electronic means. In spite of these handicaps, however, there were some trend-setting achievements, even in the first week of the service. One of them involved Walter Lockeyear, one of the new staff photographers, who took a close-up of Princess Elizabeth arriving at the Albert Hall at 2.30 p.m. The picture was rushed back from Kensington to Fleet Street and, 29 minutes after it had been taken, prints of it were on their way to the London evening and Sunday newspapers.

The national papers had never enjoyed this sort of service before, and it gave them a huge boost. But, as long as newspapers outside London had to wait for pictures to arrive by train, high-speed operations in London were still thwarted by the limitations of railway timetables. To speed things up, Truby hired planes from Mortons Air Services at Croydon Aerodrome – and so the Press Association had aircraft carrying boxes containing the photographs in envelopes to central points from which the newspapers picked them up. By and large, that was a success, but occasionally, if the weather was bad, the planes had to fly on without landing. However, most papers got their pictures on time and it was a considerable thrill for them to be able to publish pictures at the same time as the London press. It was this venture, as much as anything else, that put the PA–Reuters Photo Service on the map. It was also a tremendous test of the technical capacity of the office. Over three successive days the plant turned out 4,000 prints every 24 hours.

The anxiously awaited full photo-wire service began operations in 1950 and was at once a huge success, although a limited wired service was launched two years earlier. The *Glasgow Herald* played a major role in these early experiments to find out the best type of transmitter for a wired service.

Experimental transmissions were arranged to a number of PA centres and these in turn were retransmitted to those papers that had receivers. These trials were so successful that papers that did not possess the receivers felt obliged to equip themselves with them. In May 1948 a portable transmitter was taken

Above The Royal Family, 1965

Right The Investiture of the Prince of Wales, 1969

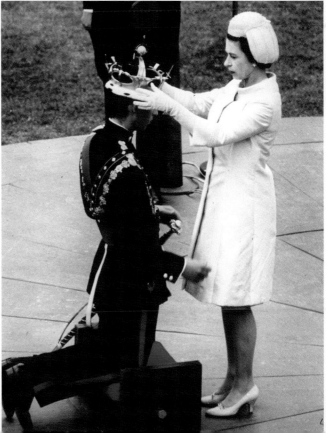

Above Frenzied Beatles fans watching the band perform, Manchester, 1963

Above Mrs Thatcher, being attacked by a woman brandishing daffodils, 1992

Left Dawn in the South Atlantic, 1982. Inside one of the hangars of HMS *Hermes* sits some of the might of the British naval task force heading south for the Falkland Islands

Right Waves crash over the promenade in Dover as storms lash parts of Britain, 2000

Above Charles, Diana, William and Harry cycling in the Scilly Isles, 1989

Left The Queen looks glum during a rainy royal visit, 1993

Above RUC officers under petrol bomb attack, 1996

Left Victorious Olympians, Steve Redgrave and Matthew Pinsent, 1996

Above Earl Spencer at Althorp where his sister, Diana, Princess of Wales, lies buried, 1997

Right The Paddington rail crash, 2000

Frankie Dettori leaps
from the saddle on
Shantou after winning
the St Leger at
Doncaster, 1996

THE LAWN
ASSOCIAT

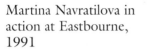

Martina Navratilova in
action at Eastbourne,
1991

to the picturesque Worcester county cricket ground and pictures of the match, between Worcestershire and the Australians at the start of their first official postwar tour, were successfully transmitted by wire to 85 Fleet Street.

This successful experiment provided valuable experience. It was, therefore, from 7 June 1950 that PA–Reuters were able to distribute pictures as news was distributed: broadcast simultaneously to the newspapers in all parts of the country. From birth to that day had taken just five years. And there was, in fact, a spectacular start to this service. At about 5 p.m. on 8 June 1950, the Birmingham-to-Glasgow express caught fire on a lonely stretch of moorland near Beattock Summit in the Scottish Lowlands. Flames from the roof of the first coach set the following coaches alight and the second and third coaches were also burned out with the loss of five lives.

When the news was received in London, instructions were sent to the Press Association's Glasgow Centre to get pictures and transmit them to London. But, because of the remoteness of the scene of the tragedy, it was well after midnight before the first pictures were received in the capital. Within an hour, however, the pictures of burned-out carriages were transmitted over the broadcast system to provincial newspapers. It was baptism by fire. The PA pictures were the first available and were widely used both in London and in the provinces.

There was more excitement in December 1951 over the epic journey of the *Flying Enterprise*, when Captain Kurt Carlsen battled for fourteen days against the worst storms the Atlantic Ocean had seen for 37 years – only to lose the ship just a short distance from Falmouth. It was a story that gripped not only Britain but the rest of the world for days on end. And PA–Reuters photos scored with publications around the world of pictures taken from a hired plane over the stricken vessel. This was one of the first occasions when planes had been used for maritime dramas of this kind.

There were some notable successes in these early years: on 3 October 1952 PA–Reuters photos of Britain's first atomic bomb test in Australia made the front pages of every national newspaper, and other big picture stories included the funeral of King George VI in 1952, and in the following year the East Coast Floods and the coronation of Queen Elizabeth. For the coronation the picture staff were on duty continuously for two and a half days, snatching sleep whenever they could on office tables.

The wedding of Princess Elizabeth and Prince Philip in 1947 had probably been the first big test for the new and burgeoning photo department. The problem was how to get pictures speedily to provincial evenings and early editions of the mornings. Reliance on road, rail and post was dismissed because they were too slow. And, with no wire service available, air was the only answer. In those days it was a big risk, as flying was not as safe as it is today – but it was a risk that had to be taken. Aircraft from a charter company, run by Alan Cobham and based at Croydon Airport, were hired and canvas wallets with streamers, containing addressed photopackets, were dropped on centrally sited public spaces or open fields, where the newspapers collected their pictures on time.

The leading picture of the wedding was taken by William Creffield as the couple emerged from Westminster Abbey and it was published in practically every newspaper across the globe and had more reproductions than any other single picture of the wedding. But in one respect the new service fell short of the aspirations of its founders. While a first-class photo-coverage service of the United Kingdom was being built up, the agency did not have a regular incoming foreign photo service. Several years were to elapse before that shortcoming was remedied.

There were many more triumphs ahead, however, such as Suez in November 1956, where the PA scored with first pictures of British troops in action. By the time the department had completed its first ten years, it possessed the most up-to-date photographic equipment, with a first-class processing service and a picture library that was then and still is today the envy of the entire media industry. Truby, who pioneered the department, said at the tenth anniversary, 'We have had more than our share of the top news pictures receiving the widest publication. For many years, time and again, we secured the top prize in the *Encyclopaedia Britannica* competition.'

The wedding of Princess Margaret to Anthony Armstrong-Jones, later Lord Snowdon, in 1960 set up another record for the photo companies, whose laboratories produced more than 14,000 prints in a single day. But it was a royal activity of a different kind that momentarily dampened the enthusiasm of two PA–Reuters photographers. They were taking pictures of the Duke of Edinburgh at the Chelsea Flower Show in 1959 when they found themselves in the centre of a series of water jets coming from sprinklers concealed in the lawn. By a strange coincidence, the duke was standing beside the button that operated the sprinklers by remote control. But Buckingham Palace officials (reportedly hard put to it to keep a straight face) vigorously denied that the duke had pressed it.

One of those photographers was Walter Lockeyear, who, during the war, had accompanied the commandos on the Dieppe raid and later, attached to Churchill as official photographer, covered the Yalta and Potsdam conferences. It was Lockeyear who, in 1958, had done outstanding work in covering the State Opening of Parliament, when he was one of only two photographers allowed for the first time into the Chamber of the House of Lords. He and his colleagues managed to operate successfully despite the restrictions of an overzealous official, no less a man than the Lord Great Chamberlain, the fearsome 5th Marquess of Cholmondeley. The marquess gave orders that photographers must take only one picture of the Queen on the throne and they were required to do that with not too wide an angle. Happily, Lockeyear ignored these restrictions and produced magnificent and historic black-and-white and colour pictures.

Truby retired on 31 December 1961 and was succeeded by Derrick Knight, who had been head of the Shell photographic unit before joining PA–Reuters Photos in March 1960. Knight, who died in 1994 aged 74, had 'enjoyed' a spectacular war career. He was commissioned in the Royal Artillery and, as a member of David Macdonald's Army Film Unit, joined the 8th Army in North Africa. Knight photographed and filmed the desert battles and was mentioned in dispatches. He then took part in the landings in Sicily and Salerno, and in 1943 was attached to the US 5th Army in Italy, where he joined forces with four other photographers, all of them eager for pictures of the action. The group made a hazardous excursion to a village near Pompeii and were cut off by a German counterattack. When night fell they attempted to return to their own lines and were negotiating a street when a German tank opened fire, killing three of them. Knight escaped and was subsequently made an MBE. He went on to film D-Day, was wounded at Caen, and followed the conflict into Holland.

So it was with this rich and astonishing background that Knight joined Shell after the war and became established as a leading industrial photo-journalist. Once he had taken charge at

PA–Reuters he transformed working techniques, disposing of the old plate cameras and replacing them first with roll film and then 35mm.

The once Dickensian darkrooms were transformed into the most modern laboratories in Fleet Street. In his era, PA–Reuters had the best equipped team of photo-journalists in Europe. And Knight, who had a sharp eye for business, saw the potential for a co-operative European venture. However, Reuters wanted no part in this, and the Press Association opted instead for a link with Associated Press. The refusal by Reuters to co-operate came as a bitter blow to Knight and it coloured the rest of his time with the PA. He finally resigned, joining the Ministry of Defence's publicity team, working first for the Royal Air Force and then the Army.

But it was in 1961 that Lord Brabazon of Tara, pioneer motorist and aviator, opened the new PA–Reuters photographic laboratories, and disclosed an illegal picture he had taken in the House of Commons. It was the historic occasion when Neville Chamberlain made his last speech as Prime Minister, with Winston Churchill also in the frame. 'Mercifully, Chamberlain was quite still during the half-second of the exposure,' Brabazon recalled. 'Since then many pictures have been taken of the House of Commons in action, but in those days it was illegal and a very serious view was taken if you were caught . . . I could have gone to the Clock Tower.'

In 1965 Reuters pulled out of PA–Reuters Photos.

Throughout its history, the Press Association picture operation has not merely kept abreast with the techniques in its field, but has kept ahead as well. Pictures can now virtually be transmitted direct from the camera from anywhere in the world. For some years, staff photographers, such as Rebecca Naden in particular, have been covering, highly successfully, overseas cricket tours. These are some of the highlights of the rapidly modernising picture service in the final decade of the twentieth century. In addition to the technical innovations, the 1990s also included the appointment of extra staff photographers in the provinces.

Regular colour was wired experimentally in 1989 and 1990 was a year of massive modernisation including the installation of an electronic picture desk with colour included on the wire on a daily basis. Dixel-Hasselblad colour transmitters and portable film-processing equipment were introduced, allowing photographers to wire in digitally from out-of-London assignments. In 1992, PA's entire picture wire output was switched to digital, although many subscribers continued in analogue. In 1994, ISDN lines were added to the Press Association Bulletin Board, which now stores the entire daily file.

Pictures, which were a relatively late arrival on the Press Association scene, have been one of the biggest success stories in its entire history. From 2001 almost all assignments were shot using digital cameras and there was a large increase in foreign cover, including royal tours, sport and spot news.

15 Out with the Old

From the first day he walked across the newsroom of the Press Association, Edward Davies, who was appointed general manager in 1948, wanted to replace the old Creed-Wheatstone system of transmitting the news. It had served the agency well since its installation after World War One. Now, however, it was time for further advance.

There was nothing wrong with the Creed system – but it simply could not cope with the PA's steadily increasing volume of traffic. It was like a single-line railway. If several stories were competing with one another in interest and importance, they could still go through only one at a time, in a queue. So some stories could miss vital newspaper editions. Therefore, on a busy news afternoon, there was occasionally a savage 'massacre' of news stories that had been prepared for evening-newspaper use but could not be sent to them in time to meet their editions. On such days, a mass of morning-paper stories would choke up the wire till late in the evening.

Important and urgent stories were naturally allowed to jump the queue and the wires were also cleared for copy that had to be sent at fixed times, such as Stock Exchange reports and racing results. But all this was by no means an ideal situation. And there was another serious shortcoming to the Creed system: everything that was sent out arrived in the form of a tape 'punched' in Morse code. This tape had to be passed through another machine to be translated into a printed message.

When Jock Newlands, chief of the Telegraph Department, retired in 1934 and was succeeded by his deputy, Leonard Warren, it was recognised that the PA must start to use more sophisticated machinery and telegraph codes, which would allow the news to be transmitted faster and over more than one channel. However, it was another fourteen years before the new VF (Voice Frequency) came into full operation – a hold-up largely due to World War Two.

By May 1949 the new system was in operation, except to Ireland, because the British Post Office could not then provide the necessary VF circuits. Belfast was added to the teleprinter system in 1953 and Dublin and Cork soon after that. Warren, who had overseen the change from Creed-Wheatstone to multi-channel transmission, retired in 1953 but sadly died only three weeks later.

The whole innovation was a huge credit to the PA telegraph chiefs and mechanics. They planned and carried through the re-equipment in London and all the provincial centres, but also gave help and advice to many of the newspapers for whom the idea of multichannel teleprinter working was a completely new and formidable proposition.

The new system was an instant success. Instead of one Morse channel working at 120 words a minute, six channels, each working at 66 words a minute, were available, providing a capacity of about 400 words a minute. Another huge advantage was that all the newspapers were now served directly from London and each received the same items of news at precisely the same moment. It also meant that racing results and special items could be sent over particular channels without interfering with other news. Eventually, the printing up of punched tape in the newspaper offices became a thing of the past. The news, by now, was printed in page form by the teleprinters at the receiving end, ready at once for the newspaper subeditors and linotype operators.

Many of these new advances were also overseen by Jack Lush, who was telecommunications manager for the Press Association for a number of years and spent more than forty years with the agency. Lush, who succeeded Warren in 1953, described his first view of the PA wire room under the glass roof lights on the top floor of Byron House in 1929, and frankly admitted that what he saw gave him a considerable shock.

He said, 'I had come from the Post Office, where the telegraph instrument rooms were a model of orderliness based on years of regulation and convention. I thought the PA telegraph room looked a very amateurish hook-up. It was not long, however, before I realised that for sheer unremitting traffic handling, the Post Office could not touch the press.

'What appeared to be disorder was in fact the result of unorthodox and sometimes adventurous innovation. I found that press communications could not function within the limits of conventional telegraphy and needed to find their own enterprising methods.'

Lush added, 'There is a long list of technical developments which owe their success to the pressures of a system which can afford no delays and carries a service which can originate anywhere in the world; can be delivered to any other part of the world, and can rise from a trickle to a flood without notice.'

In those early days, the PA worked with Morse keys, sounders and automatic Morse transmitters and receivers, delivering a perforated tape. This was fed into a printer, producing a slip that passed through an unpleasant gum-dispensing device (quite undeservedly dignified by the name of Dextrinaire) and was eventually passed on to the subeditors in page form.

Telegraph lines were more frequently than not on overhead pole routes, subject to all the hazards of wind, rain and snow. When conditions were bad, the speed of transmission was equally affected. When conditions improved the operator edged the speed up to the top limit to feed in those extra inches of tape that, over the course of the few hours, meant so much when translated into words of copy.

The Press Association's first teleprinters arrived in the late 1920s. They were American machines called Morkrum Tele-types, and were used to replace the manual Morse wires from the Central Telegraph Office to Byron House, carrying copy handed in at local post offices by provincial correspondents. They were also operated from the Law Courts.

Since those, by modern standards, fairly crude beginnings, there was a record of steady progress over the next few decades. These included the introduction of the PA's first Voice Frequency Bay in 1935, giving six channels to Manchester over one line. Then, in 1948 and 1949, came the change from Morse to teleprinters at all provincial newspaper offices, abolishing the intermediate paper-tape process and printing directly from the line-wired signal.

This coincided with the abandonment of all single-wire transmission in favour of multichannel VF systems, in which frequencies within the audible range were divided into bands of 120 cycles per second, each of which, suitably modulated, could carry a teleprinter signal.

In 1950, the Press Association started the wired-picture broadcast service. This meant that wired pictures were now elbowing their way on to the same circuits as the teleprinter channels, so that each line carried six teleprinter channels as well as pictures. This gradually increased over the years.

And, as traffic increased, delays became even less tolerable. The London DP (direct printer to national newspapers) had moved from a single small group of subscribers in 1929 to serve a second and larger group in 1941. These two were expanded to a total of about 110 machines in each service during the war.

All this was followed by the introduction of the first sports printer and ultimately the third general-news channel in 1956.

The transmitting equipment required for these four services occupied no fewer than seven 8-foot-6-inch racks. However, advantage was taken of new miniaturised equipment and all these were built into a single 2-foot-square cubicle in 1967. The following year the highly successful PA news wire service was also accommodated in the same cubicle.

The next significant advance was the start of the experimental TTS (tele-typesetting service), also in 1967. It was launched as a pilot project involving four subscribers, the *Belfast Newsletter*, the *Cork Examiner*, the *Huddersfield Daily Examiner* and the *Halifax Evening Courier*. It was a service that grew and prospered and quickly reached more than thirty subscribers, continuing to expand rapidly beyond that.

All this opened up enormous new possibilities and opportunities, starting with the introduction of the Stock Exchange prices service, and laying the foundations for a computer typesetting system from wired agency tapes. This new TTS system meant that the telegraph operator had to produce every line of a length exactly to the column width of the newspaper using it. It was around this time that the all-capital-letter, teleprinter printer traffic was refined and updated to incorporate upper- and lowercase characters.

The world had certainly moved on from single overhead wires and Morse keys to a range of highly sophisticated equipment. That in itself was a revolution. But it was only a start. What was to come – by comparison – was awesome. One of the most original ventures into what is now called new media was in 1967, when the PA's name was, quite literally, up in lights. A news service, interspersed with advertising, was installed high on the Criterion Building in London's Piccadilly Circus, flashing the main stories to the thousands of promenaders down below. The whole procedure involved the use of no fewer than 14,000 lamps. In the space of under four seconds, each letter or symbol in a message swept across the static banks of lamps that successively flashed on and off in different patterns or colours

– each tiny group consisting of one white, one red, one green and one yellow. This was achieved by switching, and the motive impulses for that came from baths of mercury up in the rooftop offices.

Although this looked dazzlingly modern, the original idea came from Continental Europe in the last years of the nineteenth century. It involved endless festoons of shiny brown paper (the sort used in lampshades), composed of strips perforated with lettering and then joined end to end with sticky tape, firmly and continuously skimming across the mercury. The mercury, being liquid metal, popped up through the holes in slight beads, humped like the top of a mercury column in a thermometer. The beads brushed below rows of contacts to make electrical circuits. It was simple in theory, but highly complex in wiring detail. On the office wall were racks of metal stencils for punching letters into the paper. The challenge was to learn how to present pithy items of news that would each last just a few seconds, yet tell the essential story. It proved a popular innovation and was extended to some of London's principal railway stations, including Waterloo.

16 Clemmie's Revenge

I N 1954, TO MARK his eightieth birthday, Winston Churchill was presented by Parliament with a portrait of himself by Graham Sutherland. The trouble was Churchill loathed it. He could see no merit in it whatsoever. 'It makes me look half-witted, which I ain't!' he told close friends. Meanwhile his wife, Clementine, said it made him look deranged.

But on the big day Churchill was anxious not to offend those who had raised the money for it. So, at the unveiling in Westminster Hall, he sarcastically described it as 'a remarkable example of modern art'. In Pitman's shorthand, alas, the forms for 'remarkable' and 'great' can be very similar. Unfortunately, the Press Association reporter who covered the event picked the wrong one and so according to the newspapers the following day Churchill regarded it as 'a great' painting. Needless to say, the great man was far from amused.

The work of art was supposed to be hung in the Palace of Westminster but in fact found a home facing the wall behind a boiler in the cellar at Winston's home, Chartwell. Then, some-time later, unbeknown to Sutherland, Clementine, who detested the painting as much as her husband did, gleefully cut it up in small pieces and gave it to the gardener to burn in the incinerator with the winter leaves. Her actions meant that years later the story of the PA mistake was to be raked up all over again and the poor reporter, who by then had just retired, had to endure a further spate of calumny over a single misread word of shorthand.

For the story did not come to light until 23 years afterwards, when, at 5.30 p.m. on 11 January 1978, a PA newsman, Geoffrey Smith, took a call from the Churchill family executors, who told him the whole sorry tale, adding that Winston had been given an assurance that it would 'never see the light of day'. With a world exclusive on the agency's hands, another reporter, Peter Beal, attempted to track Sutherland down in the South of France, only to find he was on holiday in Pembrokeshire. When the artist was finally contacted, he was in despair, describing the ritual burning of his painting as 'an act of vandalism unequalled in the history of art'.

The following day, Beal's story was splashed in most of the morning papers, one of them under the headline 'Clemmie's Revenge'. The next morning a reporter, John Shaw, also spoke to Sutherland, who was now distressed because he realised that he had no photograph of the portrait. That was soon remedied. The picture news editor, Paddy Hicks, made special copies of the presentation photographs and of the painting itself and sent them to Sutherland. The artist wrote back, saying, 'I should like to thank you and your colleagues for their great kindness when they interviewed me over the telephone and the care they took in making sure what I said was perfectly accurate: a great rarity which is very greatly appreciated.'

Meanwhile, history shows that the Press Association did manage to placate Churchill only a few months after the reporter's original shorthand error in 1954. At that time Jack Juster, who was the Press Association's parliamentary chief, and his eventual successor, Cyril Arthur, were both senior office-bearers in the Press Gallery setup. The Gallery also wanted to present Churchill with a present on his eightieth birthday – and had decided on a watercolour of him by the celebrated artist Edward Ardizzone. Arthur, employing his renowned diplomatic skills, persuaded the Commons authorities to allow Ardizzone to sit in the Press Gallery and sketch Churchill addressing the House. This was a unique privilege never before and never since granted. Earlier sketches and caricatures of political figures had been done by button-holing the subjects in the Central Lobby and inviting them to pose just for a few minutes.

When the painting was complete, some of the grandees of the Press Gallery came to the conclusion that it was not imposing enough to give to Churchill. However, that was not the view held by either Juster or Arthur. So, armed with the painting, they paid a secret visit to Churchill. The moment he set eyes on it, the former wartime Prime Minister expressed his uncontained delight. That painting was, in fact, treasured by the Churchill family and still is to this day.

Churchill always had a high regard for the Press Association. On one celebrated occasion he said, 'Because the work you do is so valuable, the responsibilities of the Press Association are heavy. Without your help, the public would be uninformed and without your integrity they would be misled and defrauded. You have since the war had to exercise a discrimination never previously forced upon a national press. Many will feel you strike a fair balance, and I believe that you will continue to resist temptation to diminish fact for the sake or sensation or to twist truth and to serve partisanship.

'That is the great thing, the great feature, and I think I may speak for all political parties, that we discern and admire in the work of the Press Association.'

One person who attended that lunch commented afterwards that it was plain that Churchill 'meant every word'. Those remarks were passed when, as Prime Minister, he was guest of honour at the Press Association annual members' lunch on 11 June 1952. But he was also complimentary about the PA in private. Once at a luncheon in his honour given by the Jamaican government at the Ritz Hotel, in London, Churchill peered over his half-moon glasses at the guest sitting opposite him and enquired, 'Where are you from, young man?'

'The Press Association, sir,' said Reg Garner, a long-serving PA reporter.

'That's a fine organisation,' commented Sir Winston.

But the Churchillian habit of lisping occasionally and of dropping his voice unduly at the end of a sentence often caused havoc among reporters. On one occasion, during the first postwar Labour government, the PA reported him as saying, 'The present government is whistling the Empire away.' After the BBC radio news bulletin that evening, Churchill came on the phone to the Press Association news desk. 'You have reported me as saying that the present government is whistling the Empire away,' he roared. 'What I intended to say was that the present government is whittling the Empire away. But don't change it, Mr PA. I like it.'

During the period when he was in the political wilderness, Churchill sometimes telephoned the PA to enquire about international news. The chief reporter, Arthur Booth, was on duty in the news room at the time Mussolini's Italy invaded Albania, when he heard Churchill's familiar voice over the telephone. Arthur told him the full story of the attack. 'This is very grave,' Churchill growled, once again thanking the Press Association for its help.

Another long-serving Press Association reporter, Dick Eccleston, was covering a series of Churchill's speeches when he went to see the legendary wartime leader at his hotel. Eccleston asked if he could have a copy of his manuscript, because, if the agency did not have it in advance, the speech would miss the first London editions. So Churchill, who always trusted the Press Association implicitly, gave Eccleston his only copy, which the newsroom was then able to file on press telegrams and return. That same weekend Ecceston went to see Churchill again about another speech and pointed out that Saturday afternoon football took precedence over everything else at the Press Association and that his speech was in danger of being swamped if it was filed during those critical hours.

Tentatively, Eccleston asked if Churchill would be kind enough, in the circumstances, to dictate his speech in advance. 'Certainly,' said the ever-obliging Churchill. 'How much do you want?'

'Three hundred words?' Eccleston suggested.

'Three hundred words!' bellowed Churchill. 'That's not three sentences.'

Then, he took a puff at his cigar and said: 'Well, it will go something like this . . .' He then proceeded to deliver the entire speech to his audience of one.

When Churchill died, a comprehensive editorial plan, which had been devised some years before, was put into action. The agency had mounted a 24-hour watch on his home in Hyde Park Gate and was first with the news. The vigil was a duty that had to be performed discreetly and also not in the best of weathers. After the lying-in-state in Westminster Hall in the Palace of Westminster came the funeral and 23 PA reporters were placed at vantage points from Westminster Hall to Waterloo Station, a piece of preplanning meticulously worked out by Jack Williamson, chief news editor and soon to become managing editor.

Meanwhile, the agency posted 18 photographers at 24 different positions, and, as it was Saturday, they also had a full sporting programme to cover. That day the Press Association was stretched to its limit. During the period of the funeral, PA photographers took 82 black-and-white pictures and by the end of the day they had distributed more than 6,200 prints as well as processing 135 original colour transparencies. The first picture issued was of the public lining the route in great numbers at 6 a.m., including crowds outside the PA's offices in Fleet Street. The last ones were of the floral tributes on the grave and people filing by in tribute. In many cases, the photographers were able to use messengers and dispatch riders to bring the pictures back to Fleet Street, but the authorities would not provide facilities for messengers at St Paul's and cameramen there had to bring their own pictures into the news centre.

Some of the London newspapers and many of the provincials used a selection of the PA colour pictures and the picture desk maintained an open wire between 85 Fleet Street and Copenhagen and Stockholm to enable pictures to be sent through during the entire period of the funeral. Afterwards, the picture desk learned that they were at least half an hour ahead of their rivals throughout the whole event and reports from Scandinavia said that the agency's photos were 'superior in speed and quality'.

The Press Association's 'intro' on one of the leads during the day was, 'Winston Spencer Churchill, the man who made history, passed into its pages today.'

It was the beginning of a story that won a sheaf of accolades, notably from the *Glasgow Evening Times*, which said that the report 'used short, evocative Anglo-Saxon words in a way which would have delighted the old orator himself'.

17 The Monopoly Game

T HE EXCHANGE TELEGRAPH closed down its general home-news and parliamentary wires to newspapers in the autumn of 1965, claiming that these services had become 'completely uneconomic'. Now, for the first time, the Press Association had to collect all the general election results on its own. But the demise of Extel raised concerns in Parliament about the 'monopoly' that PA would allegedly enjoy as a news service.

The Labour MP Hugh Jenkins, who had a special interest in media issues, asked the President of the Board of Trade, Douglas Jay, to intervene, while the Liberal Party demanded action by the Monopolies Commission 'to ensure the continuance of a competitive service'.

The militant printing unions also demanded action and an Exchange Telegraph Defence Committee was set up to fight the closures. It sent a letter to George Brown, the Secretary of State for Economic Affairs, saying:

The obvious dangers – the danger to press freedom, the danger of restricted channels for the dissemination of news, the danger of sheer commercial self-interest obliterating the national interests – have been sharply underlined.

The deprivation to newspapers of an alternative news service (the value of which was recognised by the Royal Commission on the Press) is a further step towards the contraction of ownership and a further contraction of outlet. We are convinced that such a move is vital to good public policy and that a thorough investigation is vitally necessary.

There was also a statement from the central London branch committee of the National Union of Journalists, which said:

The committee deplores the proposed closures and particular-ly the resulting monopoly in the home news agency field with attendant professional, social and political dangers. It is especially concerned at the apparent under-valuation by national and provincial newspaper managements of the Exchange Telegraph Services concerned . . .

The departure of Exchange Telegraph was, in fact, bad news for the Press Association. With no competition, there was a danger that some slackness could creep into the agency. The Press Council also pitched in, expressing regrets 'because the decision reduces the sources of information available to all newspapers'.

The closures generated a considerable amount of political heat for some three weeks. However, Jay eventually rejected the calls for the matter to be referred to the Monopolies Commission. And later still he said he was satisfied that the alternative news-gathering services that were available were adequate to protect the public from any possible detriment. But, for all the talk about monopolies, there was little that could be done. Here was a company that had been fighting a losing battle in respect of some of its key services. Enquiries by the Board of Trade showed that the Exchange Telegraph needed an extra £150,000 to carry on – and a subsidy was out of the question. Some seventy of the total Extel staff lost their jobs, but large numbers were taken on by the Press Association.

The *Guardian* newspaper, in a leading article, succeeded in bringing a sense of proportion to these events. It said:

The MPs and trade unionists who want the Government to intervene are barking up the wrong tree. Though the Press Association will now be the only major news agency supplying domestic and parliamentary news, this does not mean it will enjoy a monopoly in any real sense. Most newspapers have access to parallel and alternative news services through their own London offices or through links with other newspapers or groups.

In any case it is hard to see what the Liberal Party means when it calls on the Monopolies Commission to 'ensure the continuance of a competitive service'. If the Press Association finds itself alone, that is not its fault. Extel is giving up the reporting of parliamentary and general news of its own choice and for commercial reasons. The company cannot be required to continue a service which it finds unprofitable, in order that some newspapers shall continue to enjoy a multiplicity of news sources.

The Times took a similar view in an editorial. While the extent to which the Press Association and Extel were in competition was very limited and principally confined to London, what competition there was did certainly act as a spur. But there was really room for only one domestic national news agency in the twentieth century. However, Extel kept in operation its profitable areas, such as its financial and sporting services and its special news services channelled mainly to clubs and hotels.

Until then, the Law Courts service had been run jointly by the Press Association and Exchange Telegraph. The PA took it over from the beginning of 1966 and it became known as the Press Association Law Service. In fact, the Extel staff at the Law Courts joined the PA. Among the other key members of the Extel staff who joined the PA at this time were their diplomatic and lobby correspondents, Arthur Williamson and Edward Spencer Shew.

But perhaps the most important member of the Extel staff to come over was Don Bristow. As we saw in Chapter 11, he arrived in 1968 with a wealth of journalistic and especially agency experience behind him and performed roles in planning and industrial relations.

Meanwhile, the Royal Commission on the Press, in 1977, chaired by Professor Oliver McGregor, of London University, spoke highly, although not uncritically, of the Press Association. And it made the point that there was no room for a rival agency, however much some politicians might regret what they regarded as a monopoly – a situation that was actually denied by the Commission.

But the Commission's view was reiterated by the PA management years later when the agency was faced with the threat of UK News. This, for the record, is what the Commission had to say:

The Press Association is the only news agency providing a comprehensive service of domestic news and information. Its output constitutes such an important element in the contents of the provincial press that to a large extent the editorial standards of the Press Association become the editorial standards of many newspapers in the country.

The Press Association competes for the news with radio and television, with the national press and with the provincial press also. It is not a monopoly. Moreover the co-operative ownership arrangements of the agency give those who use the agency's services the power to influence its performance.

An error in a Press Association tape can rapidly be transferred into a large number of newspapers, where it will often not be identifiable as coming from the agency. Although the agency will put out a correction where a significant error of fact is brought to its attention, not all the papers which carried the original story or based an item of their own on it, may carry it, and it is difficult to correct a mistake which appeared in many newspapers through the correspondence columns of each of them.

We believe the Association's position is so strong that it should be particularly prompt, generous and scrupulous in correcting mistakes. The evidence which we have received about the agency speaks highly of its accuracy, and we do not suggest that there is a frequent need for correction. We received two kinds of criticism of the Press Association. The Acton Society Press Group and the Liberal Party, for example, were anxious because it faces no direct competition. We understand and sympathise, but we do not consider there is room for two comprehensive, domestic news agency services. Therefore it is not realistic to consider the possibility of an alternative.

The other principal criticism of the agency was that it has tended to go beyond the transmission of facts into interpretation, explanation and the highlighting of particular aspects of stories. An important part of this is the use of headlines. Some witnesses including . . . the Confederation of British Industry, and the National Union of Journalists, suggested that this tendency was leading to lower standards and represents a potentially dangerous imposition of a single set of news values or stereotypes.

In response to criticisms of this kind, the agency has pointed to the need for explanation or interpretation if the facts it reports are to make sense to the reader, and it has drawn attention to the rule that such comments or interpretations must be seen to be separate from the fact themselves. We have not carried out a close enough examination of the Association's output to enable us to form a conclusion about

this criticism, but we urge the agency always to make clear
the distinction between fact and comment.

And in another passage in its report the Commission, the third
such on the Press in thirty years, said:

> Following the end of the parliamentary and home news
> service of Exchange Telegraph (Extel) in 1965, the Press
> Association is now the only news agency handling national
> news, and it also transmits overseas news from Reuters,
> Associated Press (AP) and Extel to regional papers. The Press
> Association is a non-profit making co-operative owned by the
> provincial press.
>
> Any newspaper publisher outside London may be a mem-
> ber, and the publishers of nationals may be members if they
> have a Manchester edition. In addition, the London offices of
> the other nationals, the BBC, ITV and independent radio hire
> the service.
>
> The Press Association transmits an average of 200,000
> words a day, one-third of which is derived from other
> agencies. It estimates that it originates 10–20 per cent of the
> news content of provincial evening papers and sometimes
> nearly half of that of provincial mornings.
>
> Mornings and evenings make large use of its picture service.
> The principal news agencies supplying overseas news direct
> to the British Press are Reuters, AP, United Press International
> (UPI) and Agence France Presse. Reuters is a United Kingdom
> company owned by the Press Association and Newspaper
> Publishers Association, together with the Australian Asso-
> ciated Press and New Zealand Press Association. These bodies
> are party to a Trust Agreement which guarantees the indepen-
> dence of the news service supplied by Reuters.

What the Commission had to say about the Press Association
on that occasion was based in part on a twelve-page memorandum (plus appendices), which the PA submitted to them. This
submission pointed out the general purpose of the PA:

> Its raison d'être from its inception has been to supply the
> most comprehensive news coverage possible to all the news-
> papers throughout the British Isles. As other news media
> developed, the Press Association extended its services to

them, but its constitution and function have not varied materially during the past 108 years.

The PA service is not cheap, but it provides major economic benefits to subscribers who receive a service of a range and quality which could not be achieved except by a pooling of resources. This is particularly important for smaller papers in the face of increasing competition.

The document also commented on the disappearance of competitive agency services and the emergence of the PA as a de facto monopoly:

None of these news agencies operated, or tried to operate, on the Press Association's comprehensive scale. Generally, their activities were restricted to London newspapers and other media in the capital.

Like its predecessors in abandoning the field of general home news, Exchange Telegraph's services were available only in London. The cessation of their service did not accordingly affect 90 per cent of the newspapers in the British Isles, which never had access to it. At the time of Extel's cessation of home news coverage, that agency was already co-operating with the Press Association in joint coverage of the High Courts and of General Elections, of sporting results and scores, and in a number of other areas. In all these areas there was accordingly no competition between Extel and the PA. The Press Association never had covered the London Stock Exchange, but bought such news from Extel – and still does. Extel never had covered racing news, but bought such news from the PA – and still does. The areas of competition were accordingly restricted.

When Extel took this action in 1965, there was some parliamentary and public debate about the emergence of the PA as 'a monopoly news service'. The Liberal Party called for action by the Monopolies Commission 'to ensure the continuance of a competitive service'. The President of the Board of Trade, Douglas Jay, was asked by an MP to intervene. The printing and journalists' unions also deplored the action. Mr Jay said, first, he was satisfied that the case was not an appropriate one for the Monopolies Commission and, later, that he was satisfied that the 'alternative news gathering services which are available are adequate to protect the public from any possible detriment'.

His latter remark touched the core of the matter. News-papers outside London, but especially those printed and published in London, have access to a large number of alternative news sources . . .

The submission quoted editorials from both the *Guardian* and *The Times* supporting this argument. *The Times* wrote: 'Even in the reporting of home and parliamentary news the fears of monopoly are largely irrelevant to this particular issue. So far as major newspapers are concerned no press agency can have a monopoly: its role is to supplement, not to replace their own competitive service . . .'

In a passage on the use of the PA service, the memorandum said that 'in an average day, the PA transmits a total of about 200,000 words'. It continues:

Of this, a little under two-thirds was from PA sources alone; the remainder comprising material from Reuters, Associated Press, the Exchange Telegraph Company and the PA–Extel Joint Service of sporting results and scores. No single paper uses more than a fraction of this output, which is designed to meet the widely varying needs and deadlines of over 120 papers. But almost every story the PA issues gets into print somewhere. If it is not used – in the general form sent, or as the germ of an idea then applied and developed locally by a paper's own staff or as material on which editorial comment is based – the agency has failed in its role of meeting members' needs.

Frequent consultation between PA executives and those of regional newspapers helps the agency staff to gauge these needs.

It continued by spelling out the basic role of PA:

A news agency takes its editorial decisions solely on editorial judgments. It is not influenced by other considerations. The service is based on four criteria: accuracy, speed, balance and simplicity of language. It is an agency's job to report facts, not to comment or editorialise. Often such facts must be ex-plained, backgrounded or interpreted if they are to make sense to the reader. But any such interpretation must be seen to be separate from the facts themselves.

It is the agency's job to report the facts.

18 Streets of Trouble

'I F YOU WANT TO DIAL 999 you'll have to use another phone – I'm dictating a story!' Reporter Michael Day's words rang out of the copytaker's earphones as a mob surrounded the telephone kiosk in an embattled Northern Ireland hotel. It was the late 1960s and life for the Press Association's reporters and photographers like him, working on the streets of Belfast and Londonderry at the height of the Troubles, was dangerous.

But the agency was to emerge with credit and distinction from those early days when entire streets were burning, snipers were rampant and barrages of rocks and petrol bombs from rioting gangs were all part and parcel of a journalist's working day.

In the beginning it was painfully evident that Protestant extremists hated the press, and particularly English journalists. Several reporters were threatened by supporters of Dr Ian Paisley, who was to become leader of the Democratic Unionist Party. Anyone unlucky enough to be caught with a notebook would immediately have it snatched away, ripped up and tossed into the gutter. Many photographers had cameras grabbed and films of militant crowds were destroyed by exposure. What made it even worse, according to Day, was a situation where positive hostility towards journalists went hand in hand with general non-co-operation. This was a no-win situation and it was therefore virtually impossible for reporters to check the endless rumours and claims that were forever on the go.

Communications were at best difficult and at worst nearly impossible, although it is a credit to all concerned that the stories always got through, no matter what the danger or other problems. This was in the days before mobile phones existed as part of a reporter's everyday equipment. Naturally, few people would dare to open their front doors to be asked to borrow their telephones while the riots were blazing. Meanwhile, callboxes – well lit and isolated along the streets – made good targets for snipers and petrol-bomb throwers. The safest way to get stories over from the streets was to get into a telephone box, remove the light and sit on the floor with the knees well up to protect the face should a bullet shatter the glass. There was always, of course, the probability that the phone would not work.

Reporters naturally wished to avoid petrol bombs whenever possible. When a petrol bomb goes off, it can leave a trail of blazing petrol 30 feet behind it – and, since they all contained either sugar or detergent, the burning petrol would stick to whatever it hit. Day suffered a head injury when rioters hurled a shower of petrol bombs during one incident. He turned to run and smashed his head on a 'no waiting' sign!

It was August 1969 that serious rioting broke out, marking the Apprentice Boys' parade in Londonderry. A former Press Association reporter, John Shaw, tells the story: 'The worst outbreak was in Derry. It went on all night. I got there the following afternoon, when it began again and continued without a break until 5 a.m. on Monday.

'It all took place on a hill leading to the Catholic quarter of Bogside. The crowd smashed paving stones and charged down the street, throwing as they went. The police countercharged up the street and brought in water cannon. The crowd retaliated with petrol bombs. All the street lamps were smashed, and as night fell civil disorder spread through Londonderry. But, while all this rioting went on, the little family saloons that wound their way round the bottles and stones scattered across the main road still did business.'

Later that same Monday, an exhausted Shaw was joined by another Press Association reporter, Bob Peart. The Cabinet met in emergency session that afternoon and troops were moved to the outskirts of Londonderry as the rioting continued almost nonstop on Monday night, Tuesday and Wednesday.

The Press Association men kept abreast of developments but naturally grew increasingly weary. 'We were thoroughly exhausted by the end of it,' Shaw recalls, 'doing "clearing-up" stories by day and "fresh rioting breaks out" pieces by night. The emotional pitch was such that it seemed to me that the whole place would really explode when Londonderry held its own Orange Day procession a month later in August, and I did a piece on these lines for the office'.

Before these troubles, however, there were two weekends of vicious violence in Belfast. At that time Tom McMullan – who was to become the Press Association's diplomatic correspondent – was the agency's sole representative in the city.

McMullan coped alone with the first night of violence, dodging petrol bombs and stones in the Crumlin Road, across which the Catholics and Protestants were bombarding each other. During the weekend Iain Macaskill and Mike Day were flown out from London to join him. They all had long, tiring stints in the Crumlin Road until the fighting died out on the Tuesday night. The three of them then went to Londonderry for the march on 12 August. All was quiet until the parade entered Waterloo Place, where it was jeered by a small group of Catholics from the Bogside area. They were behind barriers put up by the police to keep the two factions apart.

The jeering continued and then a stone was thrown at the parade from behind the barrier. McMullan was on the spot to see the first exchange of stones, a relatively mild outbreak until riot police arrived in full combat gear. They diverted the march and sealed off Waterloo Place. As they did so, they were bombarded with stones. That bombardment was maintained for more than an hour and the three reporters watched events cautiously from shop doorways. These had been rendered 'safe' because most of the windows had been boarded up for fear of trouble.

After several police had been felled by stones and bricks, the order was given for them to retaliate – at which point the fighting began in earnest. McMullan had to return to Belfast and so Jon Churchman joined the other two in Londonderry. Day describes the subsequent scenes:

'The following forty-eight hours in Derry were sheer bedlam. During one six-hour spell there was a constant hail of petrol bombs and missiles, which we all had to dodge to get within a few yards of the fighting. Then the police decided to use tear gas. It cleared not only the demonstrators but us as well. With eyes streaming, aching chests and burning faces we were forced to stay in our hotel until the effects of the first volley had gone.

'It was a frightening and dangerous time for us. Constantly dodging missiles, we often had to cross road junctions protected by the huge armoured police wagons that continually rumbled to new areas of rioting. So much happened in those forty-eight hours that most of us thought the trouble had been going on for days. On both the Tuesday and Wednesday nights, Londonderry was lit up by major fires, started either to hamper the police or as revenge attacks against firms suspected of religious discrimination. Besides being tired, we tended to get depressed, just by constantly watching two groups of people trying to kill and maim each other. Twice I saw policemen set on fire by petrol bombs. And, in the field hospitals set up in the Bogside, there was a constant stream of people of all ages waiting for treatment for the effects of tear gas. Youngsters lay around, many of them suffering burns where they were injured by burning petrol spilled while they were throwing fire bombs.'

During one spate of fighting in Londonderry, both Day and Macaskill were trapped and unable to escape: Macaskill was in a public house and Day in a fish-and-chip shop, both filing copy.

Day recalls: 'Suddenly the police were pushed back by rioters and we were stuck right in the middle. I have never been so frightened in my life. Petrol bombs bounced off both buildings while we sat by two fire extinguishers. At one point, I climbed out on to the roof to see if we could escape should the shop catch fire. About an hour later, police armoured wagons and water carriers pushed the rioters back and, as they did so, a shot was fired through the shop window, and unofficial police supporters kicked in some of the other windows as they rushed past.

'Then after constant threats to burn down the City Hotel, where more than a hundred journalists were staying, two petrol bombs were thrown in. One set fire to the cloakroom and the other filled the hotel with smoke. Luckily, not much damage was done, but we had to ask for police protection – which was grudgingly given.'

Day goes on: 'Some people risked going to bed, but most of us stayed up all night in case of further attacks. I am convinced that those who threw the bombs in would have burned the hotel down the following night, but by then we were saved. In the afternoon we walked out of the hotel and saw in the square outside a British Army Land Rover with a big machine gun mounted in the back – and we knew it was all over.'

And, as we know now, it was by no means over. But the arrival of the British Army at least gave some respite, if only for much-needed sleep. It is hard to understand it now, but the outnumbered Republicans and Catholics fervently rejoiced at the spectacle of the British Army. It was as if they had been liberated from the Protestant mob – and that was probably the truth. The police left the streets and the troops took control.

But, while Londonderry quietened down temporarily, worse violence was starting to erupt in Belfast. Roy Albans, one of the Press Association reporters covering the city's violence, recalled: 'The Falls Road, a Republican enclave, on the morning after the worst battle, looked more like something out of the London blitz than a scene in peacetime Britain.

'I drove from one end to the other in a nightmare journey. For a stretch longer than the whole of Fleet Street, there were buildings – shops, pubs, factories – burning on both sides of the road. Some shops had collapsed across it, and there were junctions at which the whitish scorch marks peculiar to the fire bomb almost covered the surface. I had all the windows of the car closed, but even so I could feel the heat building up inside as I drove. Opposite one blazing factory was a gang of youths shouting incomprehensible slogans and throwing stones into the flames. Men were strengthening the barricades that blocked off every side street. Some barricades were of double-decker buses, just burned-out shells.

'Days later, when I drove up the Falls Road again, flames fed by the gas supplies were still leaping in some of the piles of rubble. The most troubled part of Crumlin Road was comparatively small, a section of some four hundred yards southwards from the junction with Shankill Road marked by a Catholic church. Until that day the street had been served by a dozen or more bars: I saw the systematic destruction of these and other business premises.

'On Thursday night, August 14, stones were thrown from side streets at the north end of the road, and this developed into a fire-bomb battle, although most of the bombs fell short. I was a couple of hundred yards away talking to a senior policeman by his Land Rover when I heard shots. There were single shots, possibly from a revolver, the deeper boom of a shotgun, and then the rattle of more than one automatic weapon, followed closely by the sound of heavy machine gun mounted on a police armoured car. The police officer, closely followed by me, dived for cover.

'He put on a crash helmet. I tried to present as small a target as possible, and then, after a few minutes' lull, I crossed the road to a telephone box to put over my story. I had hardly finished speaking when the firing started again. I decided the box was too exposed, and cowered behind a parked car. More police vehicles arrived, and eventually the crowds were dispersed.

'Next afternoon, at the scene of the night's fighting, a priest gazed round through binoculars: there was not another soul to be seen. I went across the road to interview a householder. While we talked, I on the pavement, he in the shelter of his doorway, there was a single shot from a rifle. Something smacked into the wall, and I hurtled through the doorway into the house.'

That night Albans said that pubs went up in smoke on both the Catholic and Protestant sides and, ironically, a neon Guinness advertising sign shone until the very last.

'Later there was more gunfire across the main road from the Hooker Street and Disraeli Street turnings. A crowd gathered in the entrance to Disraeli Street and each time a police armoured car sprayed Hooker Street with bullets loud cheers went up. Answering fire came from the shadowed windows and roofs down the street. The telephone box I had been using before was now in the battle zone, its windows shattered'.

Later, Albans was to build single-handed a radio set, which was used by the news desk for many years to come. He was described by the news editor as 'Britain's first electronic reporter' – and Albans candidly admitted that his shorthand was not as reliable as his machines.

John Shaw had one particular horrific moment in a Belfast telephone box as he was trying to file copy to London in the thick of the rioting. A mob of about two thousand, loosely termed Paisleyites, were streaming down the road towards Albert Bridge, Belfast. Young boys were armed with lengths of copper pipe, youths brandished golf clubs and middle-aged men were carrying makeshift clubs and bottles – a fearsome spectacle of an undisciplined and ferocious band of thugs, young and old. There was a menacing swagger in their step and hate in their eyes: and a large part of that unqualified hate was for the press. Shaw, to his alarm, found himself in a telephone box trying to dictate a story, right in their path. He was dictating 'snaps' direct to the deputy night chief sub, Reg Weedon. Suddenly the telephone box door was yanked open and a young thug demanded: 'Are ye a pressman?' Shaw, who was seated on the floor of the box, to his eternal credit, incredibly kept his cool and said, 'No, I'm on holiday. I'm a tourist and I'm making a private conversation. If you want to make a call, please wait outside, but at the moment I'm ringing relatives in England.'

The thug paused, uncertain whether to believe him or not. It was not a pleasant moment for Shaw. But one of the interloper's friends nudged him and said, 'Leave him. The soldiers are down at the bridge. We can have a real go there.'

And so, to Shaw's intense relief, the mob passed on, leaving him unmolested. He filed his story and later joined his colleague

Peter Robinson. The confrontation at the bridge ended in stalemate: the Army succeeded in keeping the Protestants and the Catholics apart, using manpower, guns and CS gas. Both Shaw and Robinson were gassed and got to bed at 3 a.m. – after a routine Sunday's work in Belfast.

There were incidents, however, that afterwards – if not at the time – bordered on the comical. For instance, on 30 September, the Paisley supporters, some six thousand, of them, demonstrated on the lawns in front of the Stormont Parliament buildings on the outskirts of Belfast. The three Press Association reporters, Shaw, Robinson and Macaskill, inevitably got separated. Shaw came across a television team from New York, who were threatened and called liars by the mob.

'We don't distort the news, ma'am,' one member of the TV crew told an agitated Paisleyite woman. 'We just film it as it happens, how it happens, where it happens. Then it goes back home to the US.'

'Well,' the woman screamed back at him, 'just take care not to film any lies then.'

'It was all very Irish,' Shaw said afterwards. But a little while later he saw an American reporter and his crew being beaten up, but was powerless to intervene because the numbers were so great. They left that night for New York.

Around that time, a number of soldiers were shot in unusual circumstances. Shaw actually traced a brave taxi driver who had witnessed one of these incidents in the notorious Grosvenor Road area, near the centre of Belfast. Shaw's dramatic story was widely used by papers throughout the United Kingdom and was given an accolade on the Granada television programme *The Papers*. It was also a valuable story from the Army's point of view and they thanked him for it.

This same three-man team went on to cover the weekend riots in the first fortnight in October. There were major incidents night after night for weeks, and from time to time there were changes in the team to give some respite to those who had endured the worst of the trouble. On the night of 11 October, a large Protestant crowd gathered in the Shankill Road. Police formed a cordon to stop them getting down to a predominantly Catholic block of flats on the perimeter of the Protestant 'territory'. There was a volley of shots. One policeman fell dead and his colleagues on either side were wounded. The police took cover and most of the crowd dispersed as snipers took up their positions to rain bullets on to the scene.

Mike Day takes up the story: 'Peter Robinson was first on the scene while we made preliminary check calls to the army and police. When Macaskill and I found Peter he was crouched down in a telephone kiosk filing copy. The Army was moving in and troops were lying combat-fashion on their bellies all around the box. Police were about two hundred yards in front of the Army, and the three of us started to make our way to the forward position. At first we walked single file as near to the shop walls as possible. Bullets were still coming down the road so we decided to take the back streets. We got to the police position at a road junction, and waited and watched as bullets zinged along the street.

'I had never realised one could hear a bullet. They whistled overhead almost as if they were going in slow motion. Periodic bursts of firing continued, and Peter, Iain and I in turn made our way back to the telephone to file.'

Meanwhile, a photographer, Eric Shaw, had persuaded a local man to take him up past the police position to cover near where the snipers were firing. It was from there that he got some of the most spectacular and dramatic pictures of the entire troubles.

'The night hotted up shortly after we arrived back at the telephone box,' Day continued. 'Unfortunately, it was outside that Catholic block of flats, and it was the only means of communication. Although we had used telephones in homes in the backstreets, nobody in this area dared to open their front doors while the shooting was going on. At the kiosk we took out the light and while two of us sheltered behind the box the third, crouching inside, gave copy. The Army was still fully prepared beside the box when, just after we had finished putting over copy, a shot struck the road about ten feet from it. Everyone fell flat on the ground: the soldiers took up combat positions, and we were told that one or more snipers were about fifty yards away. Other shots hit near the telephone box before we eventually crawled to safety behind a wall.'

The following night was virtually a repeat performance, although this time both the police and the Army were better prepared and there were no deaths. On this occasion, the Army moved a fleet of heavy armoured vehicles up to the 'front line' to protect everybody. During all these disturbances, the Press Association was well at the front with picture reporting as well. One of the most skilful cameramen was Nick Beer, who was later to die in a helicopter accident during a NATO exercise. Other photographers who took part, in addition to Eric Shaw, were Johnny Horton, Mark Seymour, George Stephenson, Tony Harris and Derek Millward, plus a stream of picture processors and other technicians complete with a mobile darkroom.

All in all the Press Association threw a lot of resources into Northern Ireland, and the Republic, too. Before the Troubles renewed in the late 1960s, the PA had no staff correspondents either north or south of the border. Freelances were relied on to cover both the Province and the Republic, except, of course, when staffers were sent over to cover big stories.

That was one reason why there was an immediate rethink of the situation. The reporters and photographers of the Troubles were soon to have an office, in the *Belfast Newsletter* building, rather than have to operate from hotel rooms.

19 Nice One, Harold

PHILIP SIMPSON WAS A STICKLER for detail – so much so that he once dragged a prime minister into the late-night fog to deliver a speech in an empty hall, just so that he could report it.

The bizarre event took place because Simpson, working in the Press Association's Liverpool office, had received the text of a speech by the Premier, Harold Wilson. But the speech, due to have been made in the Prime Minister's Huyton constituency on Merseyside, was not delivered because a snarl-up on the railways delayed his arrival and the meeting had been abandoned.

Downing Street, however, had given Fleet Street permission to publish the speech as if it had been delivered. But even that was not good enough for Simpson, a diminutive figure but also a person who was a stickler for getting his facts absolutely and impeccably right. He felt he could not disseminate the text unless Wilson had actually delivered the words in the appointed venue. So the intrepid reporter travelled through the blustery winds to the city's Adelphi Hotel, where Wilson always stayed when he was in town. Finally, he persuaded the Prime Minister to leave the comfort of his suite, travel across to Huyton on this disagreeable night and read his speech out loud, to the puzzlement of the cleaning lady and the satisfaction of Simpson. Honour duly satisfied, Wilson returned to his hot drink and Simpson to the telephone to file his story. But before he left Wilson grumbled, 'I would not have done this for anyone else but you, Phil!'

Wilson was always full of praise for the Press Association. At the PA centenary dinner in November 1968, he spoke highly of the agency's local correspondents. 'My experience in this whole postwar period is that you are superbly served by your local representatives,' he said. 'They are professionals. For one thing, Press Association shorthand is impeccable, even at the speed I sometimes speak.

'In an age where Britain is rapidly becoming the only nation where its professionals can do shorthand – this is why so many politicians abroad so often, not without justification, claim to have been misreported – the Press Association through its local man rightly lays claim to straight and accurate reporting.

'I know this will put me in difficulties if next week I have to say that I was inaccurately reported. But as it has happened to me only once, eighteen years ago, with PA and was due to the fact that your excellent and reliable man in Ormskirk, now sadly no longer with us, had become rather deaf, I will take that risk.'

Wilson said that the Press Association talked with kings but did not lose the common touch. 'Its photographers and reporters walk with the crowds,' he added. 'And, whatever the changes in communications over the next century, I am confident that whoever speaks at the same dinner a hundred years from now will, on your behalf, be able to make the same proud comment.'

The Prime Minister's words about royalty and the common touch rang true throughout the sixties and many times it was the everyday ingenuity of the agency's staff that brought out the best of the big occasion – such as the investiture of the Prince of Wales at Caernarfon in 1969. A memorable picture of the Queen placing the coronet on the head of Prince Charles was taken by a Manchester-based photographer, Eric Shaw, from a position on the battlements of Caernarfon Castle. The film was lowered in a bag over the walls to a messenger waiting below, who raced with it to the press centre, where it was processed by the Press Association's mobile photo team. Its transmission by wire was completed less than one hour after it was taken. This was the star picture of the entire event and was used on the front page of every national newspaper the next morning.

But these successes do not happen by magic. The way it was handled and the speed with which it was transmitted reflected the weeks of planning that went into the massive editorial operation. And the planning of this particular event was complicated by the threat posed by the so-called 'Free Wales Army' and other anti-monarchist and anti-investiture elements. The police made no secret of the fact that they were extremely worried about disruption by these elements and even the possibility of an assassination attempt. As it turned out, the event passed peacefully – but things might have been very different if the elaborate security precautions not been put in place.

Meanwhile, that same year, a Press Association reporter was 'fingered' in a telephone box by the Duke of Edinburgh. It happened after a meeting at which the duke had made some uncomplimentary remarks about several pop singers of the day whose voices reminded him of the sound of dirty bathwater gurgling down the plughole. He had assumed the remarks were off the record and that no reporters were present. But in fact the Small Businesses Association had invited the Press Association to send two reporters to attend the after-lunch discussion in which the duke was taking part. The reporters, Leonard Moxon and John Shaw, both highly experienced operators, were each holders of an official card from Buckingham Palace giving them 'facilities as a correspondent'.

During the discussion, which involved about thirty people, the duke described Tom Jones's singing as 'hideous'. Only a few days earlier he had asked the singer after the Royal Variety Performance at the London Palladium, 'What do you gargle with, pebbles?'

After a while, the duke spotted Shaw taking notes. 'He saw me sitting at the table and asked, "Who are you?" Shaw recalled. 'I told him I was from the Press Association and he replied, "What the hell are you doing here?"

'I told him I was reporting the function. There was a silence, then Prince Philip said, "Nobody told me the press were here . . . You had better not let any of this get in." '

A few moments later, Moxon was already telephoning his part of the story from a call box on the premises, and Prince Philip got wind of it. Moxon said, 'I had nearly finished when I heard the door being opened. The light went out, and somebody tapped on my shoulder. I turned round. It was the duke.

' "What are you doing? I hope you're not reporting what I have been saying," he said. I told him I was. "I don't want it," he replied. "It was a completely informal discussion, and I didn't know the press was there. I don't want anything of what I said quoted."

'I told my office to hold the line and joined the small crowd with the duke at the door. I told him I had an invitation and a Palace press card but he still seemed angry.

'I pointed out that all I had reported so far were his innocuous remarks about big international companies. The duke burst out with an angry remark about "chaps like you . . ." I didn't answer and he was edged gently to his car by officials.

'He must have been practically the only person there who didn't know that the discussion was being reported. Later I was told by Sir Richard Powell, chairman of the Institute of Directors and a top-table guest, that the duke had telephoned to apologise to me, which, of course, I accepted.'

Later, an official of the Small Businesses Association admitted that it had not informed the duke that the press was present. 'I feel we have let him down,' he added. And later still Buckingham Palace apologised to the Press Association over the incident. The Palace spokesman said the duke was firmly under the impression that no one from the press was there, and if he had known he would not have spoken in the terms he did.

A few days later Tom Jones received a letter on behalf of the duke – not an apology but an explanation. The letter said that the duke intended nothing harsh by what he had said, and the star accepted that.

The Press Association report of this incident omitted some of the bad language used by the duke. Its editor-in-chief, David Chipp, said later, 'I thought at the time that we were correct to do so and still think this, though some of my colleagues and some editors for whom I have a high regard believe we should have carried the whole text of his abuse, even though it was a private exchange, and left it to newspapers to decide on what to omit.'

There was, indeed, considerable argument within the Press Association office as to whether the story should be issued at all. However, Chipp expressed his admiration for the way in which Moxon and Shaw behaved. 'They conducted themselves with firmness and restraint under very difficult circumstances,' he said.

Prime ministers, pop stars and royalty aside, the sixties in Fleet Street will always be remembered by those who were there for the decade that played host to one of Britain's most tragic stories – the Aberfan disaster. It turned out to be probably the most harrowing individual disaster for reporters to have covered throughout the twentieth century.

On that fateful day, 21 October 1966, a coal tip plunged down engulfing a school in the Welsh village killing 116 children and 28 adults. The coal slurry had slipped in heavy rain and buried Pentglas junior school. One day later, pupils and staff would have been away on their half-term holiday. The disaster appeal raised around £2 million. What was sadly strange was that people from all over the world sent toys – for a village suddenly without many of its children.

Cliff Phillips (known locally as Cliff the Kiosk because he always appeared to be in telephone boxes dictating stories to the office) was the Press Association's Cardiff staffman and on that morning he was covering court proceedings in the Welsh capital. On the instructions of the news desk, a correspondent in Cardiff was told to contact Phillips in the court and order him to head for Aberfan as fast as he could.

Meanwhile, within five minutes of the first hint of the tragedy, the newsroom in London had managed to cobble together a story around some basic facts following a call to the emergency services in Merthyr Tydfil. Every available reporter was then put on direct calls as Phillips made his way down to the scene, quickly followed by Wilf Giles, the Press Association's Bristol staffman. Others who made up the agency team in Aberfan included Ray Smith, who had only recently joined the PA from the *Portsmouth Evening News*, where he had been the Isle of Wight staffman, and Alan Watkins.

Phillips, who was later to receive the MBE for his work at Aberfan, not only produced widely used vivid and moving stories describing the stark desolation of the scene, but, with tears in his eyes, also desperately tore at the rubble with his bare hands, to try to rescue the youngsters buried beneath it.

20 The Bigger Picture

P A PHOTOS REMAINED at the forefront of technical advancement. In 1970, it set up a new centre at 371 Euston Road, London, with drive-in studios and laboratories. The object was to build up a unique service for British industry, backed by all the experience and technical know-how gained over the years. And that know-how went on show when giant colour enlargements and display transparencies produced in the Euston Road laboratories featured in the British Pavilion at EXPO 70.

The new studios quickly built up a large and varied clientele, ranging from heavy industry to cosmetic manufacturers, who required top-quality studio photographs for their colour brochures. Martin Cleaver and Ron Bell were two of the photographers employed over the years by the Press Association. Both deservedly won awards for their work and received honours, Cleaver an MBE and Bell, who was for many years the agency's royal photographer, an MVO, which came direct from the Queen.

Cleaver's outstanding work with the Press Association came at the height of the Falklands conflict, and Bell was appointed royal photographer in 1976, at a time when it was virtually unheard of for the agency's journalists to venture abroad. Up until then, foreign picture coverage was provided for the Press Association by the Associated Press.

But Bell probably became the first PA photographer to venture outside these shores. For within a few months of taking his royal post, he accompanied the Queen on a state visit to Luxembourg. The following year – the Queen's Silver Jubilee – he went on an eight-week royal tour of Australia, New Zealand and the South Pacific.

One of Bell's most famous pictures was of the Defence Secretary, Fred Mulley, fast asleep alongside the Queen at a Royal Air Force fly-past in 1978. The photograph earned him the news picture story award in the World Press Photo competition.

Bell had already been named British Press Photographer of the Year in 1975.

One of his first jobs with the Press Association was covering the Derby. He was at the finishing post with a speed graphic camera and as the horses galloped down the final straight he removed the sheath from the lens ready for the winner to fly past. But as he did so he accidentally fired the shutter. It would not have mattered with modern cameras, since continuous shots can be taken like the rapid fire of a machine gun. But at that time a whole process, lasting several valuable seconds, had to be undergone before the camera was ready to take the next shot.

Bell panicked. Fortunately, an experienced Associated Press cameraman was at his side and realised his plight. Quickly, but clearly, he talked Bell through what he had to do to reload as the thunder of the hooves grew louder. Bell hit the shutter button just as the winner passed.

'I was in a sweat,' he admitted later. 'Without that AP photographer I would have gone to bits. What on earth would I have said to the editor?'

Bell was at the centre of an amusing incident at Broadstairs immediately after the October 1974 general election, in which Harold Wilson strengthened his position at Westminster after throwing Edward Heath and the Conservatives out of office in February of that year. Broadstairs was Heath's home territory and Bell went there to get shots of the defeated Tory leader at a birthday party. On his unannounced arrival, Bell asked if it would be all right to take photographs; the woman of the house looked at him sternly and replied, 'Yes, but on one condition – that you mow the lawn.'

This was not some suburban back garden with a grass patch the size of a tablecloth. It was half an acre. But the doughty Bell set to work manfully and, once the job was done, he was allowed to take the pictures.

On another occasion, in Venice, the Queen Mother was doing the tourist thing: a trip around the canals on a gondola. Naturally, the photographers wanted to make something special of it, and Bell hit on the perfect idea. The gondolier was an ex-waiter in a London restaurant and spoke near-perfect English. So Bell managed to get him to play a key role in a little ruse. The photographers would buy an ice cream – a Cornetto – give it to him, and he would hand it to the Queen Mother at the crucial moment. It would be a picture made in heaven.

The Cornetto was purchased and the photographers clustered around the quayside. But, as so often happens on these occasions, there was a brief delay – and the Cornetto started to dribble in the fierce sunshine. Worse was to follow. The tide came in and so the attendants were not able to get the Queen Mother aboard at the appointed spot. It was going to be 100 yards away up the quay. The inevitable mad rush of photographers to get vantage places at the new embarkation point followed.

Finally, with the Queen Mother duly boarded, the gondolier obligingly handed her a dripping Cornetto with many elaborate gestures of courtesy, and she accepted it with as good a grace as she could muster. Fortunately, in the rush to get to the new vantage point, Bell was the only photographer to be in the right position to get this vital shot. All the others found themselves clustered behind the gondolier's head and got nothing. It was a picture, naturally, that was used all around the world.

Meanwhile, when royalty are given flowers or any other gift, it is instantly passed on to an equerry behind the royal personage. This usually causes no problems whatsoever. However, on this occasion the bedraggled and fluid Cornetto was passed back to Sir Paul Greening, Admiral of the Royal Yacht Squadron, who was escorting the Queen Mother. The dripping ice cream was not the sort of object that admirals necessarily enjoy having to clutch. So, quick as a flash, he passed it on to a subordinate, who also passed it on and so on down the line of command, until it reached a point where there was nobody else to hand it to. The historic Cornetto, far from being relished by the Queen Mother, finished up in the murky waters of a Venetian canal.

During the early days, before Princess Diana was on the scene, Bell was sent to Sandringham to get a picture, without being intrusive, of Prince Charles and a girl who was reported to be spending a weekend with the royal family. Because of the Press Association's quasi-official relationship with the Palace, the instructions from the picture desk were, 'Don't stick your neck out. And don't let them realise that you're there.'

Bell duly arrived to discover that the royal party were shooting in the fields some distance away. Not far away was a road island with a large telegraph pole. 'I thought I would stand by the pole and, as they came by, peer out and if there was a picture worth taking, take it, otherwise I would not. I was determined to be very discreet,' Bell recalled.

'I had my cap pulled right over my eyes, my coat collar turned up and the camera in front of my nose. Nobody could possibly know who I was. I peered into the cars as they went by, but there was nothing much to photograph so I didn't do anything.'

Later that week, Bell was covering another event with the Queen, when her detective came up to him and asked, 'Did you enjoy Sandringham at the weekend?

'Not really,' Bell replied, but how on earth did you know I was there?'

'The Queen told me that there was an unusual amount of press activity that weekend and I told her why I thought that was – and that even the Press Association had sent someone. The Queen replied, "Yes, I know. I saw Ron Bell trying to disguise himself as a telegraph pole." '

For years the picture desk at the Press Association was a much disregarded part of the organisation, almost a poor relation. As a PA–Reuters service in the early days, it was not a section of the organisation that was brimming with enthusiasm. The photographers, by and large, were dispirited because they were effectively corralled on the ground floor of the agency in accommodation that was, to put it mildly, inadequate. The news desk was five floors away and there was, incredibly, virtually no formal liaison between the two desks. Reporters would go out on stories, not even recognising the photographers covering the same engagement. Often they would not even know if a PA photographer was present. David Chipp and Reg Evans, the executive editor, did their best to keep in close touch with the picture desk to ensure that good stories were accompanied by good pictures and vice versa. But in the past there had been precious little attempt to achieve that whatsoever.

Things took a big leap forward, however, when Paddy Hicks took over as picture editor. The agency already had two first-class Fleet Street veterans on the picture desk, Jack Richards and Dick Makin, both of whom had backgrounds in the freelance agencies of the 1930s, where the competition was rough and tough. All three men had a genuine feel for the lens, knew precisely what stories would lend themselves to pictures and above all recognised the importance of enthusing over and encouraging photographers when their work was good, something the Press Association had not been good at in the past.

Jack in particular had a fund of stories about the lengths photographers would go to in order to get the best shots. When

King Edward VIII was being driven from Windsor Castle to a Royal Navy ship at Portsmouth, which would take him to France following his abdication broadcast in 1936, Jack was an eager young man carrying the agency photographer's gear. Suddenly the two of them saw the royal car coming at them at 'a fair old lick' down the road. 'Jack, step into its path, there's a good lad!' the photographer ordered, pulling out his camera. Jack, in the line of duty, obeyed unhesitatingly. The brakes of the car shrieked, the vehicle ground to a halt, the camera clicked and Jack stood shaking. It was a classic picture that showed Edward VIII, white-faced, staring out of the window with one hand across his mouth. The caption under the picture, which appeared in virtually every paper in the land – and many overseas as well – said, 'The King acknowledges the cheers of the crowd as he leaves Windsor Castle for the last time.'

What, in fact, King Edward VIII was more likely to be thinking was, 'Who was that bloody fool who jumped out in front of us and nearly got killed?' The King never had the faintest idea that the whole incident was a high-risk stunt. No bones were broken but it was a close-run thing. Jack Richards retired in 1982. A Londoner through and through, he was a man who could see a picture in everything he touched. A colleague once likened him to Charles Dickens's Sam Weller – 'impressively worldly wise, and up to all the tricks, with a sharp and kindly wit.' That summed him up precisely. He married Hilda Down, the doyenne of the Press Association picture library, who devised a foolproof system which to this day enables even the most 'awkward' pictures to be retrieved in a matter of seconds.

It was a slow business getting the picture desk to its rightful geographical position, that is cheek by jowl with the news desk and therefore a wholly integral part of the agency's news operation. Fortunately, the technological revolution provided the solution. When that arrived, there was no need for the huge transmission department, which occupied more than a quarter of the editorial floor space. And so a new-look picture desk was born.

It was during the Chipp era that the Press Association managed to get an accredited royal photographer to match the accredited court correspondent. Ron Bell was the first one, followed by Martin Keene – later to become picture editor – and he in turn was followed at the Palace by John Stillwell.

21 On the Move Again

I N 1934, THE RENOWNED architect Sir Edwin Lutyens and H
Rogers Houchin were commissioned to design a new building, which was to be erected on the site of Byron House and
adjoining properties, which the Press Association had already
acquired. The space was there to erect a large and impressive
building that could stretch from Fleet Street almost to St Bride's.
Sir Roderick Jones was the moving spirit behind the plan.
Optimistically, those who were put in charge of the project
calculated that it would cost about £140,000 and take about a
year to build. These estimates were laughably wrong. The total
cost, including freeholds, was just under £450,000 and the period
it took to build was far longer than envisaged. The Press
Association did not occupy it until the summer of 1939, a few
weeks before the outbreak of World War Two.

In the meantime, the agency needed a temporary home while
the demolition and building were in progress. The old *Daily
Express* office in nearby St Bride Street was rented and equipped
at considerable expense. It was to be the headquarters of the
agency for nearly four years.

The new building quickly ran into problems. Sir Edwin
Lutyens, in all his grand thinking, had envisaged an edifice of at
least ten storeys and 100 feet high. He was absolutely confident
that there would be no civic objection to this. But he had read
the runes badly. The old London County Council produced an
army of bureaucrats and insisted on a maximum height of 80
feet, which virtually meant going back to the drawing board.
The plans had to be revised and the building reduced to one of
nine storeys. It was a major and costly setback and one that
accounted in large measure for the delays that followed.

Next it was the turn of the Dean of St Paul's to enter the fray.
He complained that the building, even after the architects had
bowed to the will of the London County Council, would interfere
seriously with the view of St Paul's Cathedral from Fleet Street,
a view that was described as 'one of the finest obtainable'. The

agency was sympathetic with the dean's views, but not enthusiastic about them. With reluctance the Press Association had to agree to setting back the upper floors. It was a classic example of failing to test the water with the big toe before plunging headlong in. Finally, however, everyone was satisfied and by July 1939 the building that famously became 85 Fleet Street was ready for occupation. The Press Association and Reuters moved in.

The new offices were variously dubbed 'Britain's Wonder News Clearing House' and 'Nerve Centre of World News'. Reuters leased more than half of the working space along with their 'allies' – foreign newspapers and news agencies with which it had close relations. The Press Association occupied most of the remainder. And so life began at 85 Fleet Street – appropriately on the site of a shop once run by Frederick Pitman, brother of Isaac Pitman. It had sold shorthand systems.

The move to 85 Fleet Street marked the end of an era for the Press Association and the opening of a new one. It was the first time for sixty years that the manager was not a member of the Robbins family, although there were still two members of the family working there, one as chief of the London Service and the other as head of the parliamentary reporting staff.

The retirement of Harry Robbins in 1938 was the end of the age of paternalism in the Press Association, which by now was employing hundreds of men and women with a competitive atmosphere to match. Long gone were the days of his father Edmund, who knew the names of all the staff and made sure that an employee who had a new addition to his family always got a little extra in his pay packet. As the company grew, it had to become less personal. The new general manager, Edward Davies, had come in from outside, and was not concerned about adhering to old traditions.

Davies, at the early age of 23, and after only a few years as a journalist, had been appointed secretary of the Newspaper Society, a post he held for 12 years before arriving at the Press Association. It was for him a huge contrast, since he had left a small staff. Now he had to administer hundreds of people. But his period on the Newspaper Society meant that he had a close association and acquaintance with many leading and influential figures in the provincial press – very much a plus for the agency.

At the end of 1939, Percy Shaw, who had been secretary of the agency since 1911, also retired. Shaw had been a loyal, if outspoken, servant of the Press Association. He was a man of strong opinions, both political and otherwise, and would have relished a role that gave him more scope to express them. Even so, he felt unable to contain his views and from time to time wrote outspoken letters to newspapers for publication. It was not a practice that necessarily endeared him to the agency's management and there were occasional brushes with the general manager over the years. But his departure, allied to the end of the reign of the Robbins family, helped to push the agency into a new and even more exciting direction.

However, in the last decade of the twentieth century, Fleet Street – the Street of Ink, the Street of Shame, call it what you will – was transformed from the unofficial headquarters of the British and overseas press into a mere extension of the City of London, forever moving its tentacles westwards.

Fleet Street had for centuries acted as an exciting buffer between the City tycoons at one end and the lawyers and the Royal Courts of Justice at the other. It was, without doubt, even to nonjournalists, by far the most stimulating street in London – probably the world.

The pubs were full of exuberant journalists, boasting of their derring-do, and 'inkies', the printers, with whom the journalists rarely mixed and vice-versa. And then, with the incoming tide of new technology, one by one the papers drifted elsewhere. It started dramatically with Rupert Murdoch's famous 'moonlight flit' to Wapping, a move that led to a year of sometimes violent protests. That started the exodus.

Ultimately, in the early part of 1994, the PA, which was becoming more and more isolated, so to speak, at 85 Fleet Street, decided to make a move as well. By the time it moved, the agency was the last national media organisation left in Fleet Street. Indeed, nearly all the provincial offices as well had either been moved out or closed down. All that remained, in news-paper terms, when the PA took off was the office of the *Dundee Courier* just up the street, while Reuters, of course, continued in 85 Fleet Street, using the building as their corporate head-quarters. But these were the last outposts in the Street of Ink!

Fleet Street, sadly, from a journalist's viewpoint, fell into the hands of big business. Those pubs that remained open as the newspapers took flight simply lost their character; some say they lost their soul as well. And they lost their traditional custom, too.

The idea was to sell 85 Fleet Street, make a profit on the deal, and move out. Hartlepool-born Mike Imeson, who had held many senior editorial posts on the Press Association over the years, was put in charge of the move. It took him and those who worked with him some nine months to find the right premises at the right price.

In between the early spring of 1994 and finding and signing the deal on 292 Vauxhall Bridge Road, Imeson spent days trailing London, looking at buildings, some of them old and decrepit with rotten floors, some spanking new but too small or too remote – or too pricey.

One day at the end of that year, the PA chairman, Richard Storey, along with Robert Simpson, the chief executive, Imeson and a few others piled into a minibus to look at a short list they had selected. One was in Farringdon Street, hardly a stone's throw from Fleet Street. It was an old garret place, above a cheese factory.

As Imeson said later, 'It would have been very good if we had knocked the whole thing down and started again.'

Then they looked at a building south of the River Thames, close to the IPC tower. And then, one fine June afternoon, they looked at what Imeson called a 'brilliant' building in Docklands, the area, in fact, where a new hi-tech 'Fleet Street' was starting to burgeon. It was priced at £4 million and it had twice the floor space of the building that the Press Association finally settled on. It would also have been one-third of the price. Imeson recalls, 'The weather was glorious. It was a June afternoon. We went to a pub and we looked out. The sun was glistening on Docklands and on the ships on the Thames. It was idyllic.

'Robert Simpson said, "We'll have this," and the man from Knight Frank and Rutley, the estate agents, breathed a sigh of relief.'

But in the cold, grey light of the following morning the Press Association had collectively changed its mind and the decision was taken to move to Vauxhall Bridge Road, a convenient and central area of London, close to Victoria Station. Imeson explained that the principal reason the PA did not go to Docklands, despite the attraction and cheapness of the building, was that the Mirror Group, which was already based in Dock-lands, expressed the fear that, if the PA moved there, there would be no national media presence in the centre of London, although it had been contemplated that the agency would also set up a small office in the heart of the capital, in any event. But, in the end, that did not arise. To the uninitiated – and even to those who claimed to know – it looked as though the move to

Vauxhall Bridge Road could be completed in a matter of six weeks. In fact it took eight months – even though, in the words of one PA executive, the building looked 'oven-ready'.

The reason was that every single bit of floorboard had to come up and every single bit of the ceiling had to come down, for more than 64 miles of cables had to be installed for the new telephone and computer systems. One of the first decisions was to allocate telecoms to the third floor. It may seem trivial but time was spent in choosing carpets and curtains and, above all, desks. So fierce was the competition in the market for desks that Imeson recalls that people even attempted to bribe him (unsuccessfully, of course!) with trips to California and exotic ladies in their bid to tempt him to look favourably on their products.

The move was a highly complex affair, conducted in stages. And, to ensure that there was no interruption to the flow of news emanating from the Press Association, complicated telephone links were set up between 85 Fleet Street and 292 Vauxhall Bridge Road, involving a number of telephone exchanges across London, thus providing a fail-safe operation.

The one-way traffic system in Vauxhall Bridge Road was closed on two consecutive Sundays to enable equipment to be hoisted on to the roof. 'Who would have dreamed,' Imeson said, 'that you needed backup diesel tanks to put a thousand gallons of diesel fuel in, in case something went wrong? And the generators that powered the building could not stop for a second in case they went wrong, too.'

Then there was a slight difference of opinion with the local council, who said it was contravening Westminster planning laws to have satellite dishes on the roof. Eventually, these problems were ironed out to the relative satisfaction of all the parties. So, after nearly 130 years in and around Fleet Street, the Press Association finally flew the nest. But there were no parties to mark this historic departure, nor a house-warming for the new abode. Because the very nature of the Press Association is based on the slogan adopted by London's famous Windmill Theatre during the blitz: 'We never closed . . .'

The move was, in fact, a seamless operation, thanks in large part to the direction of Mike Imeson. A subscriber to the Press Association who was unaware that the move was taking place would not have noticed anything amiss. The flow of news copy continued without so much as a single blip on the screen.

22 Crime Busters

OVERAGE OF THE BIG crimes has always been a strong point of the Press Association – and none more so than the coverage of the police bust named Operation Julie, which cracked a huge drug ring in Britain in the late 1970s. It was probably the most memorable PA achievement in the history of the agency's backgrounders.

The editorial planning involved putting reporters in dangerous situations for long periods, after the police uncovered a £100 million drugs find in a cottage in Mid Wales on Christmas Eve 1977 – a discovery that the PA also broke to the world. The task of unearthing the background facts to the case was clouded, not only by danger for the reporters involved, but also by various legal strictures imposed by the courts. This meant that some of the material had to wait for more than a year before it could appear in print.

The story starts on 26 March 1977, when more than eight hundred officers raided addresses all over Britain and arrested over ninety people. The chief news editor, Peter Freeman, was so impressed by the scale of the swoop that he set in train one of the agency's biggest background operations. A Bristol staff reporter, Allan Smith, quickly confirmed the potential. He attended the lower court hearings in Swindon and although they produced very little copy – reporting restrictions were not lifted – he spoke to police officers, and, when the Swindon hearings were completed, he was able to provide the Press Association with a detailed account of Operation Julie as told by the prosecution to the magistrates. This was the key document on which the PA based all its subsequent enquiries.

Bernard Scarlett, the agency's crime correspondent, had been following his own lines of enquiry at Scotland Yard. At this point, a conference was held and John Shaw, a background reporter, was brought in, along with a photographer, Alun Jones, who, as a Welshman, was a definite advantage. There were two main drug factories, one in Seymour Road, Hampton

Wick, west London, and the other in a mansion in Carno, Mid Wales. Shaw and photographer Jones spent several days in and around Carno, and were astonished that no other journalists had been seen in the area. So the pair were able to secure exclusive photographs and interviews – and just in time, because people subsequently refused to speak to or allow anybody else into their homes. And they found precisely the same situation at Hampton, becoming the first – and the last – on this trail.

Meanwhile, Scarlett's contacts among chief constables and other leading police officers opened many official doors to the PA. Both he and Shaw were given long in-depth interviews, not only by senior officers involved in Operation Julie, but also by those who had infiltrated the gang. So, by the end of 1977, the Press Association possessed a bulging file of material, all of which was entirely exclusive. The trial date was set for early January, and the plan was to have the entire background material prepared by then – so that it could be sent by post to newspapers, ready for use the moment the go-ahead was given.

But it was by no means the end of the road for Shaw and Scarlett. Like Topsy, the background material just grew and grew. More and more first-class stories emerged, all of which, of course, had to wait until it was safe to use them. But the situation was further complicated by the way the trials took place at Bristol. The judge, Mr Justice Park, decided to divide the indictments into several counts, calling them the Welsh conspiracy and the London conspiracy, involving more than thirty individuals in the dock at one time or another. So, instead of one grand trial, there were a series of smaller trials, each cross-referring to others. It was a nightmare from a media point of view, and caught the Press Association temporarily off guard. And there were yet more legal complications to come. The judge ruled that some of those mentioned in the smaller trials could not be named by the press in case the larger trial to come was prejudiced as a result. It was, as Peter Freeman said at the time, 'a hair-tearing business'.

Another reporter engaged in covering the trials was Rob Gibson. The PA had heard whispers about a number of police resignations, and through various contacts the news desk was able to give Gibson six names. He watched them giving evidence in court and afterwards took them to one side. Some of those who had been infiltrating deeply into the conspiracy chose to resign partly because, in some cases, of the hostile reception they received when they returned to their home forces and partly because they felt that the painstaking and often danger- ous work they had undertaken to smash the gang had not been properly recognised or rewarded. Others resigned because they felt that a future of mundane police work was too tame a prospect compared with their exciting life as vital parts of the Operation Julie team.

There was also a feeling of distaste among these officers at the 'unseemly scramble' for glory in the case among the top police brass – the people who had not actually been at 'the coal face'.

Piece by piece, like a jigsaw puzzle, Gibson put his story together. When he filed it, the Press Association had another exclusive under its belt waiting for the green light. Later, one of the policemen involved wrote to the PA and said of Gibson, 'I would like to say that the way he approached his task and the end result which was published is a credit to the Press Association.' But the judge still had not finished – even at the end of the final trial. For, when all the guilty verdicts had been reached, usually the moment when the legal restraints are removed and the background can be released, the judge an- nounced that he would not be passing sentence for some time – possibly weeks later. Faces fell on the press benches.

Normally, a professional judge would not be thought likely to be influenced by background details, but in this case Mr Justice Park issued a detailed warning about the publishing of certain background material before he had passed sentence. It was not, he said, because he would be influenced by the background material when he came to pass sentence – but because other people might think he had been. This was the signal for hurried and flurried activity at the Press Association headquarters. All the material that had been sent out in advance had to be combed in exacting detail to ensure that it did not clash with the judge's ruling. Legal advice was sought on what could or could not be used. It was a tangled web and much of the copy needed to be heavily rewritten.

The process could hardly have been more frustrating. But, at the end of the day, a substantial amount of the background could be sent, topped off by Gibson's story of the police resignations. This gave many papers their front-page splash with a cross-reference to big background features inside. But there was still more work to be done in the period before the sentences were passed.

Gibson did a 'ghost squad' story of the undercover detectives and Scarlett went to the Home Office forensic science laboratory at Aldermaston, where the drug factories had first been identified. Then he also turned in a story about the drug godfathers starting up from scratch again in the United States.

Finally on 8 March 1978, the sentences were meted out – seventeen people were jailed for a total of 124 years – and the go-ahead was given for all the other background stories to be published. They included lurid biographical details of the drug dealers and their henchmen and -women, the fascinating accounts of the police officers who infiltrated their world and the astonishing story of how the detectives pieced the huge operation together.

The Press Association team subsequently received a commendation at the British Press Awards for their work on Operation Julie and later received a special Witness Box Award for Crime Reporting – an engraved silver vase.

Five years later, a crime of a different sort exploded on to the national scene – the IRA bomb blast that killed five people and injured scores of others at Harrods on 17 December 1983. And for one Press Association man it was to be a story of journalistic endeavour.

Harry Aspey, then the agency's night chief sub, was shopping at the Knightsbridge store with his wife Christine and their two children Charles and Camilla on that fateful Saturday afternoon when the bomb went off. In spite of personal shock and fears for his wife and children who were taken to hospital, Aspey, 'with blood trickling into my shoes', filed the most dramatic account of the outrage.

He graphically described the scene:

I scrabble around in a sea of glass, thinking is that what happens when hydrogen-filled balloons ignite. Then I see the rest of the family, sitting or lying in the road. Police picked them up and rushed them away. I followed them and we ran across Knightsbridge. It was complete chaos. There was a great cloud of smoke and a terrible smell of explosives. Strangely, I do not remember anyone screaming. There seemed to be utter silence except it seemed I could still hear carol singing.

We ran to a doorway and as we were cowering in it I noticed blood on Christine's dress and dripping from my hand on to my shoe and realised for the first time we were hurt. Police were saying, 'Don't move, don't move, there's another one somewhere'. So we carried on cowering. From then on, irrationalities. We cower in the doorway of an exclusive diamond shop in Knightsbridge. The owner arrives.

He wants to go in to open the windows. Should I ask him if I can use his phone? The blood from my wife's cut head is seeping on to her coat and the children are crying. The interminable wait in the ambulance. All around us dazed and bloody faces. Then the journalist's nightmare. I don't have a pen. I don't have a notebook, and I don't know where there's a telephone.

At the hospital they reassure me there is a phone in casualty. I borrow writing materials. I speak to Cardinal Hume. 'You can have that quote for free,' he says with a gentle smile.

Aspey said that his pen had been acquired 'from somewhere' and that his notebook was a pad of someone's old parent-teacher association raffle tickets. But in spite of this motley and makeshift assortment of a reporter's necessities and his shock and injuries, Aspey's graphic account of the explosion was carried in full, and bylined, in all the papers the following day – and again on Monday.

23 War Zones

THE FALKLANDS CONFLICT was not only a major triumph for
the British forces: it was also a story of enterprise, great
privation and danger for Press Association journalists 'at
the sharp end'. And behind the scenes there was a rich tapestry
of frustration and anger at what was considered unnecessary
bureaucracy and frequent obstruction in the corridors of the
Ministry of Defence at Whitehall.

So difficult was the ministry at times that the agency's defence
correspondent, Bob Hutchinson, wrote:

> Never in the field of human conflict have so many tried to
> report a war with such a conspicuous lack of success. The
> Falklands conflict was a private war, albeit undeclared both
> politically and militarily. With a tasteless cocktail of incompe-
> tence and conspiracy, the Ministry of Defence in London
> sought to ensure that the harsh facts and horrors of modern
> warfare were as divorced from public perception as the
> disputed islands were from the British homeland.

But in spite of all the handicaps and the seemingly insurmountable hurdles the Press Association emerged from the war with
flying colours and accolades from news centres around the world.
Two abiding memories of these momentous months was the
historic and award-winning picture taken by the photographer
Martin Cleaver of HMS *Antelope* exploding like a massive fireworks
display and the dramatic shot showing the panoramic view of the
preparations for war taken below the decks of the carrier HMS
Hermes. Cleaver took the *Antelope* picture after waiting for nearly
three hours, numb with cold, on the superstructure of RFA
Stromness. Elsewhere, and at different periods, two reporters,
Peter Archer and Richard Savill, each experienced great danger but
succeeded in filing some of the most graphic copy of the conflict.

Back home, however, the Press Association went into another
battle, with the Ministry of Defence, which had to contend with

two very tough and determined characters, the editor-in-chief, David Chipp, and Hutchinson. They adopted a firm policy of 'no surrender'. Whatever obstacles the ministry tried to throw in the path of the agency, Chipp and Hutchinson managed to over-come them, and turn what looked like being impossible situations to their advantage.

In his memorandum to the House of Commons Select Committee, Chipp pulled no punches. He said, 'Inevitably and unfortunately, the Ministry of Defence presented the press with an image of obstructionism, an attitude which was not necessarily always there, but which laid the foundations for the loss of credibility. The MoD never recovered from it.'

The phoney war began even before the British Task Force set sail on its historic mission. First there was trouble over the number of journalists allowed to sail with the troops. With only hours to go before accredited journalists were to be on board, Chipp went into action and after heated exchanges won the first skirmish.

On another occasion Hutchinson, a heavily bearded and fearsome-looking fellow (although in reality a gentle and friend-ly soul), became so infuriated at what he regarded as the total lack of ministry co-operation that he ripped up his defence correspondent's accreditation card and tossed the fragments at a leading civil servant, to the alarm and astonishment of onlooking bureaucrats. As he did so, he shouted, 'It's not worth the paper it's printed on.'

It was a daring gesture that paid off. The civil servants gave in to his demands. But it was not long before the ministry saw the funny side of what had happened. The following day, a package awaited Hutchinson at the press centre. It contained a red-backed war correspondent's pass dating from the late 1940s. Inside, Hutchinson found he was now authorised as a 'field correspondent with the British forces in Whitehall'. His physical description on the pass was 'robust'. The same ministry joker also sent a package of pictures of the Task Force warships to the picture news editor Colin Macer. On top of the pile was a photograph of HMS *Victory* coming back into service 'after the longest refit in the Navy's history'.

These jokes were all very well, but there was also the very serious business of reporting a war to be done. CARELESS TALK COSTS LIVES was the World War Two slogan emblazoned on billboards throughout the country. It was no less relevant during the Falklands War. In this conflict, the Press Association was acutely conscious of the fact that, with the speed of modern press communications, one mistake in judgment in what was transmitted would not only jeopardise the success of the British operations and British lives, but also, conceivably, the lives of the agency's own men at the front – Savill, Archer and Cleaver.

Hutchinson explained, 'It was for this reason that we sat on much of the information we gleaned from unofficial sources about what was happening. Throughout, the ministry refused to give us any guidance on what to print, either attributably or unattributably. So often, we had to decide ourselves what to put into a story.'

There were periods when Chipp seemed to be spending more time at the ministry getting pictures and copy back from the Task Force than at the Press Association in 85 Fleet Street. Such were the difficulties and frustration of working against censorship. The hot, stuffy and usually acrimonious press centre was staffed by the Press Association around the clock – and joining Hutchinson was reporter Alan Jones and a team of long-suffering journalists culled from the general news pool, the Law Courts and Parliament. Sometimes it was difficult to find anybody in the ministry who had the faintest idea of what was going on – or, if they did happen to know anything, they would not talk about it.

One night, at the height of the conflict, the Press Association team were startled by the appearance of a top general in the press centre. He asked them, 'Do you know what's going on? How are the Paras doing?' When an incredulous agency reporter asked him whether he was not himself up to date on the progress of the conflict, the general replied, 'Oh, no. Nobody ever tells us anything!'

As the conflict dragged on, covering the ministry patch gradually degenerated into a series of set-piece arguments with officials, ending in confusion and disorder. Principal target of the press was the ministry's deadpan spokesman, Ian McDonald, the deputy chief of public relations, described by one reporter as 'the warm-up man for the Lutine Bell'.

McDonald's sombre regular appearances on television transformed him into an unlikely national figure for the duration of the conflict. After that, he disappeared into the deepest recesses of the ministry, never to be seen on TV again. On one celebrated occasion, McDonald was walking to the ministry alongside

Hutchinson, who was haranguing him furiously about the lack of information and press facilities.

'And where is our interview with Defence Secretary John Nott?' Hutchinson demanded. 'People will forget what he looks like.'

At that precise moment, a tourist made Hutchinson's point far more telling. He rushed up to the wordless McDonald and shook him warmly by the hand. 'Ah, Mr Nott,' he exclaimed, 'I think you are doing a wonderful job . . .'

'See what I mean?' said a triumphant Hutchinson. McDonald typically refused to show any sign of embarrassment. Hutchinson, despite his manful efforts, still did not get the interview. He was later to protest, to a Commons committee, about the behind-closed-doors nature of some of the briefings.

He recorded:

On one occasion, defence correspondents were told unattributably of the return of some of the Task Force ships in varying degrees of battle damage. The ships were named and the information was duly published.

Later we began to receive calls from distressed wives and families of one frigate who had rung the Navy at Plymouth for more information to find the story had been denied.

When we approached the Ministry about this, we were told that as the discussion was unattributable it had never taken place and therefore officially the Ministry of Defence or the Navy could not comment on it. So the Ministry's reluctance to impart information again unwittingly caused undue distress to its own families.

Although Hutchinson spent more time at the Ministry of Defence than any other Press Association reporter during the conflict, it was Alan Jones who secured most of whatever big breaks were available from Whitehall. It fell to him to cover the first action from London: the recapture of South Georgia after the raid on Grytviken. It was this event that later caused Margaret Thatcher famously to proclaim 'Rejoice!' outside 10 Downing Street.

When the news broke, Jones had to chase down three flights of ministry stairs, and out past the Ministry of Defence policemen demanding to see his security pass, even though he was leaving the building.

Jones, fortunately a lithe, fit man and a demon squash player, sped across Whitehall, vaulting over crowd barriers and bursting through a startled protest march, all with the purpose of finding an empty public call box that contained a working telephone. He was lucky not to get arrested. Some police officers, seeing him crash through this disciplined march, sending banners flying, assumed he was a troublemaker, trying, single-handed, to wreck it. It was only when they saw him disappear into a telephone kiosk, that they realised he was a member of the press and left him alone.

The end of the war provided one of the most incongruous scenes witnessed in the Ministry of Defence. Argentina had already announced that she had surrendered, but the British were saying absolutely nothing. Plainly, Margaret Thatcher wanted to make the official announcement in Parliament.

'You will have to wait for the House of Commons statement later tonight,' was all that officials would tell the frustrated reporters, despite the news coming from Buenos Aires. That evening Chipp walked into the press room at the ministry to show a senior figure from the New Zealand Press Association (NZPA) the Press Association at work. Suddenly John Nott looked in, returning from a party at 10 Downing Street. He paused at the entrance – a fatal mistake. He was at once surrounded by half a dozen clamouring journalists, Chipp included, notebook at the ready.

'It's all over, chaps,' Nott said cheerily. And after that he proceeded to give them some more details, adding, 'Of course, that's all off the record.' But this was a classic case of shutting the gate after the horse has bolted. 'Oh no it's not,' piped up Hutchinson. Nott tautened and looked taken aback.

'What do you mean?' he asked, panic appearing to set in. Hutchinson explained that, while Nott was talking, Press Association reporters, Chipp included, were filing his words on the agency's dedicated telephones.

'Well, you'll have to get it back,' Nott said, by now really worried. 'Can't be done,' said Hutchinson cheerily. 'It's already been twice around the world.'

Nott, a beaten man, withdrew in confusion. What happened ruined the impact of Margaret Thatcher's statement to the Commons that night. The general view in Fleet Street that evening was that Nott was almost certainly at the receiving end of a particularly nasty handbagging.

On another occasion, McDonald was poised to announce a major event in the Falklands, and was insisting that he wait until 9 p.m. so he could do it live on BBC television news. It was then 8.55 p.m. and the incorrigible Hutchinson insisted that was not good enough. So he snatched the text from McDonald's grasp and phoned the words over to the Press Association. By the time he had finished, the countdown to the news was already in progress, and McDonald, normally so cool under pressure, was getting frantic. Hutchinson had to crawl on his hands and knees towards McDonald to return the script out of sight of the TV cameras. If McDonald appeared a little less than composed during that broadcast, he had good reason to be.

But the phoney war did not end with the cessation of hostilities in the South Atlantic. The Royal Navy and Chipp were still at loggerheads even though the guns were silent on the Falklands. The next drama for the Press Association emerged as HMS *Invincible* was returning in triumph to Portsmouth with Prince Andrew aboard. Inexplicably, the Royal Navy had excluded the Press Association from the press party joining the carrier on the final stages of her voyage. Repeated appeals were made to the Ministry of Defence for a change of heart, but they were all refused.

However, 'Admiral' Chipp, as he was dubbed by the media trade paper *UK Press Gazette*, swung into action. He sent a memorandum to all evening paper editors, saying:

> For your information Royal Navy has excluded PA from press party joining *Invincible* on Thursday, though ample facilities given to television and radio. Have made repeated representations without effect, pointing out that if our reporter can only join Friday morning we shall be unable provide adequate early story for your first editions.

Chipp then cheekily added, for good measure, the Royal Naval press officer's telephone number at the Ministry of Defence. The broadside hit home. The Royal Naval press office was inundated with calls from evening paper editors across Britain. There was a swift change of tack, and just two and a quarter hours later Chipp was able to send a victory signal to his fleet.

It said, 'Many thanks for your support over *Invincible* return. PA now has reporter on vessel from tomorrow and there will also be a pool photographer.'

The reporter was Paul Harris. His story, which began, 'Prince Andrew came home from the Falklands war today to a kiss from the Queen and a share in a hero's welcome', was splashed in morning and evening newspapers throughout the land.

Weeks after the conflict, Chipp and Hutchinson claimed to the House of Commons Defence Select Committee that the mutual trust, confidence and sense of credibility between the Ministry of Defence and the media had been damaged, possibly irrevocably, as a result of the Falklands conflict. Both men were in bullish form when they appeared. The committee was investigating the handling of press and public information during the crisis. Chipp had already issued a written and highly critical memorandum, but had done so in a constructive spirit looking ahead, and saying that attempts should now be made to 'mend fences' with the MoD. The committee chairman, Sir Timothy Kitson, a Tory MP and a former parliamentary private secretary to Edward Heath, questioned Chipp's statement that the Navy had been 'particularly obstructive' towards the media during the conflict.

Chipp stood by his point, saying, 'I believe they did not have the experience that the Army had in Northern Ireland, and I think they did not want us there. They found us a nuisance and perhaps an embarrassment and I think they were mainly obstructive.'

The memorandum also complained that, throughout the campaign, the MoD was continually caught between premature disclosure of information by the field correspondents and the timing of the release of official announcements in London.

'Initially, the Falklands correspondents' copy was vetted on board ship, and then transmitted to London for collection or passing on by or from the MoD. After the landings at Port San Carlos, we had double censorship in effect. The copy was cleared by the Falklands operational forces and then vetted by military officers in London, with "requests" to omit this or that. There were inconsistencies.'

Peter Archer, in an appendix to the memorandum, vividly described the 'inconsistent nature of procedures for vetting copy by the censor'.

On board HMS *Hermes*, the captain initially insisted on vetting all copy before it could leave the ship. Later, vetting was delegated to the senior education officer, his deputy and to the Admiral's secretary. In practice this meant vetting was erratic. Copy was being censored twice, sometimes three times, and each censor seemed to have different ideas about what could or should be published.

Archer recalled that on one occasion a mystery man censored a colour piece describing flying exercises. He struck out adjectives, altered the style and took out passages already passed by the Ministry of Defence representative.

'When I complained and asked who was responsible, I was told that nobody knew who had defaced the copy. I took my complaint to the captain and the story was reinstated.'

Archer also found that he was barred from sending the sort of stories from HMS *Hermes* that reporters on HMS *Invincible* were allowed to file. On another occasion, he handed copy to the *Hermes'* MoD man who was sitting in the wardroom drinking a glass of port. 'I told him the story was urgent and asked if it could be dealt with immediately. I returned half-an-hour later to find the unvetted copy soaking up port and other spilt liqueurs on a wardroom table. The copy had to be retyped and was delayed for over an hour.'

His suspicions that he and others were fed misinformation during the conflict was confirmed by the Chief of Defence Staff, Sir Terence Lewin, who also added for good measure that newsmen were 'most helpful with our deception plans'.

It was only when Archer and Savill returned to London that they discovered that some of their stories – often obtained at great personal peril – had either not been transmitted at all, or had disappeared into the stratosphere.

Meanwhile, Martin Cleaver's dramatic shot of HMS *Antelope* exploding was the picture of a lifetime, and it demonstrated more than any other the patience and endurance to which photographers frequently have to submit themselves in the course of their work.

Cleaver recalled: 'I was on RFA *Stromness* having an evening meal when we heard a loud explosion. We rushed on deck and saw that a small fire had started on *Antelope* and it seemed to be spreading. I took some pictures of the fire, caused by the detonation of a previously unexploded bomb, but they did not "make". I thought about what was likely to happen and decided that that the ship would probably explode because of the aviation fuel and missiles aboard. So I stood on the superstructure and waited.

'After about two and a half hours, with my hands going numb from the cold, the worst happened and it did explode. I caught the moment with one frame. I knew that many men had escaped, which was some comfort, but I felt physically sick as the explosion had torn the ship apart. I processed the shot the following morning and did just one print because I was still feeling very upset. But I knew exactly what I had got.'

That was by no means Cleaver's only triumph during this testing assignment. Among others was his historic split-level pictorial shot on HMS *Hermes*, the flagship of the Task Force, and another telling shot of the ground littered with helmets, ammunition and water bottles, where more than 1,200 bedraggled Argentinian troops had surrendered. These pictures, and others by Cleaver, dramatically told the story of the Falklands War more graphically than a thousand words.

Later, in an editorial, the *British Journal of Photography* heaped praise on the Press Association photographer, saying, 'It was fortunate that UK press photography was represented by someone of his calibre. With the outstanding split-level pictorial shot on Hermes, he showed at the outset that his photographic eye was developed far beyond the straight record.'

Archer filed his first lead as the Task Force left Britain. He set the scene: 'The Fleet is on its way. Britain's aircraft carriers HMS *Invincible* and HMS *Hermes* slipped away from the dockside at Portsmouth today to an emotional farewell.'

It was the opening of a story that was splashed across the front pages of newspapers throughout Britain – and beyond. And it was the start of a challenging period for a domestic news agency reporter who was subsequently to see scores more of his graphic dispatches appear untouched in papers all round the world. On 2 May, almost all the Sunday papers gave massive bylined coverage to Archer's dispatch on Britain's aerial assault on Port Stanley. A few days later, he was filing an eyewitness account as British sailors abandoned the blazing destroyer HMS *Sheffield*.

It was this tragedy that led to one of the most unbearably sombre moments anyone can remember in the House of Commons, when Nott reported the loss of the *Sheffield* to MPs late one evening.

Later, Savill, who was sent on to the Falklands after Archer, was present to report what he called 'the sudden and dramatic end to the bloody fighting'.

Savill had earlier experienced a hair-raising day. The previous night he had spent hours journeying perilously through a minefield, walking heel to toe along a white tape laid down by the Royal Engineers. A misplaced foot could have meant death. Then, as the troops ringed Port Stanley, he walked with two other journalists for half a mile along the snow-covered track of no-man's-land.

He said, 'We removed our camouflage clothes and set off, tentatively awaiting possible sniper attack at any moment . . . we clutched our National Union of Journalist cards and note-books to identify ourselves.'

As they approached Port Stanley, there was a brief moment of panic. They could see ahead of them two Argentine soldiers. Savill and his colleagues waved their accreditations at them. But the Argentines were in no mood to fight. They were cold, dirty, dishevelled and dispirited with the deathly look of defeat in their eyes. All they wanted to do was to shake hands.

Savill's own arrival in the Falklands was not encouraging. After seven days of travelling, with barely any sleep at all, he discovered that his arrival on HMS *Bristol* had been preceded by a signal by Sir John Fieldhouse, the fleet's commander-in-chief, warning the Task Force to be careful of him. It read:

HMS *Bristol* personnel to avoid discussion of any operational matters with Savill, who can be expected to take full advantage of his environment to glean newsworthy information. Speculation on possible courses of action, operational capability of Task Force, individual units and state of readiness must also be avoided. Names of ships and individual units should not be specified.

Flattering, no doubt, for an enthusiastic reporter, but not really what he wanted to hear. Savill said that this warning made him all the more aware that the Press Association's tradition of immediacy in its news gathering was going to be hard to maintain. He spent a week acting the role of dummy casualty on HMS *Bristol* as she sailed to the exclusion zone. Then he was transferred to the aircraft carrier HMS *Hermes*, where he spent a few days with repeated air raid warnings. He recalled: 'The alerts were nerve-racking but not without humour. On one occasion, during dinner, everyone dived under the table. When the alert was over and I returned to my chair, my fork was still in a potato, a sign of the panic.'

A day or two after he arrived on *Hermes*, survivors from the sunken merchant ship the *Atlantic Conveyor* were brought ashore with dramatic accounts of their rescue. As Savill was the only reporter there, he had a major story to himself. He filed 1,000 words, only to be told by the Ministry of Defence censor to cut it to 500 words as the signal could take no more. When Savill returned to London two months later, he discovered that not a single word of that exclusive had reached the Press Association office.

'It was a difficult war for correspondents,' Savill reflected. 'In the Falklands, correspondents dug their own trenches, and cooked their own food from ration packs. There were no beds, no baths and no whisky. Getting copy back was always a struggle. Reports could only be sent through MARISAT [maritime satellite] ships inshore and through a satellite communications system set up on land in a tent at Ajax Bay. Most of the time reporters were dependent on a friendly helicopter pilot putting handwritten copy in an envelope and taking it to Ajax Bay.'

A Ministry of Defence minder would read the copy but it would be by no means certain that it would ever reach London.

'When I returned to the office after the war, at least five stories had gone missing, including an account of the surrender after the fighting had finished,' Savill added. It was plain that if the Ministry of Defence wanted to shift copy, and it suited it to do so, then it was a very different story. In one particular instance, Cleaver and Savill were flown out to an air strip at Goose Green, after the battle, to be shown tanks of napalm that were to be used against British forces. They were given the instructions for use and allowed to spend time examining them. Savill wrote the story, which was in London in a matter of hours, making the front page of the London *Evening Standard*.

Similarly, the Ministry of Defence gave every assistance possible when it came to transmitting copy detailing the mindless vandalism by Argentine forces on local houses in Goose Green. But, when it came to reporting British losses, it was virtually impossible. Invariably, any such losses were announced in London, and, by the time copy arrived from the reporters on the spot, it was out of date.

One of Savill's best memories of the war was the first person he met when entering Port Stanley ahead of the British troops. The Roman Catholic priest, Daniel Spraggon, greeted him and two colleagues at his garden gate with the words, 'Thank God for Mother Thatcher.' Said Savill, 'It made for a good headline.'

Meanwhile, the Gulf War brought out the best in PA. And it was the defence correspondent Charlie Miller who led the way. After Saddam Hussein's invasion of Kuwait, Miller was among a small group of six journalists selected as the first media team to be granted access to Dharan, the coastal city in northeast Saudi Arabia where the Royal Air Force was deploying Tornado FE-3 fighters.

The reporters were crammed into the rear of an ageing RAF VC10 transport aircraft, so their role was far from glamorous. But Miller's pooled stories, virtually from the front line, near the Kuwait border, were the start of the PA's key role in reporting the build-up to conflict and the war itself.

As the UK forces' involvement increased, so Miller shuttled back and forth between London and Saudi Arabia, reporting on the large strategic and political picture – the military build-up and human-interest stories of the men and women on the front line.

In true PA style, one of Miller's dispatches created such ructions that it led to questions in the House of Commons. Miller had innocently asked some of the British soldiers how they planned to celebrate Christmas in the desert. The answer was that an edict had gone out from on high that 25 December had been 'banned' because of concerns about upsetting their Saudi Arabian hosts. The story made huge headlines in the newspapers the following day. Some MPs were furious and said as much in the Commons. However, the Foreign and Common-wealth Office and the Ministry of Defence swiftly got on the case and ultimately, common sense prevailed. The troops celebrated Christmas in the Gulf – albeit quietly – and it was thanks to Charlie Miller and the PA that they were able to enjoy even that modest concession.

Three weeks later hostilities began. But one of the most scary moments occurred before the fighting started. After a whistle-stop visit to the political leaders of Saudi Arabia, Bahrain and Oman, the Defence Secretary Tom King and his entourage arrived back in the Saudi capital, Riyadh, where King Fahd had granted an audience. However, only Mr King and his immediate advisers were allowed out of the RAF VC10. The small group of accompanying defence correspondents, Miller among them, were compelled to wait for four hours in the plane in the middle of the tarmac, as the broiling noonday sun nudged the shade temperature towards 130 degrees F. Finally, at 1300 hours, with King back on board, the VC10 rolled forward to begin take-off with its fuel tanks full. It is a fact of aerodynamics that the hotter the conditions, the longer the take-off. That fact was only too obvious to the passengers as the VC10 reached the end of the runway. The plane staggered no more than 20 feet into the air, where it fought to keep airborne. On board, the experienced defence correspondents – a quiet, normally fairly macho group – exchanged rare glances of concern. An *Independent* reporter, Chris Bellamy, a relatively new member of the team, leaned over and anxiously asked Miller what was going on. As the wings waggled dangerously close to the ground, Miller replied, 'I think we've run out of airstrip and we're still trying to get up enough speed to take off. We've left it a bit late.'

The engines screamed and the vibrations worsened. Concern turned to fear and fear to something like suppressed panic. 'Saddam Hussein could not have planned it better,' was the thought running through Miller's mind. The minutes passed and seemed like hours as the VC10 strained every sinew to gain speed. After what seemed an interminable time, the plane inched slowly higher. The concern and fear began to ebb once the 100-foot mark was passed. Yet it was some considerable time before King ventured to the back of the aircraft to brief Miller and his colleagues.

As war became inevitable, the Press Association drew up its own battle plans, deploying its own manpower. David Mason was dispatched to Riyadh, Finlay Marshall to the RAF base in Bahrain and Ben Preston to the Royal Navy fleet afloat in the Gulf. Miller was ordered to co-ordinate the PA battle plan from Fleet Street. They all acquitted themselves, often in the most difficult and dangerous conditions, with great skill and professionalism. Within minutes of the first Allied strike on the Iraqi capital, Baghdad, PA was the first to run reports that RAF aircrew had been an integral part of the initial strikes in their Tornado GR-1 fighter-bombers. It was a lead that the agency was to maintain throughout the conflict.

The Press Association was the first media reporting team to reveal the military inoculation programme against biological and chemical weapons, the first with the Allied air attack plan and the first with the start of the land attack.

Miller was also deeply involved in the coverage of the Bosnia conflict, which, little by little, the United Kingdom was sucked into. The Royal Air Force was given the task of flying the first

England win the World Cup, 1966

Above Crumlin Road, Belfast, 1969

Top right Red Rum wins the Grand National, 1977

Right Bill Beaumont plays for The Calcutta Cup, 1981

Above 1,200 Argentine soldiers surrendered to the British forces here. Goose Green, Falkland Islands, 1982

Top left The Brixton riots, 1981

Left The Queen Mother in Venice doing what all good tourists do – eating ice cream in a gondola, 1984

Above The PA's Chris Moncrieff, with John Major and Chris Patten

Top left The *Herald of Free Enterprise* at Zeebrugge, 1987

Left The Kings Cross tube station fire, 1987

The PA's current home in Victoria

relief flight into the besieged capital, Sarajevo – and Miller was on board the C-130 transport plane. He was aware of what lay ahead when he discovered the aircraft was from No. 47 Squadron – the special-operations flight that specialises in behind-the-lines work with the Special Air Service.

The crew were veterans of the Gulf War, anxious but confident. Diving at what seemed to be an impossible angle into Sarajevo, the aircraft fired off missile-confusing chaff and flares, and landed successfully with the first load of supplies to launch an operation that was to last for years. PA had unrivalled access to this historic event.

A few months later, British peacekeeping forces started to move into the area and the Press Association decided to dispatch Miller and a photographer, John Giles, into the war zone. As the military were in the process of setting up bases, the two PA men were forced to travel around Bosnia without the security of a military escort. It was a highly risky operation, travelling along loggers' tracks through the forest-clad Bosnian mountains in a hired Citroën BX With no four-wheel-drive vehicles available, they filled the car boot with spare tyres, petrol cans and other essential survival equipment. They were forced to negotiate their way through armed roadblocks and maintain a constant watch for notorious criminal gangs along the tortuous route.

Accommodation was never easy to find and on one occasion they were forced into accepting lodgings with the local Croat godfather, who provided a much-needed supper in a large dining room surrounded by the local hoodlums, who tested the PA men's nerves by bouncing hand grenades on the tables and explaining why they thought Hitler was such a great man.

The next test for the agency was Kosovo. Bob Roberts, deputy political editor, and a photographer, Tim Ockenden, travelling with the King's Royal Hussars, were among the first British journalists to enter Kosovo with the army. Roberts crossed the border after dawn with the advance guard of the British Army. He was confronted by 'an eerie country inhabited only by the ghosts of ethnic cleansing'. For hours, during a painstakingly slow advance, they did not come across a single civilian – and not a single inhabited home. The only signs of life were heavily armed Gurkha troops sent ahead to secure the first few miles of road. Private cars lay abandoned, all pointing in the direction the refugees had fled weeks earlier. Most had bullet holes and shattered windows. One had an axe casually lying by an open door. Roberts saw home after home, burned out, empty and ransacked. Then, in the ethnically cleansed town of Kacanik, eighteen miles inside the Kosovan border, he and Ockenden edged on foot through silent streets behind a paratroopers' unit. Not a soul could be seen. Yet old washing fluttered on lines and, outside, tables were laid for barbecues that were never eaten. 'The identity cards of ethnic Albanians lay discarded on the streets,' Roberts recorded, 'along with cartridge shells.' He continued:

> On a dusty summer day in June, it seemed the most desolate place on Earth. Yet as the day progressed there were signs of life. At first it was just movement in the distance. Then, as we rounded a corner approaching a town called Urosevac at around 1 p.m., we saw a few dozen people lining the street. Waving and smiling, they were chanting, 'Nato! Nato!'
>
> As we rounded the next bend hundreds of women, old men and boys who had emerged from cellars and mountain hiding places were cheering and shouting welcome. As the Warrior armoured cars slowed down they swarmed over them. Soldiers were being hugged and kissed by people showing an almost desperate joy at being alive. Women pressed small, purple flowers on to soldiers. Roses and garlands were hung from tanks. A barefoot boy cartwheeled in the middle of the road ahead of the armoured column. One elderly woman dressed all in black mistook me for a soldier. She embraced me and would not let go. With tears streaming down her face she kept hugging me and talking in Albanian. The words meant nothing to me but when she looked into my face the meaning was clear: this was their liberation day.

Roberts said that even for journalists 'who pride ourselves on cynicism' it was an emotional journey. 'There were however hairy moments when angry and drunken Serbs cruised around in cars letting off bursts of AK-47 gunfire,' he added, 'but most seemed to be aimed in the air. And on the discovery of the first mass grave, soldiers warned us against crossing a field to see it because it might be mined and booby-trapped. We all looked at each other before going on, but none of us stayed behind.'

Roberts told how, on a drive into the mountains in the first few days of the liberation, he walked up a dirt track to a ruined house where he had seen some people:

I thought they were refugees returning to their homes and I was keen for an interview. As I got within 50 yards of the building, the people inside stood up. They were notorious Serb paramilitaries and I found myself looking at half-a-dozen rifles pointed at me. Deciding they were perhaps reluctant to be interviewed, I waved, gave them my friendliest smile and tried to walk back casually to our vehicle. It seemed a long, long way.

There were some grim sights, but there were also moments of humour:

On the first full day in Pristina, Ockenden and I were on foot patrol with the Paras when there was the sound of gunshots and shouts of 'Sniper! Sniper!'
The Paras threw themselves on the ground and I followed, hurling myself behind a soldier armed with a heavy machine gun. The unflappable Tim, as calmly as if on a Sunday stroll, wandered over to us and asked: 'Should I be lying down?'

Later, on a night patrol in northern Kosovo before all the Serbs left, they were camped high in the hills with a reconnaissance unit. Roberts again:

We were in a tense mood as gunfire could be heard nearby. Suddenly we saw a tiny light moving down a rough path. The soldiers cocked their weapons. We took cover. The light seemed to be moving from side to side and suddenly I recognised what it was from my days growing up in Africa. It was a firefly, a harmless insect which gives off a light to attract a mate as it moves. I shouted 'firefly'. However shouting anything with the word 'fire' in it is not a good idea when you are standing among a group of soldiers. Half a dozen tough squaddies dived for cover thinking they were being shot at. By the time I had explained myself and they had dusted themselves off, I was not the most popular member of the squad.

Surprisingly, and unlike the case in most countries that are relatively backward compared with the industrialised West, filing copy did not prove a huge problem. To the amazement of the reporters covering the war, mobile phones actually worked in Pristina. 'As you came over a hill with a bomb-ravaged city below, the mobiles burst into life,' said Roberts. 'The news desk was usually on the phone within minutes.'

The nearest there was to a problem about filing was when they were with troops moving into one of the northernmost parts of Kosovo during a massive rainstorm. Roberts was using a satellite phone to try to send copy, but the satellite dish had to be held up by hand to get a signal.

'In the middle of a crowd of joyous ethnic Albanians, I got one to hold up the dish and tried to make him understand that he had to stay still to maintain a signal,' Roberts recalled. 'Unfortunately the dish became a trophy of the day and was paraded up and down the road to shouts of celebrations. After half-a-dozen attempts at persuading people to stay still, we gave up and headed back to Pristina.'

The biggest practical difficulty for the reporters was coping without water, electricity and light for days on end. 'We could charge our equipment off car batteries and army generators but as for washing in hot water, using a toilet which flushed or having a decent meal, forget it,' said Roberts. 'After what seemed like an age – probably about a week – of living rough, we'd had enough. We persuaded an army lieutenant to drive us back over the border to Macedonia and booked into what passed for a good hotel for a night.

'Never has a hot shower felt so welcome or a cold beer tasted so good . . .'

24 Disasters

T WO OF THE WORST soccer disasters of the twentieth century happened in front of the Press Association lenses. And today the harrowing pictures of the Hillsborough and Heysel tragedies record the chilling, heartbreaking moments that are part of our history.

At Hillsborough on 15 April 1989, the Press Association came in for a considerable amount of criticism for issuing photographs by David Giles of the victims of this terrible tragedy. It has now been widely accepted, however, that this was misplaced criticism. The Press Association is a news wholesaler. It had the pictures and it distributed them to customers. What happens then is for the newspapers who take the service to decide. Most of them took the decision to use them.

Giles was sent to Sheffield to cover the FA Cup semifinal between Liverpool and Nottingham Forest, along with his Leeds-based colleague, John Giles. As chance would have it, he was at the crucial end of the ground as the tragedy started to unfold within a few minutes of the kick-off. But it was not until some considerable time later that he discovered the scale of the disaster.

'We saw the police pulling a few people out of the crowd, but that is routine at these sorts of matches,' he said.

> Then we realised it was more serious. There was only one small gate open and people were being pushed towards it, while the police were dragging arms and legs. It was quite horrific. As I was taking pictures, a man jumped on my back and shouted that he wanted to beat me to pulp. I know it sounds callous, but when you are working, you are not conscious of what is really happening. It was only some time afterwards that it all sunk home when someone said to me: 'Do you realise that many people were killed in that incident?' At the time I just did not believe them.

That tragic day, 95 Liverpool supporters were crushed to death.

John Stillwell was the darkroom technician at Hillsborough on that fateful afternoon. The Press Association darkroom was situated underneath one of the stands and, when Stillwell realised that something was wrong, he ran to the top of the stairs and looked down at the crowds, catching sight of David in the thick of the chaos. Still keeping his eye firmly on the photographer, so as not to lose him, he raced on to the pitch and over to his side. 'What have you got to give me?' he shouted in the din – and David thrust three rolls of film into his hand. Stillwell raced back to the darkroom and within minutes the dramatic and heartbreaking shots were zinging down the wires.

Peter Went, the Press Association's chief football writer, described his feelings that day: 'I noticed a huge swell in the crowd behind the goal at the Leppings Lane end minutes before kick-off and I soon realised there was a major problem as fans climbed over perimeter fencing and collapsed on the pitch. My first thought was: Oh no, please, not another Heysel. The tie was abandoned after six minutes and I vividly recall filing the first news of the fatalities. I told the London news desk: 'I've seen nine bodies carried off the pitch on stretchers with their faces covered by blankets or coats. As far as I am concerned that means they are dead.

'Unlike Heysel, the scale of the disaster was immediately apparent and I will never forget the desperate attempt to revive one young fan in front of the main stand. Those attempts seemed to go on forever before finally hundreds of watching fans let out a huge cheer as the lad at last showed some sign of life. I often wonder whether or not he made it.'

The scenes at Heysel in 1985 had been no less harrowing. Went takes up the story: 'Liverpool flew to Belgium to defend their European Cup title against Juventus, at the end of a month that saw their Merseyside rivals, Everton, inherit their First Division crown and triumph in the European Cup Winners' Cup final. The first story I filed on the tragic day of May 29 1985 was a lunchtime piece confirming that Joe Fagan was to step down as manager of the Anfield club after the match against the Italians.

'We arrived at Heysel about ninety minutes before the 8.15 p.m. kick-off and I immediately noticed that some Liverpool supporters were sharing a large section of terracing with rival fans. It was to become a battleground that left thirty-nine people dead and scores injured when a wall collapsed after a surge by the Merseyside supporters.'

PA's editor-in-chief, David Chipp, was in Essex when the story broke. He drove back to Fleet Street to take charge of the operations as, minute by minute, the full extent of the horror unfurled and the death toll mounted.

Went continued: 'The area beneath the main stand, where I sat, became a makeshift mortuary while helicopters buzzed overhead, ferrying the injured to hospital. UEFA officials decided that the final would go ahead, eventually after a delay of eighty-five minutes, but having reported the carnage I had little appetite for the required running match copy.

'It was an apathetic, irrelevant affair and Juventus won with a Michael Platini penalty. Liverpool had booked to stay in Brussels after the final and the following morning I returned to Heysel with my media colleagues and saw at first hand the run-down state of the stadium, the demolished wall and the personal belongings, including shoes, that still littered the terracing. It was a heartbreaking scene, one that I will remember all my life. On the flight home – we always travelled with the team – Liverpool announced they would be holding a press conference at Anfield, to announce that Kenny Dalglish was succeeding Fagan as manager.

'At the team's ground, I began to file my copy on the appointment when I was interrupted by a colleague who told me that I was among journalists who had been summoned to Downing Street the following morning to brief Prime Minister Margaret Thatcher.

'The Prime Minister had already launched an anti-hooligan crusade after riots at a Luton-versus-Millwall FA Cup quarter-final two months earlier, which I covered, and she listened intently as we gave our version of the tragic events at Heysel. She showed great compassion but also an "iron" touch as she spelled out in no uncertain terms the draconian measures she wanted to introduce, including membership cards, a ban on away supporters and no alcohol sales within grounds.'

Went gave evidence before Mr Justice Oliver Popplewell, who was already reporting on the fire at the Bradford ground and a riot at Birmingham that year. His remit was extended to include Heysel. Went's vivid stories from both these disasters deservedly received top treatment not only in the British press but in newspapers around the world.

Geoff Meade, the Press Association's man in Brussels, also recalled the coverage of the Heysel stadium disaster. He was involved in the tortuous months of trials of Liverpool supporters in the Palais de Justice. Meade was on 'hooligan watch' and the match was just another game for him – he was not interested in the play or the result. He had been on the trail of hooligans all over Europe and his lack of interest in football was a big advantage to him. He had no team loyalties and was totally focused on the job in hand, travelling to France, Luxembourg, Germany and elsewhere to await trouble, which very often came.

But nothing had prepared Meade for the Heysel tragedy. He spent the day of the match in Brussels city centre, where a small group of troublemakers had already smashed a jeweller's window. But Meade and other reporters thought there would be no more trouble that day. They decided to go to a restaurant closer to the ground while the game was on and monitor the Liverpool fans as they left for the railway and coach stations afterwards.

'We thought we would all be home with our cocoa soon after ten p.m.,' he said. How wrong they all were. For Meade recalled: 'Shortly before kick-off, the area around the match was filled with blue flashing lights and sirens. But the Belgian police were notorious for overreacting and I well remember remarking on their usual panic approach to crowd control. Then it dawned on us all that perhaps we should take a look across the road. We left our steak *frites* on the table and set off. At the ground the doors were locked and a large official refused to let us in.

' "There's a man in there who's gone crazy with a knife," he said. We sped through a gap and round the outside of the stadium. There was little to see and so we split up. Minutes later I found myself approaching what looked like a pile of sandbags against a retaining wall. As I looked, two men carried another sandbag and dropped it on a double-width pile. Then I realised that they weren't sandbags. They were bodies, purple from asphyxiation. In the ground the pre-match tension was as it normally would be – nobody knew this awful crush had happened, apart from those in the immediate area.'

It took time for Meade to piece together the facts. 'There was no man with a knife of course – and the Press Association news desk was already aware of what was going on through the live television coverage. In my mind's eye, I can still see the vivid yellow ball of the setting sun going down behind the crumbled stadium wall as more bodies were pulled out.'

Finding a telephone was a major problem. The Heysel area of Brussels was not the wealthiest and the nearby shopkeepers had pulled down their shutters for fear of rioting, unaware of the real cause of the police activity. 'The restaurant where our meal was uneaten and unpaid for had closed down,' Meade recalled. 'I went from one block of apartments to another to find someone to let me in to use a telephone. Many had no phone, and many others were not going to let a manic foreigner in with lurid tales of bodies everywhere.'

Finally he did find a telephone to send his descriptive piece – then he returned to the scene of the disaster to collect his thoughts and report on the clear-up operation through the night.

'It's difficult for a solitary Press Association reporter to compete directly against international agencies with teams of staff at such events. But by concentrating on the domestic priorities one can often produce a more focused account than those with a worldwide audience to satisfy,' he said afterwards.

Two years after Heysel came another tragedy, this time at sea. And the tragedy brought a special sadness into the Press Association newsroom. For two of the agency's secretaries, Janet Turner and Jacquie Virtue, and their husbands were among the victims on the *Herald of Free Enterprise*, which overturned at Zeebrugge on that fateful day of 6 May 1987. The Press Association's personnel manager, David Thomas, even though he did not have a passport at the time, was sent over to Zeebrugge to look after the families' affairs. This enabled the agency's reporters and photographers on the scene to concentrate totally on the story, without feeling they ought to be attending to the personal tragedies that afflicted the company.

Finlay Marshall, who flew over the wreck with a photographer, Mike Stephens, described it as 'like a discarded child's toy, bathed in hazy sunshine' – a description that was widely used in the national and provincial papers. Some of the nationals also splashed Ray Massey's exclusive interview with the *Herald* captain, David Lewry, who spoke about his 'night of hell'. Massey secured the interview, an emotional affair, in the garden of the skipper's home in Sandwich. It recorded the personal and mental suffering of one man and the heroism involving him and many more.

Meanwhile, a reporter, Linda Pullen, flew from Heathrow with the Transport Minister, John Moore. The original plan was that she would return with him that night, but in fact she stayed on and helped the growing team of reporters, including Peter Woodman, Alex Scott, John Aston, Geoff Meade and Ingrid Morris, and the picture news editor, Colin Macer. By coincidence, three Press Association reporters were crossing the English Channel, independently and privately, on the day of the disaster, in which 193 people died. Meade was returning to his Brussels base after a family holiday in Devon; Morris was on her way to a skiing holiday; and Aston, from the Law Courts staff, was off on a weekend break in Amsterdam.

Meade heard the news flash on his car radio as he drove into Calais. Even though his wife and children were in the back, he at once headed for Zeebrugge. On the way he tried to tell the news desk in London that he was heading to the scene, but all the roadside telephones were out of order. Then he faced horrendous traffic problems on the approaches to the port. The news had spread and fearful relatives were already gathering in the cold, gloomy night. Meade threaded his way through the seething mass of people, as far as he could along the sea wall. He then abandoned his car, leaving his surprised family inside, strode to the end of the sea wall and stared out into the dark.

'I vividly remember it was bitterly cold and my ears were burning. All I could see were lights around the area. I assumed the boat had gone down, but it was all pretty useless,' he said. Then, for him, as for other reporters who had descended on the scene, it was a case of trying to find, amid the chaos, someone in authority who knew even the slightest thing about what was going on. Meade finally managed to alert the office that he was at the scene after queuing 'for hours' for the single telephone in the terminal. Then he heard that a makeshift press room had been set up somewhere outside the port area. He found it – and chaos too. It was full of reporters who had virtually no information, and a single telephone for which there was another massive queue. Meade's only hope was to join the queue for the phone and pray that, by the time he reached it, he would have something worth filing.

But he was dogged by the thought that his wife and two children were still languishing in his car outside in the freezing cold. Finally, he found a colleague who was happy to drive them back to Brussels and let Meade have use of his own car 'for the duration'. Eventually, Meade set up a headquarters for the Press Association contingent. One of them, Linda Pullen, even managed to get into a memorial service for the dead, which was officially closed to the press. She did so by telling the forbidding but highly impressed minder on the church door, 'But you've got to let me in: I'm from Her Majesty's Press Association.'

There was at this time the added dimension of press intrusion. And Zeebrugge was just the kind of story during which it was difficult to avoid this accusation. Meade recalled: 'The problem of press intrusion was evident. I remember cringing as Tim Ockenden, our photographer on the spot, balanced his telephoto lens on my car door to get a full-face shot of a grieving relative coming out of that service. Although we were a considerable distance away and not intruding in any physical sense, Tim and I both felt uncomfortable.'

The Press Association team on the spot was helped by Thomas. Over breakfast one morning, Meade suddenly became aware that Thomas was inadvertently giving them full details of the procedures for leading relatives and friends of the dead through the grim task of identification, strolling through the lines of bodies in the makeshift morgue.

'I started asking him to describe the building, the numbers of bodies, et cetera, et cetera, and I think he found it a little distasteful. But so did we all.' Meade and Pullen stayed at the scene for weeks afterwards and witnessed the operation to turn the vessel upright again. But, before that happened, there was one curious incident. Meade was drinking coffee with a Townsend Thoresen press officer in the Zeebrugge departure terminal. She told him that there was a very good story right under his nose and that all he had to do was to look out of the window.

'I looked and looked and couldn't see anything except ferries coming and going. And then it slowly dawned on me. Instead of the familiar white and orange TT paintwork, there were boats in a new white and blue livery, which I hadn't noticed before.

'The press officer confirmed that Townsend Thoresen were repainting the entire fleet, virtually overnight, in a bid to erase the image of the white and orange hull which, at that time, still lay a few hundred yards offshore . . .'

25 Royals

A T 04.41 ON SUNDAY, 31 August 1997, a newsflash went out on the Press Association wire. It read, 'Diana, Princess of Wales, has died, according to British sources, the Press Association has learned this morning.'

Behind that sad announcement, which devastated an unbelieving world, lay a fascinating story of professionalism, tenacity, team effort, trust and good luck. But in the end it was journalistic professionalism that counted for more than anything else.

The newsflash that shocked the world had been filed by a Press Association journalist standing on the tarmac of the Manila military air base in the Philippines. PA's defence and diplomatic correspondent, Charlie Miller, had woken up early that morning in his hotel room in the Philippines capital and, as usual, monitored the international TV news while shaving and packing.

What he heard stopped him in his tracks: Diana had been injured in a Paris car crash and her close friend Dodi Fayed was believed to be dead. Miller was accompanying the Foreign Secretary, Robin Cook, on a tour of the Far East, which had already taken in Malaysia and Indonesia. The visit to Jakarta and the Suharto regime had been seen as the focal point of the trip, because it was the first acid test, since the general election earlier that year, of New Labour's so-called ethical foreign policy.

'As soon as I heard the news, I grabbed the internal phone and rang the head of the Foreign Office News Department, who was staying in the same hotel,' said Miller. 'He confirmed the details and suggested I got the other journalists together for an impromptu press conference with Cook in the hotel lobby. Cook acted as the government spokesman and told of his concerns for Diana and her family. At that stage we all believed she was still alive.' As Cook headed off to meet the families of the British Embassy staff, Miller and the other journalists filed their stories, finished packing and left for the military air base, where an RAF VC10 was waiting. But Miller was restless. He could not settle in his spacious aircraft seat, so he went outside and spoke to some of his Whitehall contacts as they arrived at the heavily guarded base. It was at that moment he heard for the first time that Diana had probably died, and Cook would probably be making a statement.

'I immediately found a quiet corner, pulled out my mobile phone, which thankfully worked with a full signal, and rang through to the London news desk,' he said. 'I explained the situation was serious and that Cook was going to make a statement. I then started checking the facts and talking to my contacts again until I was convinced I was right. I then suggested to London that we put out a newsflash which would alert the media about the critical situation. Consequently, I filed a short flash which read, "Foreign Secretary Robin Cook's official aircraft has been delayed in the Philippines as he prepares to make a statement amid mounting speculation that Diana, Princess of Wales, is dead."'

On the basis of that short paragraph, several of the London-based Sunday newspapers pulled their final editions and awaited further news from the Press Association. It was still a mystery to them where this news had come from. Meanwhile, Miller, assiduous as ever, continued checking the facts and finally, aware that an official announcement would have to come from Paris for diplomatic reasons, was satisfied that the agency could go live with the news. So he telephoned the executive editor, Mike Parry, who had come into the newsroom in the middle of the night, as soon as the news broke of the crash, to take charge of the news desk.

Miller told Parry that he thought the Press Association should go ahead with the newsflash. 'To an outsider it might seem like a monumental decision,' Miller said, 'but to me – and to Mike – it was straightforward news judgment. I shall always be grateful to him for his handling of the event in London. Someone with less stature might have suggested waiting for the official announcement. We didn't.'

As a result, the Press Association gave the media what they needed, and when they needed it. Papers were able to publish the full story in their final editions – which were still rolling off the presses at daybreak and beyond on that fateful morning – and radio and TV had the news the world needed to hear. This historic PA newsflash beat the rest of the world by sixteen minutes.

PA's editor-in-chief, Paul Potts, spent an anxious time in those minutes before the death of the Princess of Wales was officially confirmed in the French capital. For Miller in Manila, the work continued. Cook gave his statement and the full story was filed.

Four hours later, the VC10 touched down in Singapore and the results of Miller's handiwork were everywhere to be seen: banner headlines, nonstop TV and radio bulletins. The world was in mourning. 'Those moments will stay with me for ever,' said Miller. 'My feelings were a strange mixture of extreme sadness and excitement. It was an awesome experience like no other I have known. As I dictated the final newsflash I suddenly realised that that single phone call was going to turn the world to grief.'

For his efforts, Miller deservedly received the London Press Club Scoop of the Year Trophy in 1997. But, as he acknowledged, Mike Parry played a no less crucial role in deciding to release the tragic news – a daring operation since, although he trusted Miller absolutely, there was not a single official word to confirm the news.

When Parry arrived in the newsroom at 12.30 that morning, he believed that only Dodi Fayed was dead. 'At that stage, everybody believed Diana had a broken arm, lacerations to her thigh and concussion,' he said. 'The crucial enquiry at that time was just how badly injured she was. For the next three to four hours we tried to find out the extent of her injuries.' Then suddenly Parry realised that a bad situation was incalculably worse than he had feared.

'At about 4.20 a.m., my phone rang and it was Charlie Miller on the tarmac beside Cook's plane. He told me the aircraft had been delayed and, from discussions he had with Robin Cook's people, it seemed as though the Foreign Secretary was going to make a statement about the condition of the Princess of Wales – and that it was a serious statement.'

Parry believed that Miller had been 'using his experience and contacts he had built up over a decade of doing his job' and as a result he told his executive editor that he believed the situation with Diana might be very much more serious than was first thought. This was the first spoken suspicion that the princess was dead. Ten minutes later, Miller was back on the phone. He could say with certainty, he told Parry, that Diana was, in fact, dead.

'Sitting in London in the early hours of the morning and getting a telephone phone call from the other side of the world telling you the Princess of Wales is dead is a somewhat daunting experience,' Parry admitted. 'There are probably not two or three journalists in the whole of the world whom I would have trusted so implicitly to act on that information. But, because of the reputation Charles Miller has, I decided we would put out a newsflash – time 4.41 a.m. I accepted what Charlie told me – you don't interrogate your own people. Then there was a gap of sixteen minutes until 4.57 a.m., when the official announcement came from France.

'It was a nerve-racking sixteen minutes,' said Parry, 'easily the most dramatic moment of my journalistic life – telling the world the Princess of Wales was dead and doing it before an official announcement. It is a tribute to Charlie Miller and to the accuracy and integrity of the Press Association that I was able to do that.'

Later, Parry fully justified what Miller and he had done in response to critics who said the information should have been held to await the official announcement. 'On reflection, we acted absolutely properly,' he said. 'There were some detractors later who claimed it was irresponsible to have done that. But we were in charge of that information and it would have been irresponsible not to have divulged it. There were other media organisations speculating on all sorts of issues and, as we knew the absolute truth of the matter, we were right to issue it.'

Nerve-racking it certainly was. If it had been wrong, it would have had incalculable effects on the Press Association's reputation. But the people at the hub of this tingling drama were 100 per cent sure of their facts.

Indeed, some of the most beautiful and moving pictures taken by the Press Association were of the 'island of flowers' at Althorp House, where Diana, Princess of Wales, was buried. Just two days after the funeral, photographer David Jones was permitted to visit the scene by her brother, Earl Spencer.

Jones was rowed out to the island by the gamekeeper, Adey Greeno. Afterwards, Jones said the entire island was carpeted with the flowers, millions of blooms, which became a spontaneous symbol of a nation's grief.

'It really was very peaceful and extremely moving,' he said. 'It is the peace and solemnity of the scene which really strikes you. There was nothing but the rustle of the leaves in the trees, the sound of ducks swimming on the lake and the birds singing. In the distance was the sound of agricultural machinery. It really is a tranquil haven, a place of calm. If you had a special place where you would like to go and sit for a while and be silent, it was just like that.'

The sadness felt in the Press Association over Diana's death is still there today. For the agency had a long association with the Pimlico kindergarten beauty who became a princess. But there were ups and downs along the way. For on one occasion the agency was at the centre of a controversy over an interview with Lady Diana Spencer, as she then was, shortly before her engagement to Prince Charles.

A Press Association reporter, Roger Tavener, secured an interview with her while she was working at the New England Kindergarten in St George's Square, Pimlico, London. She was quoted as saying, 'I would like to marry soon. What woman doesn't want to marry eventually?'

Next year? was the next question. 'Why not?' the future princess said. 'I don't think nineteen is too young – it depends on the person.' And, when asked if Prince Charles had proposed to her, Lady Diana blushed and giggled nervously: 'I can't say "yes" or "no" to that. I can't confirm or deny it.'

Inevitably, the interview got huge play in newspapers under Press Association bylines. Later, however, Lady Diana was to deny having talked about marriage. Her mother, Frances Shand-Kydd, also protested about allegedly inaccurate reports and harassment of her daughter by the press since Lady Diana's name had been linked with Prince of Wales.

But Tavener firmly stood by his story. He said, when the denials emerged, 'I am astonished and a little upset by these reports. The interview was very friendly and ended after about twenty minutes only because I had exhausted my fund of questions. I had a full note of the interview, which contains dozens of questions and answers. The subsequent story is an accurate and faithful report of what Lady Diana said. I take very seriously my role as a Press Association reporter, and the agency's reputation for accuracy.'

David Chipp also backed him up, saying, 'Roger Tavener is an experienced reporter. He has full notes of his interview with Lady Diana. I have no reason to doubt the correctness of our story.'

And, as if further proof were needed, other reporters who were present and within earshot of Tavener's interview confirmed that his account of the conversation was accurate in every detail.

The marriage of course did take place – and the wedding on 29 July 1981 was one of the most memorable days in PA's history. Even so, to Chipp's great regret, the Press Association did not get the historic picture of Charles and Diana kissing on the balcony of Buckingham Palace. Otherwise, it was an impeccable operation. This is how it was described by the associate editor, Reg Evans, who was in charge of the operation:

Adjectives in the PA file fell as thickly as the confetti that showered down from the tall buildings on either side of Fleet Street. And why not? The heir to the throne doesn't marry a stunning beauty every day. For most of us in the agency it was the colour story of a lifetime. The satisfaction came from seeing Press Association royal wedding pictures and copy massively used in evening and morning papers throughout the country. It was like that all the way through the Royal romance. The agency was first with the engagement announcement. Court correspondent Grania Forbes, eight months pregnant, was called from maternity leave to conduct the first interview given by Charles and Diana. Ron Bell's engagement day pictures, as well as making every newspaper, later smiled from millions of posters, postcards, tea trays, pottery and lapel badges. Throughout the engagement period the Press Association kept ahead with news and pictures.

Meanwhile meticulous planning and research was going on for the day itself. Picture editor Paddy Hicks spent months of political in-fighting to get the positions he needed along the route and in St Paul's. For the Press Association gets nothing as of right. Every position had to be bargained and sweated for.

Grania Forbes was extensively by-lined for a question-and-answer session with Diana – a talk which beat the wedding eve TV interview by two days. And 24 hours before the wedding, newspapers received from the agency a full descriptive story written in the past tense and sent under embargo for early editions of evening papers.

The Press Association's main wedding story began to roll as the first coaches jingled out of the Buckingham Palace gates. Forbes, filing from St Paul's, wrote a glowing description of a bouncy, beaming, winking Prince Charles on 'clearly the happiest day of his life'. And it was all summed up by Alastair Percival in a morning-paper round-up widely used the following morning. His first two sentences put it all together:

> He raised her slim white hand to his lips and then, on the balcony of Buckingham Palace, kissed her on the mouth – Britain's future king and queen in moments of tenderness for all the world to see. The kisses summed up the enchantment of the most public wedding in all history.

That day the picture desk produced 16,300 black-and-white wedding prints. From the colour laboratories came six thousand colour duplicates – but, alas, no kiss.

And so came extensive coverage of the royal couple and of course pictures of their sons William and Harry. But the Press Association was involved in a bizarre incident over the christening of Prince Harry in St George's Chapel, Windsor, on Friday, 21 December 1984.

The court correspondent, Grania Forbes, much experienced and much trusted, had filed a story implying that Princess Anne had snubbed Charles by not attending the christening. She had, it was alleged, gone rabbit shooting instead. The story was issued along those lines but, when Chipp came into the office shortly after it ran on the wire, he took a different view over the slant. The story was eventually withdrawn and replaced by another one, which made no mention of a snub or of a family feud, both of which had appeared in the original story. The new version simply pointed out that Princess Anne and her husband were not present and had left their home Gatcombe Park, 'dressed for shooting'.

Prince Charles had actually telephoned the Press Association personally about the first story. Chipp insisted that no outside pressure was applied on the Press Association to withdraw the report and stressed that he had personally decided to replace the first story and put out a substitute. 'When I came back and saw the first story I decided that it suggested more speculation than an agency ought to make,' he said. Others, including Reg Evans, strongly disagreed with Chipp's decision.

Buckingham Palace later said that it was 'a matter of regret' for Princess Anne and her husband that they had not been able to attend, but it had been understood right from the start that this would be the case. Absolutely no advance information was given out about the christening, which the royal family regarded as an entirely private occasion. So Forbes, like the rest of the press pack, was waiting on the pavement outside Windsor Castle, watching people as they went in – and trying to construct a story from that.

The associate editor, Reg Evans, was in the office that morning and, to use his own words, was 'foaming at the mouth' because there was still no story from Forbes. But when her story finally dropped, some time after midday, Evans was elated by what he saw. The line about going rabbit shooting in Gloucestershire had been, according to her, entirely verified. Indeed, there had already been a good deal of speculation in the press earlier, suggesting that Princess Anne was displeased that she had not been invited to be a godparent.

After the story was distributed, Chipp came into the office and Evans left. Chipp took a different view about it and then there was a call from the Prince of Wales, who had seen the story. The Prince told Chipp that it was not true to say his sister had snubbed the christening and indeed they had known she would not be coming, because her list of engagements had already been fixed.

Having received this personal assurance from the Prince, Chipp could hardly suggest he wasn't telling the truth. The editor-in-chief then took the very unusual step for the Press Association of actually cancelling the story and putting out a substitute. But Chipp continued to insist that it was the speculative nature of the story that caused him to withdraw it. However, it was effectively all too late. The newspapers angled their story the next day on the fact that the agency had cancelled the story after Prince Charles had been on the telephone. The sad outcome of all this was that the PA was subjected to pressure over a considerable period from senior officials of the royal household, who wanted Forbes withdrawn from her post as court correspondent.

In fact Forbes did herself ask for a change, having worked as court correspondent for some nine years. Chipp told the Palace that that he had agreed to this and that she would be moved to other important work. Chipp also pointed out to the Palace that, throughout her period in this post, she had acted at all times with discretion and had never revealed or gossiped about anything she may have heard or seen because of her special and privileged position.

Later, the Prince of Wales was to make clear that neither he nor the Princess of Wales had any doubts at all about Grania Forbes's loyalty. Even so, there is a widespread view that the Queen, who was very fond of Forbes, had nothing whatsoever to do with this decision. This is perhaps demonstrated by the fact that just before the reporter left, the Queen invited her in for a private audience – an event of great rarity – and spoke glowingly about her work, giving her a signed photograph.

Chipp then appointed another court correspondent, Tom Corby, who had been devastated that he had not been given the job when Forbes was offered it nine years earlier.

Corby was to win the hearts of the royals, especially the Queen Mother. On her ninetieth birthday he was camped outside Clarence House with scores of other media people, waiting for her to emerge and acknowledge well-wishers. This she did, and, as was her wont, she came back to do a 'curtain call'. But by this time Corby had been forced, by the pressure of the scrum, into the gutter, from which he was totally unable to move. When the Queen Mother came out again, she looked pityingly at this unfortunate, dishevelled and totally trapped figure and said, 'Oh dear, Mr Corby. You look terribly hot and terribly thirsty.'

Corby replied, 'Ma'am, I am wedged in here and I cannot move. I am terribly thirsty.'

The Queen Mother returned to Clarence House. And, a few moments later, a powdered footman appeared, bearing a bottle of champagne and a glass on a silver salver, which was formally presented to Corby in his gutter.

Corby was also a principal figure in the saga of the Duke of Edinburgh and his 'slitty-eyed' remark while on a visit with the Queen to China in 1986. The Press Association man was one of the two pool reporters covering a meeting by the royal couple with some students from Edinburgh University, who were in Xian in Central China, as part of a student-exchange arrangement.

The reporters were not expecting any excitement, or even anything at all, other than run-of-the-mill material. However, one of the students, Simon Kirby, approached Corby and said, 'The Duke of Edinburgh's a bit outspoken, isn't he? He said that Peking was ghastly and that if you stayed here too long you would get slitty-eyed.'

The question facing Corby – who had to check out the accuracy of what the student had told him – was: Do we wreck the most important royal tour the Queen and the Duke of Edinburgh have yet embarked on. Do we get fired? Or what?

Anyway, Corby and his colleagues decided to 'go with it'. It was one of the most spectacular of the duke's litany of recorded gaffes. But Corby had to be virtually bullied by the news desk into filing the line. Corby was anxious that his story did not wreck – as it possibly could have done – the Press Association's unique relationship with the Palace. Happily it did not.

Corby's first overseas assignment as court correspondent was in 1985. It was to the Caribbean. In Belize, Michael Cole, the Queen's press officer before he joined Mohamed al Fayed at Harrods, approached Corby and asked him if he had studied the menu for that night's state banquet. He would see on it an item called 'Mascal roasted gibnut.'

'Go and see the chef,' Cole said to him. 'And he'll tell you what it is precisely.' Corby duly went to the kitchens, where the chef confessed to him, 'A gibnut is a member of the rodent family . . .'

When, a hopeful Corby ventured, 'Is it a rat?' the chef merely repeated, 'It is a member of the rodent family.'

What Corby desperately wanted was for someone of sufficient standing and knowledge to admit that it was a rat. He had visions of wonderful headlines throughout Britain: QUEEN EATS RAT.

He put it to a senior official at the High Commission: 'Can I say it is a rat?' The official looked thoughtful for a moment, then muttered something about its being a great delicacy on the island. But the official's wife chipped in: 'You know very well,' she said, 'it's a bloody great rat.'

That was enough for Corby. He dashed off to a telephone and all the papers the next day splashed QUEEN HAS RAT FOR DINNER. But that wasn't the end of it. In the middle of the night, there was a beating on Corby's bedroom door. It was the distraught photographer from the *Daily Mirror*. His picture desk wanted a picture of a 'bloody great rat' like the one the Queen had consumed at the banquet. But the problem was: where would they find a gibnut in the middle of the night? A hotel employee told them, unhelpfully, 'There are plenty in the jungle if you know where to look for them . . .'

Then another hotel worker revealed that there was a cage full of gibnuts in Belize Zoo. It was at this point that Corby's undoubted diplomatic skills came into play. He successfully managed to persuade someone to open up the zoo gates at 4 a.m. so that a picture could be taken.

The man who held the keys for that zoo deserves a medal from Fleet Street for being so astonishingly obliging. And Corby deserved no less for sweet-talking a man out of his bed in the middle of the night so he could visit a rat.

One of the most famous, historic royal stories is of course the abdication of King Edward VIII – and no book on the Press Association would be complete without it. For the agency played a major role in the events leading up to that momentous occasion. And the man who effectively broke the story that shocked the nation and, indeed, the world, received the magnificent sum of £10 for his trouble – a reward that he generously shared with a colleague.

The irony was that Dr AWF Blunt, the Bishop of Bradford, whose diocesan speech sparked off the crisis, had not actually heard of Mrs Wallis Simpson when he wrote his words criticising the King. Even so, Dr Blunt, who had absolutely no intention of creating a crisis, was the man who 'lit the cigarette end which started the blaze'. Rarely has a bishop accidentally ignited such a constitutional conflagration.

The reporter at the centre of the crisis was Charles Leach, who was on the staff of the *Bradford Telegraph and Argus* and eventually became its editor. He was also the Bradford correspondent of the Press Association, a post he was trying to divest himself of. But the PA successfully persuaded him to stay on.

At this time the so-called Establishment – in those days including the principal Fleet Street editors – were aware of the King's romantic association with the American divorcee Mrs Ernest (more commonly called Wallis) Simpson. But, unlike the case today, such momentously delicate matters were denied what Margaret Thatcher was to later call 'the oxygen of publicity'.

Indeed, it was the Bishop of Bradford, who did not know half what was going on, who forced the issue into the public spotlight. It should be remembered that throughout most of the first half of the twentieth century, right up to the late 1950s, any public criticism of the royal family – however mild and oblique – was virtually unheard of. It was not the done thing, in any stratum of society, to speak of royalty in anything but the most laudatory terms.

That was why the bishop's diocesan speech, gently and indirectly criticising the King for not turning up at church except on special occasions, became such a catalyst for the tremendous events that were to follow.

In that fairly innocent but certainly very bold spirit, the bishop wrote his remarks about the King needing grace. No one except his secretary knew he had written it – until it was delivered. He was moved to write this speech because of a businessman's remark to a fellow bishop that while the clergy were building up the coming coronation 'the chief actor doesn't care tuppence about it'.

However, some time before the bishop made his remarks, he attended the Church Assembly. The Bishop of St Albans, sitting next to him, asked sotto voce: 'What's all this about Mrs Simpson?'

The cloistered Dr Blunt had no idea what he was talking about. The Bishop of St Albans then showed him some cuttings from American newspapers, which, unlike the British press of the day, were totally uninhibited about printing scandal concerning the royal family.

This momentarily caused Blunt to rethink what he was going to say in his diocesan speech. He seriously considered deleting the passage, saying he hoped the King was aware of his need for God's grace. But he nevertheless decided to go ahead with it at the diocesan conference as prepared.

He said later, 'I said to myself, That has nothing to do with Mrs Simpson, and so I left those sentences in.'

On the day the speech was delivered, 1 December 1936, Leach returned to the *Telegraph and Argus* office, to be greeted by Ronald Harker, who had been sitting on the press seats and had taken a full note of what the bishop had said. He told Leach, 'There's something good for PA here. The bishop has criticised the King. Stokes [the editor of the *Telegraph and Argus*] has decided to splash it.'

Leach had a strong feeling that the PA would not use the story. The *Yorkshire Evening Post* of that day also published the criticism of the King but, surprisingly, did not particularly highlight it. However, if the *Telegraph and Argus* were splashing it beneath a seven-column headline, Leach thought he had better give it to the Press Association as well as to the other national news agency, Exchange Telegraph.

He spoke to Extel first. The Extel copytaker took the copy but, when the agency wired the story, the vital sentence about the King needing grace was inexplicably omitted. Afterwards, Leach filed it to PA. There was understandably some delay in disseminating the story, while the agency's executives considered its massive implications. Ultimately it went out, intact, with all the relevant and controversial elements included.

This was the first that Fleet Street heard of it. Their immediate reaction was that the bishop was referring to the King's relationship with Mrs Simpson. The King's 'secret' was out and public property. And it had been unearthed as a result of an inaccurate assumption of the bishop's motives. Leach eventually received a cheque for £10 from the Press Association, which he shared with Harker. They also received a letter of thanks from the PA editor, Henry Martin, who called for a complete verbatim report of the bishop's speech and a carefully prepared summary. Quotes were also added from the editorials in the provincial press.

On 8 October 1936, before the bishop spoke, Martin had issued a private and confidential instruction to his staff, headed 'Mrs Ernest Simpson'. It said:

The Press Association's attitude regarding mention of Mrs Ernest Simpson may be governed by the following conditions:

(1) Do not mention if she goes to Buckingham Palace privately or if the King visits her. If it is desired that her presence at the Palace be known the Court Circular will notify.

(2) Do not mention if there is any real doubt about the taste of doing so. In any event, do not mention unnecessarily.

(3) On the other hand, if she is at a public function with the King and both Press and public are in a position to note her, her presence may be indicated. For instance, if she went with the King to open a public building or accompanied him to the theatre, there is no reason for suppressing the information even though it may have been obtained in advance of the Court Circular.

(4) It would have been in perfect order last week to have announced that she got out of the train on her return with the King from Balmoral.

The position of the PA during this constitutional crisis was tricky, to say the least. There was already a problem for individual editors or newspaper proprietors to decide whether or not to give wider currency to the rumours and gossip that had been in circulation for months in newspapers in the United States and the farthest reaches of the Empire.

There would be no such inhibitions today, whatever the consequences. But then the thinking was that no individual newspaper or agency wanted to get the blame for precipitating a crisis – which was going to happen anyway. It was more than that. The proprietors of many of the newspapers – and indeed, it has to be said, some of the editors as well – were all members of 'the Establishment' and would probably have been happy to have seen this affair kept under wraps for ever, an unthinkable situation half a century later.

The Press Association's position was unique in that it was the servant of the entire British press, and it was no part of its responsibility to act as the censor of news. It has been written since that the PA – in common with the whole of the British press – conducted itself with a 'restraint' that in the eyes of some observers, both at the time and later, was barely distinguishable from self-censorship.

But, even when the story was out, the nervousness with which Fleet Street treated it was interesting. Throughout, it seems, they took their cue from the altogether bolder provincial papers. It was the leading article in the *Yorkshire Post* that was extensively quoted by the Press Association and that, according to contemporary accounts, dealt 'soberly but portentously' with what the paper described as rumours but what in truth were well-known facts in Fleet Street. It was this editorial that was often credited with having particular significance in the story of the pressures and events that led up to the ultimate abdication.

The editorial was variously described as dignified and moderate in tone, but ultimately censorious and apprehensive. However, other newspapers outside London also commented on these momentous events. But even the *Yorkshire Post* did not decide to go ahead with its editorial until its editor, Arthur Mann, had consulted on the telephone with the editors of the *Birmingham Post* and the *Manchester Guardian*, both of whom also decided to comment. In particular the *Birmingham Post* editorial was highly outspoken. Other papers quickly followed suit, including the *Leeds Mercury*, the *Yorkshire Observer*, the *Northern Echo* and the *Nottingham Journal*.

But it was because the Press Association issued a quotation from the *Yorkshire Post* before all the others that this editorial gained the reputation, more than any of the others, of having precipitated the crisis. For it was when the Fleet Street papers, in all their timidity, read the extract from the *Yorkshire Post* when it came over the Press Association wires that they decided – or at least some of them did – to take the plunge, but even then they did not do so straightaway. They actually waited for 24 hours after publishing the agency's story before daring to comment themselves on events.

The Press Association earned golden opinions throughout the abdication crisis. The Speaker of the House of Commons read the King's message at 3.43 on the crucial day – and that was the precise moment the agency's fast printer clicked out the vital news in London offices. From the PA headquarters, a Morse slip was placed in the transmitter, a red light went up, and similar lights automatically switched on in the Leeds, Manchester, Birmingham, Glasgow and Bristol centres: the sign that a rush message was on the way and nothing must interfere with its transmission. These centres radiated it to newspaper offices by feeding into adjacent circuits. London flashed it to offices in direct touch.

At 3.44 London and the provinces learned that the Duke of York had succeeded his brother and was becoming King George VI. The Prime Minister Stanley Baldwin's speech describing the circumstances and events leading up to the abdication was being received in newspaper offices up and down the land at a rate of 140 to 150 words a minute – about the speed Baldwin was speaking – and the words were spilling out across the country within a few minutes of their being uttered.

Even with today's modern electronic equipment, computers and all manner of gadgets, it is still the reporter with his fast shorthand who rules the roost at the House of Commons. Indeed, throughout the ten days of the crisis, every link in the Press Association chain of organisation was tested to the limit. Every department – the news desk, subeditors, parliamentary and telegraph – knew what was expected of it, and delivered.

Another important service performed by the agency during the crisis was the issuing of a mass of background and biographical material within the first two days, all of which was a godsend to newspapers when the storm broke. Then, on 5 December, provincial evening newspapers took the unusual course for a Saturday of remaining in Creed circuit (i.e. switched on, to be able to receive the Press Association output) until 10 p.m. at the agency's invitation. It was the first time the Creed system had remained open until a late hour on Saturday since the illness of King George V the previous January.

In London, the direct printer remained in constant touch with Fleet Street throughout Saturday night and Sunday. In the provinces, newspapers, both evening and morning, with few exceptions, responded to the PA's invitation to 'come in on Creed' at 10 a.m. on Sunday, to receive whatever information was available. From the beginning of the week the main interest centred on Parliament, where the PA had keyed up its reporting and transmission. Normally, the agency's parliamentary staff would telephone news flashes direct to head office, with the full report going on Creed from Westminster, and relayed from the temporary premises in St Bride Street (85 Fleet Street was then in the process of being built) to the provinces.

It was an operation on a grand scale. In fact, the resilience of the Press Association was demonstrated when Henry Martin decided to discard the Creed at Westminster and have every line of Mr Baldwin's speech telephoned directly to the editorial department. For the actual abdication speech, the PA created a double record. A long sequence of concise snaps was transmitted to London and provincial offices in alternation with the full report: in effect two services. This was probably the pioneer effort of a system that the present-day Press Association parliamentary staff operate, on a far more streamlined basis, as a matter of routine.

Reporters were telephoning from Westminster direct from their shorthand notebooks, while the agency's general-news editorial staff were divided into two sections, one taking the snaps and the other the full version. These vital words were then dictated by reporters direct to the Morse 'puncher' at the other side of the room. It meant the world knew what the Prime Minister was saying within seconds of the words being uttered from his mouth.

The Press Association had already scored a notable scoop with the announcement, 34 hours ahead of the event, that Edward would broadcast on Friday evening. Some newspaper offices were sceptical about this, but the PA stuck to its guns and was proved right. It was also through the efforts of the PA that the London office of the American agency, the Associated Press, were able to secure a one-minute beat to their 1,500 newspapers in the United States, with the official announcement of the abdication. Thanks again to the PA, they had a five-minute beat with the full text.

The PA scored yet again immediately after the abdication. A tip had been received that Edward was to leave the country from Portsmouth, and so the star reporter of the time, Richard Eccleston, was sent hotfoot down there. Others had tried to trail the royal car but had lost it. Eccleston, however, had taken care to stay at a hotel only a few yards from the main dock gate. At around one o'clock in the morning, he wandered outside to see if he could get any information from the guards. Just at the moment he was talking to them, he was caught in the dazzling glare of headlights from a car heading for the docks. It pulled up, fortuitously, within a few feet of him and he saw the tragic figure of the ex-King inside it.

Needless to say, Eccleston rushed a story over to the PA reporting that Edward had left his country. Within minutes, other Fleet Street reporters were receiving telephone calls from their news desks, which had just seen the PA rushes. But, by the time they had reached the docks, Edward was already halfway across the English Channel on his way to France. The bird had flown – and the PA had scooped again.

If one discounts the rumour and gossip – although it was to prove accurate – that had been appearing for months in the American papers and elsewhere in the world, it was the PA who secured a complete exclusive on the authenticated story. Reuters circulated the PA copy worldwide and as a result of that there were numerous 'herograms', including a particularly generous one from the Associated Press.

Before those historic events, the Press Association's dealings with royals such as Edward VII had early beginnings. Buckingham Palace, after the Palace of Westminster, was probably the greatest single source of news in the Empire. And, right from the start, the agency built a unique relationship with the royals. With the exception of the Exchange Telegraph, it was the only arm of print journalism to have an accredited court correspondent, enjoying special facilities and privileges and used by the Palace to break important announcements.

On one occasion, the Press Association actually wrote an important declaration which the monarch subsequently signed and issued to the agency for publication to the world at large. This was down to the PA's first court correspondent, George Smith, who in 1899 was put in charge of a special office over a public house near the War Office to deal quickly with communiqués from the Boer War. Smith was a versatile man who enjoyed many years with the agency, which he joined in 1891, although he was never formally on its staff, preferring to be paid for the stories he actually produced. Before entering journalism he had been a schoolmaster. He was also registrar of births and deaths for Finchley and Friern Barnet in North London, and worked for a time as an insurance agent as well.

Only two years into his new appointment, Smith was one of scores of journalists who travelled to the Isle of Wight, where Queen Victoria was lying on her deathbed in Osborne House. She died just after 6.30 p.m. on 22 January 1901, having reigned for 63 years. The news was held back for ten minutes so that the Prime Minister could be informed. And then this simple message was read to the crowd of reporters and local inhabitants at the gate: 'Her Majesty the Queen breathed her last at 6.30 p.m., surrounded by her children and grandchildren.' Records are scanty, but Smith, who was in a crowd of reporters, ran for his bicycle as the news broke, then he hurtled down the hill into Cowes just ahead of the pack, also on bicycles, who shouted out to everyone, 'The Queen is dead!'

It was pandemonium as the reporters scorched along the pitted track, each one hell-bent on being first to reach what telephones there were at the start of the twentieth century. Smith made it first. When Edward VII was taken ill years later, Smith was practically resident at Buckingham Palace, with a royal telephone placed at his disposal. The intrepid court reporter was to hold the post for 33 years – and a message George V sent to Mrs Smith when her husband died demonstrated that the relationship between him and the royal family had matured into a more than professional one. He became their trusted friend.

Smith's crowning achievement concerned the Peace of Vereeniging, in the early 1900s. It was the treaty that ended the war in South Africa. Smith travelled to Windsor to obtain what he believed would be the inevitable proclamation of King Edward VII to his people on this historic event. But it had not occurred to the King that such a proclamation was necessary. Lord Knollys, the King's secretary, a master of hauteur, was in an icy mood when he told Smith that this was the position, and there would be no proclamation. Smith, however, enraged Knollys, who was not accustomed to being challenged by reporters, by telling him bluntly that this was not good enough and that the King was bound to send a message.

Sniffily, Smith was told that the King was taking tea with a lady in Windsor Great Park and was likely to be back late. Undeterred by Knollys's increasing irritation, Smith decided to stay put. 'I'll wait!' he announced. And, in the hours that went by in the hallway, he composed a formal message to the nation, couched in regal phraseology. The King finally returned with just enough time to hurriedly dress for dinner, and dinner was being served when Knollys approached Smith again, this time virtually ordering him to leave the premises. But it took more than that to budge the intrepid court correspondent. Smith brightly announced, 'I have drafted out something, perhaps you would be good enough to submit it to His Majesty!'

Knollys, by now speechless with rage at the audacity of the fellow, reluctantly agreed to take the piece of paper to the King. After a brief interval it was returned – bearing the signature 'Edward R' at the bottom. For Smith it was a triumph of patience. For Knollys it was a moment of humiliation.

26 Exclusives

T HE DEATH OF Donald Campbell, while attempting to break the world water speed record in *Bluebird* on Coniston Water in 1967, was a moving chapter in the history of the Press Association. The agency's reporter, Keith Harrison, had covered previous attempts by the speed ace and the two had become close friends.

Harrison was at the first attempt on Ullswater in the Lake District in July 1955. He recalled, 'It was a glorious summer that year, and the job was most agreeable, lying in the sun on the banks of the lake while Campbell sweated the bugs out of the boat. Later that month he put the record up to 202 m.p.h., going through the so-called water barrier of 200 m.p.h., which was thought at the time to have killed John Cobb in his jet boat, *Crusader*, on Loch Ness.'

But there would be nothing to celebrate on that fateful day in 1967. Before he left London for Coniston, Harrison was studying for his A-level in English, a course he had undertaken in order to see if his 'brain still worked'. A women student on the same course just happened to mention that she had to wait until the muse was upon her before she could write. Harrison, who had experienced a 'funny feeling' that day, replied that he was about to attend the world water-speed record attempt, and, if anything happened to Campbell, he would have to write about it then and there, muse or no muse, and whether he felt like it or not. 'I must have been psychic,' he recalled.

On all the previous occasions, Campbell had asked Harrison to join the team, but the news man had always refused, saying he was there as a reporter and no more. 'But this time, when he asked me again, I said I would take charge of the rescue arrangements, which involved looking after the fleet of small, fast boats and being on the water whenever *Bluebird* was on the move,' he said.

'The weather was, as usual, bloody awful. An engine change was carried out on the boat, a water-brake was fitted and, amazingly, neither of these two things was properly tested.'

Campbell's HQ was a caravan by the lake. Harrison was in possession of the crucial top-secret telephone number, which he passed to Noel Richley, the Press Association news editor in London. Richley was himself a Windermere man who had a sister living in the village. Some weeks earlier, during the Christmas break, Campbell had launched the boat with the help of a lad from Coniston village, and, while travelling at great speed, had hit a seagull. This had put a large dent in one of the sponsons (a sponson is a projection on the side of the boat, usually to give extra lift or to mount accessories), so Campbell obtained a supply of 'shrapnel' rockets from the Standard Fireworks company to scare the birds off before another attempt was made.

Harrison said, 'We all went on the water at around 5 a.m. and *Bluebird* was launched at 7.30 a.m. The rockets were duly fired and Campbell made the first run, which turned out to be just under 300 m.p.h. Normally he stopped at the far end of the lake to refuel, but on this occasion he turned straight round and came back. To set up an average speed of 300 m.p.h. he had to return at just over that speed, but, when he came past the boat carrying myself and Manchester-based photographer Eric Shaw, he was going faster than I had ever seen him go before. As he went by, his starboard sponson lifted out of the water, and he went on only two planing points for a couple of hundred yards or so. Then the sponson dropped back into the water as he continued at an unbelievable speed, and, almost immediately, *Bluebird* took off, somersaulted and crashed.'

Despite all the efforts of heartbroken Harrison and Campbell's team members, Campbell's body could not be found. 'We just located his helmet, shoes, gloves and mascot, Mr Woppit,' Harrison said.

Meanwhile, Richley, fully aware that Harrison could not be on the telephone until the attempt was over, put a call through to the secret number. Just before 9 a.m., he asked someone at the other end if there was anything to report. The reply he got was, 'Please get off the telephone, there's been a terrible accident.' Richley then took a chance – and put out a rush saying that Campbell had crashed. Harrison, desperately trying to find his friend, broke off the hunt and Shaw dropped him at the pier of Coniston Old Hall. 'The squire got his Rolls out because his phone was out of order,' said Harrison, 'and we drove to Torver, where there was a public telephone box.' Harrison got through to a PA copytaker, who helped him through the ordeal of filing a story involving the death of a close friend. The report was highly personal and emotional, but to their credit the subeditors issued it unchanged. It was a piece of writing that was widely used – byline and all – in all the national newspapers the following day.

Then the high drama of that day turned into low absurdity for Harrison. About three hours later, when he emerged from the telephone box, he realised that he was in the middle of nowhere, without any transport, Shaw having sped off to process his pictures and wire them.

'I was stuck with no car,' said Harrison. 'I must have looked a wreck, because no one would stop for me – until a Mother's Pride bread van pulled up. The driver offered to give me a lift to Coniston on condition that I helped him with his bread deliveries. So, in the face of one of the biggest stories of my life, I finished up having to unload two-pound loaves of bread to the local shops.'

Bluebird was eventually located in 2000 and winched from about 150 feet below Coniston Water on 9 March 2001 to be towed ashore for preservation work to be carried out. In May 2001, human remains, believed to be those of Campbell, were also recovered from the lake.

The story of the jewellery boss Gerald Ratner and his 'crap' speech is just one of a series of scoops that form the rich tapestry of Press Association history. For the report turned out to be an example of how the agency's policy of covering events that others may not think worthwhile pays off.

Ratner, a multimillionaire, was due to be the final speaker at the Institute of Directors' annual convention at the Albert Hall, in London, in April 1991. He had been asked to 'spice up' his remarks to keep the audience interested, for they already had to endure some heavyweight speakers earlier in the day. So it was a relief to them, and to the Press Association reporter Alan Jones, to have something more light-hearted to contend with – and Ratner already had a reputation for delivering provocative and entertaining speeches.

However, Jones managed to get hold of a copy of Ratner's words two hours before he was due to deliver them – and, in the time-honoured tradition, filed his PA story under an embargo until Ratner was on the platform.

Jones admitted, 'I didn't really comprehend, at the time, how newsy the speech was, but a couple of things happened. Firstly, several national newspaper reporters turned up at the Albert Hall after reading my story, then Bob Newton, the Press Association's city editor, came up to me and cautioned, "He'll never say those words."

'So by the time Ratner went on stage I was a nervous wreck, already drawing up excuses about why I'd filed such a sensational speech without first checking that it was actually going to be made. But Ratner calmly strode to the rostrum and read out word for word the speech I'd been given hours earlier. The rest is history – front-page stories everywhere for days. It was amazing how someone as streetwise and switched on as Ratner just totally misjudged such an important speech!'

Ratner had described one of his products as 'total crap' and said that some of the gifts in his stores were in the worst possible taste. Later he tried desperately to backtrack with a £70,000 advertising campaign, even calling on Paul Gascoigne to recommend his wares. He said, 'My remarks were meant as a joke and I would like to apologise for any offence they have caused.' But it was all too late. The damage had been done and thousands of Ratner's customers felt insulted and cheated.

A scoop with a happier ending happened in the Algerian desert in 1981. Mark Thatcher, son of the former Premier Margaret Thatcher, had gone missing on a car rally. When the news broke, the Press Association's European correspondent, Geoff Meade, was attending a meeting of European Union agricultural ministers in Brussels. He was soon on his way to Africa, however – and a village called Tamman Rasset in Algeria, near the spot where Mark Thatcher was last seen.

When he arrived at Algiers he explained his needs to a taxi driver in broken English. To his dismay he was ushered back inside the airport and directed to the ticket desk, where he had to book a three-hour flight on a wide-bodied jet into the Algierian interior. It took a lot of bartering to get on the flight – and even more to get a taxi to the village the other end. And the only hotel was in a street of dusty, ramshackle buildings, where camels hitched to a rail chewed their gums incessantly throughout the night.

The problems for Meade were immense. The telephones were in appalling condition and there was only a tickertape machine in the hotel. But at first there was little to report. Denis Thatcher, in a gloomy mood, arrived by ITN jet and talked to reporters. Meade filed the story of his arrival. He said, 'I screamed at the telephone operator not to let my call go at any costs and to put me through to copy, where I yelled at the copytaker just to type down everything I was saying as fast as possible before the line went dead – and not to worry about headings and catchlines or anything else. The line did go dead, never to be regained, but only after the vast bulk of the tale had been dispatched.'

The search for missing Thatcher, much of it conducted by the Algerian Air Force, went on relentlessly over the sands. By nightfall there was still no news. Everyone had filed stories about Denis Thatcher's remarks and the fact that a full-scale search was under way. In the early hours of the morning, however, Meade and a colleague, Rob Gibson, a former PA reporter turned *Daily Express* man, were the only ones still up, chatting away in the hotel restaurant. Suddenly, a man whom he and Gibson had hired to drive them around came rushing in. 'Thatcher, Thatcher, he come. He come now! He come here!' he cried. Meade thought he was merely talking about Denis Thatcher, but the driver insisted that he meant Mark. The Prime Minister's son had apparently been found and a fleet of cars was coming through the desert 'at a rate of knots'.

Meade said, 'We leapt into the man's van and careered through the desert, swerving all over the place. Eventually, we saw headlights coming towards us. A fleet of cars sped past and in one of them was Mark Thatcher. We did a U-turn and chased them back to the hotel, where we persuaded him to stage an impromptu mini press conference just for us. Mark said that the only things he wanted were a meal, a bath, a beer and a good sleep. That was the intro on the story of the lost heir who emerged from the desert intact.'

Meade painstakingly tapped out his story on the hotel's dusty telex machine. 'I just prayed that it had gone through to the right place,' he said. 'I don't know how I managed to work it. I'd never been near one apart from seeing an identical Reuter machine in Strasbourg.'

To his delight, however, the story arrived in time for the British nationals to change their front pages.

A not-so-happy ending happened in the case of Lord George-Brown, Labour's one-time 'volcanic' Foreign Secretary (as mere

George Brown), who brought his own mercurial political career to a sad and humiliating end. But for the Press Association it was a triumph. On Tuesday, 2 March 1976, clearly the worse for drink, he blustered out of the House of Lords chamber, and said, 'I want to speak to PA!'

One of the Press Association parliamentary press gallery staff, Richard Billinge, interviewed him and got the exclusive story that he had decided to leave the Labour Party. Although, in a sense, Lord George-Brown was a political has-been, he was, in Fleet Street terms, still a very hot property indeed. It was, therefore, a major story. The BBC interrupted its radio programmes to flash the Press Association report and the story was used everywhere. But it was the agency's picture of this event that created even more controversy.

Lord George-Brown had stumbled and fallen. The picture, by photographer Jimmy James, showed him being helped up out of the gutter. It made the front pages of several national newspapers and many of the regional morning papers. Nothing could have been more demeaning, and, unsurprisingly, there were those, including *The Times*, who found fault with the agency's decision to circulate such a picture.

But the editor-in-chief, David Chipp, stuck to his guns. It was, he insisted, relevant to the story and 'above all we are in the news business'.

The Press Association had also been first with the German surrender of the Channel Islands through its war correspondent, Frank Albert King, later to become diplomatic man. But, because the Press Association's remit in those days confined it to the United Kingdom, King had no overseas wartime assignments. However, as the Channel Islands were UK territory, King sailed in the destroyer HMS *Bulldog* when it set out to relieve Guernsey, while HMS *Beagle* went to Jersey.

The surrender was signed on the quarterdeck of the *Bulldog* at 7.14 a.m. on 9 May 1945. Two small German craft were then called alongside, and, after their swastikas had been hauled down and replaced with White Ensigns, the small advance party went ashore to hoist the Union Jack. Although there were a number of journalists aboard HMS *Bulldog*, only King and a reporter from an American news agency were nearby when the advance party put off for St Peter Port. They got aboard one of the small boats and on landing they commandeered a vehicle and headed for the German headquarters. On their way they passed a cart taking cream to the German officers' mess, and so they drank a toast to the King in Guernsey milk.

Then, having got ahead of other rivals, King and the American reporter pulled off a world exclusive with their report of the day.

Some years later, King, now diplomatic correspondent, was upbraided at the morning editorial conference for a mistake. Minutes later, after he emerged crestfallen from the conference, the cry went up around the newsroom: 'King's dead!' His colleagues momentarily thought that Frank had jumped out of the fifth-floor window at 85 Fleet Street. It was, in fact, the day King George VI died. Frank King himself died in 1964, only three years after his retirement, having worked for the PA for some thirty years.

The rioting in London in 1986 took its toll of Press Association reporters. Two parliamentary staff, John Mason and Liz Light-foot, working on the general desk during the recess, were among those caught up in the violence when they were drafted in to cover the Brixton riots. John Mason was beaten up, fortunately not seriously, and Liz Lightfoot had her handbag stolen. Meanwhile, a photographer, Chris Bacon, received a severe cut to the neck when trouble flared at a subsequent anti-apartheid rally. But Peter Woodman, who became transport correspondent, suffered the worst of all. He was shot and wounded at the Tottenham riots of that year, during the troubles that culminated in the brutal murder of PC Keith Blakelock.

Woodman said, 'I remember a stinging sensation in my chest and face and blood dripping from a cut over the eye. Whittington Hospital was all geared up. It had cleared a ward for the injured PCs and me. News – most of it bad – filtered through as the night wore on: fifty or more police hurt, journalists taken to hospital – and then the senseless and tragic murder of PC Blakelock.

'I thought I must file something – anything. With the hospital in a full emergency, it seemed hardly likely they could supply me with a phone. But, sure enough, a beaming sister duly wheeled one in. She plugged it into the socket – and it didn't work. No matter. Within minutes she was back with one that did, and I was able to file.'

Woodman said that, after the operation, he woke to find most of the pellets still where they were. 'No doubt they'll clank out in the bath in years to come,' he said.

* * *

Back in 1947, unusual tactics had been employed by Press Association reporters to get the story of three survivors from the Whitehaven pit disaster, in which 104 men died in an explosion under the Irish Sea. The three surfaced from the pit, having been trapped for more than twenty hours. They were taken straight to hospital, without reporters having the slightest chance of speaking to them, let alone getting near them. But the Press Association's Harry Stone had an ingenious plan. He was an imposing, suave and smartly dressed individual, with a sometimes haughty manner. So he hired one of Whitehaven's glossy Rolls-Royce taxis, complete with liveried chauffeur. The car purred up to the hospital and came to a halt in front of the main entrance. The hospital porter was so impressed with this spectacle that he put Stone in immediate touch with the house surgeon, who gave him an exclusive account of the ordeals of the three survivors, and how they had escaped from the horror.

It was almost certainly a much more coherent story than the three men themselves would have been able to tell. Needless to say, this exclusive was splashed in all the papers the following day.

The Press Association scored, too, at the Old Bailey trial of Jeremy Thorpe, the former Liberal leader, and three others on charges connected with conspiracy to murder, in 1979. And although Thorpe walked away a free man from the court, his political life was in ruins and his health was deteriorating. He had already, in the run-up to the trial, lost his seat at North Devon.

The Press Association rush at 1438 on Friday, 22 June, telling the world of the acquittals, was the signal that unleashed a flood of agency copy and background material, which had been sent well in advance of the verdict, covering all permutations. For more than six weeks, the Press Association's trial reporting team – the chief Old Bailey reporter Ken Dennis, chief southwest reporter Allan Smith and London staffman Paul Harris – had written thousands of words of evidence, speeches and summing up on what was arguably the most sensational trial of the twentieth century. They had also secured, for the agency alone in advance, the statement from Thorpe that his solicitor, Sir David Napley, was to read outside the court after the acquittal. And an added bonus was an 'instant' interview with Thorpe by the PA's senior background reporter, John Shaw, who had talked with the former Liberal leader before the trial.

This interview, in which Thorpe expressed confidence in his acquittal and being vindicated, was transmitted immediately after the first 'not guilty' rushes and made evening paper front pages alongside the court report. What made the performance all the more remarkable was that the Press Association was, at the time, in the throes of industrial action.

The background stories – now an important feature of the agency's coverage of big court cases – dealt with every conceivable aspect of the scandal. It was a big achievement, and recognised as such by the Australian Associated Press (AAP) in a service message from Sydney: 'PA's cover was invaluable to AAP, especially as first copy of the day from London landed at a vital time for first editions of Australian morning newspapers. Throughout the trial we used PA for nightleads, running cover and sidebars.'

One way the Press Association gets its scoops is by 'staying there' after everyone else has gone, or by covering events that others believe do not warrant their attention. One such was the old Employment Appeal Tribunal (EAT). When it was set up in 1976, its first president, a High Court judge, Sir Raymond Phillips, expressed a desire that the institution should remain in low profile. At the official opening, he said, 'If after today the court does not hit the headlines I will regard that as a testimony to its success.'

But his aspirations were quickly dashed. The Press Association found the tribunal a rich source of stories, and in the first few months had these exclusives, all of which 'hit the headlines': 'Ruled unlawful to let women workers out from the factory five minutes before men'; 'The lady cannot be a lord'. A peer's daughter had unsuccessfully sought to inherit her father's title under the sex equality legislation. And a pregnant woman who was sacked could not bring a sex-bias suit because there was no such thing as a pregnant man.

John Morecroft, a reporter who for years was at the Old Bailey, spent many an evening covering dinners. And at one he secured a highly unusual scoop. It was at the Dorchester Hotel in the late 60s.

The main speaker, a top surgeon, had perhaps ill-advisedly described in graphic detail an operation he had recently performed. The result was that ten women guests fainted, like ninepins, one after the other. They were all laid out in a row in the hotel foyer. Morecroft capped this incredible story with a quote from a waiter: 'We were told to leave them out here, because it would be more than our jobs were worth to carry them into the powder room.'

Meanwhile, on August Bank Holiday Monday in 1979, a day regarded in Fleet Street as representing the epitome of the silly season, a world-beating flash suddenly dropped on to the news desk. Chris Parkin, the Press Association's man in Dublin, had scooped everyone with the murder of Lord Mountbatten. Parkin had received a tip from a highly reliable contact. It referred to 'some sort of explosion' on the earl's boat. Parkin swiftly checked it with the Garda, the Irish police, and filed it – well ahead of everyone else. And throughout the day he remained ahead of the game.

The first PA flash went out at 1322 and within minutes five more flashes were on the wire. A 2,000-word story was running within ninety minutes of the first flash and Parkin's contribution provided provincial evening newspapers with an in-depth story from sources in London, Belfast, Dublin and the scene of the assassination in Mullaghmore, County Sligo, in plenty of time for later editions. And it was a PA reporter who broke the news to Lord Mountbatten's staff at Broadlands, Southampton.

On the same day, 18 British soldiers were killed by an explosion at Warrenpoint in Northern Ireland. So much for Bank Holiday newsroom torpor.

On another sombre note, the news of the last, fatal illness of Sir Winston Churchill was broken through two women talking over the garden fence. By chance the former Prime Minister's personal bodyguard and detective lived next door to a Press Association correspondent in north London. Chatting in the garden one day, the detective's wife remarked to the reporter's wife that Sir Winston had been very ill for several days, but she had seen nothing about it in the papers.

When the reporter came back home, his wife told him what had happened. He told the news desk – and the story broke.

Another veteran reporter, who secured a byline many years before this became official Press Association policy, was Alfred Browne, who served in many editorial capacities in the newsroom, including science correspondent and weekend editor.

In 1966, the Home Office, in response to a number of enquiries from newspapers, decided to allow one reporter, and one reporter only, to go inside Durham Prison to conduct interviews with the members of the Great Train Robbery gang. The Newspaper Proprietors' Association and the Newspaper Society had no difficulty in agreeing that it must be a Press Association man. Browne was given the assignment because, as the agency explained at the time, 'he just happened to be the only senior reporter who was available'.

And because of that Browne, who had joined the Press Association as an editorial office boy (known in those days as phonists, because they held open telephones for reporters), found his name used on the front pages of virtually every London and provincial newspaper.

A similar instance had happened six years earlier when the Press Association's chief reporter, Arthur Booth, conducted an interview with Aneurin Bevan, the founder of the National Health Service, in March 1960. It was the first interview Bevan had given since his major, abdominal operation, and the PA also had exclusive pictures.

It was a first-class read and again meant that an agency reporter's name was emblazoned throughout the land. As it turned out, Booth was also the last reporter to see Bevan before his death.

The nature of scoops by the Press Association was summed up by Norval Graham, chairman of the *Wolverhampton Express and Star*, in 1935. His words then apply with just as much force today.

'The editor-in-chief's records show a remarkable list of first-class scoops,' he said. 'Unlike, the big London newspapers, who lose no opportunity of advertising their achievements day by day, the Press Association has no chance of blowing its own trumpet and indeed has no wish to. Its reward is that a scoop is everybody's property. Provincial subscribers probably never pause to think how often the Press Association, during its 24-hour vigil, snatches a first-class story from under the nose of a single newspaper which fondly imagines that it is going to have it exclusively. Where big news is, the PA is invariably to be found.'

And how right he was a year later in 1936. On Monday, 20 January, that year, more than seventy reporters had gathered around the picturesque Norfolk village of Sandringham as the life of King George V drew to a close. The reporting conditions were chaotic. Only one telephone was available – in the local inn of a nearby village. The three British agencies, PA, Exchange Telegraph and Central News, pooled resources, booking a private line from the Post Office at £80 a month, but by nightfall there were still four miles of wire to be laid and the Post Office made it clear that the circuits could not be completed until the following day.

When the news came at 9.30 p.m. that the King was dying, the atmosphere among the journalists became frenzied. Newspapers and agencies rushed to put in continuous calls both to and from their London offices. The PA had also booked a line from 10.30 p.m. until 10 a.m. the following day and one of its reporters, Dick Eccleston, held on to it throughout the critical period. But, ironically, the news of the King's death was not given to the London news desk by him. It came in another call to the editor, Henry Martin, although surviving records do not make clear who made it – and Martin never divulged that to anybody. He wrote at the time: 'At 12.04 a.m., I received a certain call. It was a link arranged in advance but upon which I had not relied in case it failed, as was quite likely. The line was very bad; a voice spoke from far away. Yet the caller could hear my urgent questions. The reply revealed unofficially that the King had died at a few minutes to midnight. I took the decision to use the information and told newspapers that it was unofficial.'

The *News Chronicle* acted on the news flash and issued an edition with the lead prepared. The *Daily Express* editor, Arthur Christiansen, rang the Press Association to ask if he could rely on the news. On being told he could, he went into action with a special, black-edged edition – the first to reach the West End of London.

Chrstiansen said later, 'There are times when one thanks God for the Press Association.'

The agency still possesses the original punched tape of that historic newsflash that went out at 0005, saying simply, 'King Dead – The King is Dead.'

Meanwhile, on the matter of the Great Train Robbery . . .

The Press Association secured an unusual scoop in 1981 involving the train robber Ronald Biggs – an exclusive that irritated some of Fleet Street's finest camped out in Barbados, from where they believed the escaped convict was going to be extradited to Britain to complete his thirty-year sentence. Biggs had been kidnapped in Rio de Janeiro by a gang of adventurers and smuggled to the Caribbean island by boat. Their aim was to take him back to Britain. The pack of Fleet Street reporters and photographers were waiting for the decision of the Barbados High Court. But the Press Association, in its wisdom, decided not to send a reporter. Instead, PA man Paul Fuller made regular calls from London to the police station where Biggs was being detained, to ascertain whether a decision had been reached, and, if so, what it was.

His seventh call was timed to perfection. The police officer told him that the High Court had come to the conclusion that the rules governing extradition to Britain had not been properly put before the island's parliament. Biggs, therefore, had pulled off another Houdini-like escape. He was to be allowed to return to Rio. Fuller had netted a first-class exclusive. But he could scarcely believe his ears when the officer said, 'We have Mr Biggs here, if you would like a word with him. Just a minute. I will go and fetch him.'

Fuller got another great exclusive interview and the Biggs story and interview was on the wires and round the world within five minutes. Several hours later, the frustrated pack in Barbados got their first sniff at it.

Ronald Arthur Biggs is now back in Britain after his 35 years on the run, having given himself up in May 2001.

The importance of an exclusive picture can never be underplayed. It can often say more than a thousand words. And that is no more the case than at the Press Association, where its award-winning team of photographers have over the years created a social snapshot of the life and times of Britain.

In 1989, in conditions of the utmost secrecy, a Press Association photographer, Ron Bell, secured a magnificent scoop picture of the Prince and Princess of Wales and the two Princes, William and Harry, cycling through Tresco on the Scilly Isles. It showed the family in relaxed mood, far from the paparazzi's long lenses. Buckingham Palace had offered the Press Association exclusive facilities to photograph them – but strict secrecy had to be observed.

Bell had to be on Tresco by the Thursday morning, the photography had to be completed quickly, and the pictures, monochrome and colour, should be available to subscribers on the same day. But, above all, not a word. It was another 'first' for the agency and demonstrated its ability to bring black-and-white and colour to subscribers at short notice from a remote location. The operation was complicated by a strike on the London Underground, which left the capital in a state of chaos. However, a Dixel Hasselblad wire machine was borrowed and a technician employed to oversee the operation. He booked a flight from Heathrow to Plymouth and hired a Cessna air taxi to an airstrip at Land's End, where he waited for Bell to arrive on a scheduled British Airways helicopter flight from St Mary's, the principal island on the Scilly Isles. When Bell touched down, the film had to be processed at a local chemist. Four black-and-white pictures were transmitted into London and broadcast straight out. The colour was then transmitted into Associated Press and broadcast on their UK colour circuit, before being looped back into the Press Association for regional evenings to take on Friday morning. That day and the following day, Bell's pictures were splashed over virtually every paper.

The following year, Impact, the Press Association's new electronic system for the receipt, editing and distribution of pictures in black and white and colour, went on line at the beginning of July, marking the most radical change in the way the photographic department had served subscribers since it was created 46 years earlier.

The project, which was designed and supplied by technicians from Agence France-Presse and refined by the Press Association's own experts, took twenty months from conception to birth. The first picture to be issued was a colour shot of the Prince of Wales – his arm in a sling – accompanied by the Princess of Wales as he left hospital in Cirencester, where he had been receiving treatment for a riding accident. The picture had been processed on site and squirted digitally from the negative in three separations in six minutes from a transmitter in a hotel room near the hospital.

Five years before the Tresco pictures were transmitted from Land's End, the Press Association gained an exclusive of Hollie Roffey, the eleven-day-old baby who became the world's youngest heart-transplant patient. The picture was taken by the award-winning Martin Cleaver, who had to face the difficulty of shooting through two thicknesses of Perspex – the window of the isolation room and the bubble in which Hollie was kept.

London's National Heart Hospital, where this historic operation took place, had scores of enquiries from papers who wanted to take pictures. But, as often happens in these cases, the hospital administrator, Tom Cosgrove, thought the best thing to do was to invite the Press Association to cover for everybody. And there was not a chequebook in sight. Not a penny was paid for the pictures, but, in an unusual move, Cosgrove invited those papers that used Cleaver's pictures to make a donation to help defray the 'very high cost' of the operation for which the hospital had no specific funds.

Two years later it was a Press Association picture that was responsible for the conviction of a petrol bomber during rioting at Handsworth, Birmingham. The picture showed James Hazell, brother of the then Reading footballer Bob Hazell, carrying a petrol bomb, which he subsequently hurled into a building supply shop. Hazell, who was jailed for five years, was identified from the Press Association picture, even though he had attempted to change his appearance since the incident.

A little later on, the Press Association was subjected to some good-natured ribbing from some newspapers over a picture of the Queen meeting Sheikh Zayed, the visiting ruler of the United Arab Emirates. The picture caption, making sure there could be no possible confusion, said, 'The Sheikh is the one on the left in brown robes . . .'

Accidents can happen in even the best-regulated families. In 1993, Harry Taylor climbed Everest without oxygen. He took pictures of himself at the summit and sent them off to be developed in the Press Association darkrooms. But there was a terrible and uncharacteristic mistake. The negatives were immersed in the wrong chemical. Fortunately, one roll of film escaped. As one PA darkroom employee observed at the time, 'It looked for a moment as if we were going to have to ask Taylor to pop up Everest again . . .'

It has more than once been the Press Association's misfortune to get involved in disputes that are none of its concern. In 1994, Newcastle United banned the *Newcastle Journal* from covering its matches in the wake of some critical articles written about the club by the newspaper's executive sports editor, Tim Taylor. When PA pictures of a Newcastle United home match appeared in the *Journal*, the club manager Kevin Keegan banned the agency as well. Naturally, the Press Association had rejected Newcastle United's improper request to stop supplying pictures to the *Journal*.

The Press Association picture editor, Mike Riches, said at the time, 'We would never, ever pull the plug on an individual newspaper. The dispute has nothing to do with the Press Association or pictures. I think it is unreasonable and frankly rather worrying that a club should encourage us to break a contract, and to attempt to dictate what parts of our service go to what papers. I just hope this is not the shape of things to come with the introduction of Premier League photographic licences.'

One of the Press Association's most famous pictures was the world scoop of Margaret Thatcher being attacked by a woman brandishing a bunch of daffodils, while she was campaigning for the Conservatives at Marple Bridge, Stockport, during the 1992 general election campaign. It was taken by Malcolm Croft and it was a case of far more than his simply being in the right place at the right time. It involved a surreptitious 'battle' to outwit the bossy minders who were in charge of the event.

Maggie's minders had effectively banned photographers from the Marple Bridge visit, and warned them that, if they turned up, the walkabout would be cancelled. That unnecessary threat amounted to an irresistible challenge on the part of the picture brigade: how to outwit the Establishment? Croft hid in the crowd, but was spotted and ordered away. He then concealed himself in an electrical contractor's shop after being asked by the owner, 'Have you got a bomb?' and then, 'Are you from one of those left-wing papers?'

The search for 'illicit' photographers was thorough, and as they were found, crouching out of view, they were sent packing by the authorities. But Croft remained undiscovered. He was concealed in a back office, which was missed. When, after half an hour or so, Thatcher arrived, Croft emerged gingerly, fully expecting to be pounced on by her detectives. Inexplicably, they did not and he got several shots of her shaking hands, including one alongside a massive Irish wolfhound.

Then out of the blue, Thatcher was 'daffed' by an irate woman in the street – and Croft was the only photographer present to record the dramatic and bizarre scene.

'The gods smiled on me,' he said.

One of the saddest events in the history of PA photography was the death of its picture man Nicky Beer, in a helicopter accident while photographing a NATO exercise off Portland Bill in May 1971. He was one of three cameramen drowned in the tragedy. Nicky was described by the editor-in-chief David Chipp as 'quite one of our best and nicest photographers'. Tributes to him poured in from all over the country. But the one he would probably have valued most of all was the accolade paid to him by a couple of young Press Association reporters. They said that there was no one they preferred to be with during the troubles in Northern Ireland – for he was calm, cheerful, encouraging and prudent.

The year after the tragedy, Nicky Beer's colleagues ensured a continuing memorial to him as well as to Don Royle, of Associated Press, one of the other photographers killed. They purchased a silver salver that became one of the British Press Pictures of the Year Awards, to be held annually for the photographer adjudged to have the best portfolio from a member of the Council of Photographic News Agencies. The third cameraman killed was a freelance, Guy Blanchard.

Nicky Beer was 53 when he died. He had joined the old PA–Reuters photos company as one of its original dispatch riders in 1946. He turned cameraman in 1952, specialising in car-racing pictures and aeronautics. He once flew with the Red Arrows.

27 Share and Share Alike

THE TREASURE HUNT was on! The news that the search was on for a group of missing PA shares that could be worth up to £9 million sparked off a frenzy of activity. The PA telephone lines were red-hot and sackfuls of letters arrived at 85 Fleet Street from people who thought they might have a claim to this unexpected fortune.

It was the projected flotation of Reuters in 1984 that transformed what were once virtually worthless shares into something like a bonanza overnight.

Jack Purdham was the PA financial controller and secretary at the time, and spent months of his life working on this and the related issue of the flotation of Reuters – what was to be the biggest flotation in the City of London for a hundred years. Purdham was dubbed by one newspaper 'the Sherlock Holmes of Fleet Street' for his assiduous detective work on the missing shares.

Purdham had explained that there was never any reason for these people to reply to letters since the PA had never paid a dividend. The PA had, in fact, lost track of them a hundred years earlier. He said at one stage during the hunt, 'Many of the applicants seemed to think we had a treasure chest into which they could dip if they had an ancestor with the same name as one of the original owners.'

But it was not so simple as that – not by a long chalk. In fact, the whole affair was one of the most complicated legal and financial problems ever to face lawyers, tax experts and financiers.

For a start, no claims to shares could be registered unless claimants produced documentary evidence that the shares had passed to them by an unbroken chain of transfers.

PA had never paid dividends and traditionally its shares had been of little financial value. But now they had suddenly rocketed in value because of the agency's holding, at slightly over 41 per cent, in Reuters, which was to be floated on the stock market with an estimated £1 billion valuation.

The PA was set up as a news co-operative in 1868 and its shares were held by newspapers that were either involved in the formation or had succeeded those that were. All were accounted for with the exception of 1,800, which the original owners kept in their own names.

Oddly, the Press Association barely covered the story of the flotation and the 'Great Treasure Hunt' over the months, even though it attracted massive attention in many papers, broadsheet and tabloid alike, and not merely on their business pages.

However, the PA did issue a story on 17 January 1984, saying that more than 150 letters were on their way to people claiming 'part of the £9 million Press Association shares bonanza'.

Purdham said he hoped the letters would save many people time and money if their claims for the windfall were 'flimsy'. He said, 'We do not want to push people into the hands of lawyers or genealogy experts when they have no proof of interest.'

The missing shares – which were all subsequently found – were in four blocks in the names of Charles Amesbury Whitley Dundas, owner of the *Western Daily Telegraph*, Bristol, in 1868, who had 1,200 shares; Charles Bayley and George Bradley, the owners of the former *Wrexham Advertiser* (200 shares); EH Jones, former editor of the *Hereford Journal* (200 shares); and GH Bowyer, owner of the *Investment Review* of Bristol (200 shares).

Dundas, incidentally, died of alcoholic poisoning. The last mention of him in the PA files was a letter, dated 1886, in which he was described as a 'gentleman of fortune' who may have been the illegitimate son of the Earl of Zetland.

Two newspaper groups which owned the *Wrexham Advertiser* and *Hereford Journal* titles claimed the Bayley–Bradley and Jones holdings respectively, asserting that the shares were the property of the newspapers and not the individuals.

And within a week of the story breaking PA had received more than two hundred enquiries from hopeful would-be applicants.

Purdham dispatched letters to the claimants on the steps they had to take to pursue their claims, and also explaining that the PA lawyer, Robert Fawssett, had been appointed as trustee to preserve the interests of the untraced shareholders.

There were some bizarre and quaint claimants. The shortest claim received came from a Mr Dundas, living in Caithness, who simply stated, 'Dear Sir, I wish to know the amount of money I have inherited. Yours faithfully.'

Another claimant was a mercenary serving in the Congo with 'Mad' Mike Hoare. Another was an old woman aged about ninety from Bristol. And, in another case, a family living in Purley, Surrey, were met by PA representatives at Gatwick Airport as they returned from an overseas holiday to be told that they had 600 shares worth something like £1.5 million to them.

Purdham recalls, 'I was besieged by everybody, every sort of person who thought they could trace a family tree. It was a constant battle, although we finally got them all.'

One day, a man in his seventies, wearing a crash helmet and motorcycling leathers, presented himself at the PA offices at 85 Fleet Street. He had arrived on a motorcycle from the West Country and carried into the office under his arm a parcel about 3 feet wide by 18 inches. It was very heavy.

And when it was unwrapped it revealed itself to be a tombstone, which this man had removed – with the permission of the vicar, of course – from the entrance to a local church.

It marked the grave of a baby aged eighteen months. This man tried to claim that this was the missing link in the search for a 'Jones' from the *Hereford Times* in Wales. The man refused to let Purdham examine the stone, which was extremely bizarre since he was presumably producing it as evidence that could, eventually, lead to his becoming a millionaire.

However, he did consent for a photograph to be taken of the stone, although not in the most minute detail. After that, he picked it up again, motorcycled back to the West Country and presumably returned it to the vicar.

'We just knew that this was part of the jigsaw,' Purdham said. 'It was not my job to do family trees on everybody. I just wanted to find the people who held the relevant pieces of paper.'

Then there was the case of the Croom-Johnson family, of Chipstead, Surrey, who suddenly found themselves in line for a fortune. One George Bradley, who was editor of the now defunct *Wrexham Advertiser*, had Reuters shares in his own name. His great-grandson, Brian Bradley Croom-Johnson, heard the news early in January 1984 as a result of a telephone call to his wife Pamela. He said at the time, 'At first it just didn't ring any bells, but my second name is Bradley so I dug out the family tree and it took off from there.'

The original George Bradley had eight children, two of whom died young, leaving six children who could potentially inherit the shares, one of whom was Croom-Johnson's grandmother.

'She had three sons and a daughter, one of whom was my father,' he said.

The flotation also brought a huge and unexpected bonanza to four charities in 1992: Dr Barnardo's, the Royal National Lifeboat Institution, the Royal National Institute for the Blind and the Royal Society for the Prevention of Cruelty to Animals. They each benefited by some £375,000 from an estate that, up to then, was considered to be worthless.

This resulted from an intriguing story based on a thirty-year-old love affair between a divorcee and a pillar of the staunchly Conservative Carlton Club in London. A big-spending Londoner and man-about-town, Charles Kenneth Preston-Cole, who died in 1956, left small bequests to servants and staff at his club. The outcome was that there was only £6 7s. 2d. (£6.36) left, plus 300 apparently worthless shares which were ultimately found to be worth some £1,500,000.

The key to this was his love, Amy Gertrude Deans-Dundas, who provided the cashline to the massive charity windfall. On her death in 1944, Preston-Cole assumed ownership of 300 original shares in the Press Association which Deans-Dundas had inherited from her father and grandfather.

Until the early 1980s, Press Association shares were assumed to be valueless except as an entitlement to the news agency's services. But, because of the projected Reuter flotation, each of those shares was suddenly worth around £5,000 – and in this case, in total, £1,500,000.

It was *Burke's Peerage* that traced the entitlement of the four charities from Deans-Dundas's will.

The tale of how the four charities came to be beneficiaries of this windfall is one involving high living, divorce, scandal and the secrets of an upper-middle-class man and woman who lived together as man and wife.

The legacy dates to the will of a West Country newspaper proprietor, Charles Amesbury Deans-Dundas, who died in 1874. His 1,200 Press Association shares passed to his son, Charles Frederick Deans-Dundas, who on his death in 1938 left half to his son and a quarter each to his two daughters.

One of the daughters was Amy Gertrude Deans-Dundas, who in 1891, aged twenty, married Oswald Robert Mounsey. This ended in divorce. They had a son, Guy, who went to the Far East and was last heard of in Singapore in 1929. He was officially presumed dead, without issue, in 1962.

Mrs Mounsey, in 1902, married James Dalzell Niven. The couple had no children. Later, she began to live in Malvern, Worcestershire, with Preston-Cole. She was never divorced from Niven, but in 1926 she took Preston-Cole's name by deed poll.

Preston-Cole was a bon viveur and a regular habitué of the Carlton Club, and the couple lived a luxurious lifestyle, often in the South of France.

On her death Amy left her estate, valued at a mere £359 11s. 8d (£359.58), including the 'worthless' PA shares, to her lover 'in slight recognition of his great kindness to me'.

Preston-Cole continued to live in a lavish manner until his death, almost penniless, in 1956. He earmarked the residue of his estate – which appeared to be worth hardly anything – to the four charities, which, a quarter of a century later, were to receive such a welcome bonanza.

But 'Sherlock Holmes' finally managed to resolve all these problems. That was a prerequisite to further action. Flotation could then go ahead. But that was when the problems really started. There followed months of protracted, complicated, mind-blowing meetings involving the finest City and legal brains in the land, and, of course, the spectre of that ever-present demon, the tax collector, who was both ferocious and voracious in his demands for his pound of flesh – and the rest.

Many, many hours were spent trying to convince the Inland Revenue that the peculiar nature of PA and of Reuters should exempt them from what were regarded as their more outrageous demands.

And at the end of the day – after seemingly endless, sometimes acrimonious, always complex sessions – the various tax authorities, in London, Dublin and Australia, as well as New Zealand, were by and large convinced, if reluctantly so, that the great bulk of their demands were 'inappropriate', to use the expression of one person who helped to see this whole fatiguing exercise through.

The negotiations were further complicated because of the PA structure. It was not simply the PA and Reuters who were involved, but the London daily newspapers and the Newspaper Proprietors' (later Publishers') Association.

The PA retained the shares in PA Ltd on behalf of the member newspapers, not the NPA. They divided them between the various London dailies and Sundays in ratio to circulation. This meant, of course, that each of the newspapers concerned required its own experts, tax advisers and so on to sit in on these meetings.

Purdham recalls sitting at one of these particularly unwieldy gatherings with Nigel Judah, his opposite number on Reuters, along with about 120 other people. For instance, each of the London dailies was represented, with a front man and a team of five or six behind him. 'And this pantomime went on,' Purdham sighed.

'The problem was that the Inland Revenue had stepped in and seen this bonanza, which had been talked about in the City, and they wanted their bite of it – and a very big bite it was too.'

The Inland Revenue made the telling point that if the flotation was carried out and the shares were distributed to the NPA, and they passed them on elsewhere, including to the PA, who might or might not pass them to their member newspapers, it would – in the jargon of the tax collector – rank as a distribution, which, at that time, carried a tax cost of about 50 per cent, a horrendous sum of money.

To put it at its bluntest, whatever they floated for, the Inland Revenue wanted a cool half of the booty. This revelation caused not only a corporate intake of breath, but was also, in the view of some of those who were involved at the time, in danger of putting the skids under the whole operation.

All this was going on throughout 1979 and 1980. Then, early in 1981, Purdham suffered a heart attack – from which happily he eventually made a complete recovery. This illness was, of course, a very serious personal matter, but it also posed a considerable problem for the flotation negotiations.

Purdham was a relatively important figure in this affair, and much of the vital material in connection with it was not down on paper but in his head.

He underwent a heart bypass operation towards the end of April 1981, and did not return to work until early in 1982, after almost exactly a year of absence. But during that period there were one or two meetings, no more than that. The whole project remained virtually at a standstill for those twelve months. It meant that Purdham pretty well picked up the reins at the point where he had had to let them go a year earlier.

The 50 per cent demand by the tax collector was still the bugbear and nothing had happened over that twelve months to resolve the issue. And, although the PA set up a number of committees in a bid to clear it up, it actually became more of an accountants' problem – not to say nightmare – than anybody else's.

However, a decision was taken that they should immediately try to have a very private word with the tax inspector. This, hardly surprisingly, the taxman was reluctant to do. He could see the perils for him of being involved in secret negotiations that could prejudice, in his view, the entire affair.

However, the PA persisted, on the basis that, for instance, parliamentary life and huge areas of big business all flourish and prosper to a large degree on the nod and the wink.

After a while, 'some strings were pulled' – to quote someone who was in the thick of it at the time – and the proposal to hold a joint and highly unofficial meeting was agreed, although still not with any enthusiasm by the man from the Inland Revenue.

He would not meet them at the PA offices or indeed anywhere where there was any possible link with the deal. Finally the parties agreed to meet in the Price Waterhouse building at London Bridge. This was considered by the taxman to be neutral territory because Price Waterhouse remained the one firm of big-time accountants in the City who did not have a finger in this particular pie.

Price Waterhouse gave them the use of the boardroom and they all trooped off there. The Inland Revenue contingent was quite affable, although utterly correct. They would not take lunch, or even the most trivial hospitality for fear of being compromised.

The entire encounter was off the record and not a single note was taken, as they battled with the problem. The PA took the view that for them to be on the attack was a far better attitude to adopt than to be defensive. The tax officials were bluntly told that, if they were determined to stick to having their 50 per cent cut of this deal as a distribution tax, then the deal would simply not happen. That would be the end of it. Finish.

The taxmen were, to say the least, startled by the stark and uncompromising nature of what they were being told. But the PA representatives, along with those from Reuters and the NPA, argued that the very structure of the PA, which was almost certainly unique, was a compelling argument against the seemingly immovable stand being taken by the Inland Revenue.

The tax people argued that the PA's 'clients' must surely pay for the PA services. The PA replied that this was indeed the case, but they did not pay the true amount for the service, because it was a co-operative organisation.

For instance, it was argued, if the PA ran into a deficit situation the subscribers had to foot the bill. It was therefore reasonable that if the PA had a surplus the subscribers would themselves get something out of it.

The tax authorities then realised for the first time that they were here not dealing with a routine flotation but a 'one-off' involving businesses that did not conform to orthodox company structures.

There was a certain amount of head-scratching among the Inland Revenue team. It was now beginning to look as though the tax officials were moving on to the defensive, and the PA representatives, sensing this, raised another matter that was designed to make further inroads on the Inland Revenue's demand for 50 per cent.

They said that if there was still some means for the flotation to go ahead with PA still holding the 41 per cent plus – which was highly unlikely, but if by chance it did happen – the PA would receive dividends from the newly formed Reuter company, and these dividends would increase the PA surplus, which would be returned to subscribers, either by reducing the cost of the comprehensive service or in some other way.

In that case, PA argued, there could be no question of paying a distribution tax on any of that, because it simply could not be identified. The Inland Revenue recognised – even if they did not admit it at the time – the force of that argument.

They went away saying they would have another look at the situation. But – and they made this point yet again – they could not be held to anything that had been said that morning. It had been like one of those parliamentary lobby meetings of a few years earlier: meetings that did not take place in rooms that did not exist at an hour of the day that did not occur.

So no one, on either side of the argument, could publicly call in aid anything that was said at that very clandestine occasion. However, although the Inland Revenue were 'having a think' about what was for them a novel situation, the PA were still exploring what were optimistically described as 'various gateways' in the taxation laws. But, each time the PA thought they would get through, they found a blockage at the last moment.

Victory was to come, however, or perhaps 'breakthrough' would be a better description, since there were many more daunting hurdles to clear and obstacles to overcome before this complex marathon was over. The Inland Revenue agreed that the processes that would be involved in and result from the flotation would not be classified as 'distribution' in the jargon of taxation law.

Purdham told them that they need not worry as 'they would get their slice of the cheese by the dividends that were paid each time'. This was, no doubt, telling them something that they were already determined to do anyway, but it demonstrated that the PA was in no way shirking from paying its due burden of tax.

But they accepted, which was a major advance.

The action then moved across the Irish Sea to Dublin, where more problems had to be confronted. The tax authorities in the Irish Republic would not accept the deal. Their involvement came about because the PA had as members the *Irish Press* and the *Irish Times*, both Dublin-based newspapers, as well as the *Cork Examiner*. These papers had a vote in the flotation. And, if they did not vote for it, then it would be scuppered again.

The Irish Inland Revenue, at first blush, did not appear to be very co-operative.

However, Purdham, a very astute and practical business operator, suggested another off-the-record meeting, in Dublin between him and a senior figure from the Irish taxation system, at which the issue could be thrashed out in a private, friendly 'without-prejudice' atmosphere and with no one party bound by what was said during the session.

The official responded that he happened to be in London on the day in question and that he would be happy to 'pop into' the PA office to thrash it out. And pop in he did. Purdham thrashed out to him precisely and in great detail what had happened between the PA and the Inland Revenue in London. The official accepted the same arrangements, but he did not want it to be said that he had accepted simply because the British had accepted. They were, he pointed out with some emphasis, a separate country with their own laws and practices. Purdham promised him that he recognised that.

So another hurdle had been surmounted. Now the scene was set for the flotation actually to start. But yet more problems arose because, in the meantime, Reuters had decided they wanted to float not only on the United Kingdom Stock Exchange but on the New York Stock Exchange as well. Without that, they said, they would flounder.

Now it was the turn of the Americans to come over to London. They were noisy and argumentative as they met NPA and PA people, with Richard Winfrey as the chairman, one Sunday morning in an office off London Bridge. The meeting seemed to drag on and on interminably, with no resolution apparently in sight.

Then, as the day wore on, one of the Americans declared, 'My plane leaves at three o'clock and I want this thing settled.' Somebody, unidentified, down the line whispered, 'Tough.'

The man who was anxious to catch his plane admitted what the problem was. 'We have to decide on a price that is realistic. There's no point in fixing on a price where if you float it nobody wants the shares.'

Arriving at a price to float a company must involve a situation where the person who buys the shares and the person selling them both feel they are getting a good deal – and there was now pressure on them to find a figure.

The American was now getting distinctly tetchy and said since they were talking about 130 pence and 140 pence a share, let's make it 130 pence, adding 'I've got a plane to catch . . .'

The argument raged on and it reached about two o'clock, and the American was getting ever more anxious about catching his flight. Others were getting quite grumpy with him, saying that that was a matter of no importance whatsoever.

Even so, there was considerable anxiety to reach a decision that afternoon. The time of the American's flight came and went. He then started to talk about catching a four o'clock and then a five o'clock plane.

By late afternoon, the float price was fixed at 195 pence. Everybody was reasonably happy about that, even if somewhat drained, having spent the best part of Sunday thrashing it out. What was now of vital importance was that the figure should not be divulged to anyone. All those who attended the meeting were sworn to secrecy, because the whole affair could have been blown to smithereens if the Stock Exchange got wind of it.

The situation was rendered even more difficult because the flotation of Reuters had become a news story in its own right. It meant that City correspondents on the Fleet Street newspapers, and from elsewhere as well, were ringing up Purdham for information. To each enquirer, Purdham had to say he had not the faintest idea. They pressed him hard – 'Come on, Jack, you must know: is it 150 pence?' – but he still did not submit to their blandishments.

The flotation eventually went ahead in mid-June 1984, but the problems were by no means over. The Australian Associated

Press and the New Zealand Press Association became involved because they were both part owners of Reuters. And Des Anderson, who was a senior accountant with the *Melbourne Herald*, was sent over to London to keep a watching brief on behalf of AAP and NZPA. The tax problems that had caused such a headache in both Britain and Ireland were now rearing their heads in the southern hemisphere.

The AAP and the Press Association had by this stage decided to work together, and to present what was described as 'a united front on matters of control'. Both organisations felt they had to overcome major tax problems before selling any of their holdings in Reuters.

Anderson spent much of his time in Purdham's office in the Press Association. At first he stayed at the Savoy Hotel, but his visit became so prolonged that in the end he got himself a flat.

He kept commuting between London and Melbourne and – to Purdham's considerable embarrassment – returned from time to time with presents, including great mounds of Australian cheese and a toy koala bear which played Waltzing Matilda when pressed in the right spot.

Purdham insisted that Anderson should not bring him gifts because people 'might think'. But Anderson, who was a noisy but generous and honest man, insisted that these were simply things between friends.

There were one or two spats between Purdham and Anderson but these were over peripheral matters concerning how the bonanza from the flotation should be distributed.

Anderson appeared to want to intervene personally with the PA board, demanding that some of the cash be distributed among the PA staff – which was, of course, none of his business. Purdham instantly vetoed the idea and told him not to get involved.

'Anderson was most upset and uptight about the whole thing,' Purdham reported later.

In fact many of the provincial newspapers who benefited from this flotation used the cash to re-equip what in many cases was old-fashioned and in some cases even creaking machinery.

But although the flotation appeared to be going swimmingly, the Australian Associated Press, in the early 1990s, suddenly found themselves at odds with their own taxation authorities.

They came under severe attack and it looked as though they were going to be in real trouble. They were being accused of collusion with the Press Association. It was, in the words of Purdham later, 'looking very sticky'.

This latest situation also caused Purdham to make sure he had no skeletons in his own cupboard in his dealings with Anderson. 'I was pretty certain he had received no information from me that was privileged. It was just a meeting of two like minds trying to solve a problem with a mutual interest.'

But the taxation authorities in Australia were very terrier-like, not to say aggressive. And the AAP were absolutely desperate to prove that there had been no collusion with the PA – which indeed there had not been.

Then, suddenly, Purdham received a call to go to London to speak to two men who had arrived from Australia and who wanted to get the full background to what had happened, and also to enquire into Purdham's connections with Anderson. When he arrived at the meeting, Purdham was not in the least expecting what he saw. He assumed it was going to be a friendly chat with a couple of Australians whom he had got to know – on the other end of a telephone – while the flotation negotiations were in progress. But, to his intense surprise, there were not simply two people there, but about ten, with tape recorders, who engaged Purdham in a penetrating grilling which lasted all of three hours. Among the inquisitors were some of the top legal brains in Australia.

They made no comments during Purdham's 'evidence'. They just confronted him with streams of questions and took a full note of every answer. When the ordeal was finally over, the interrogators had a little whispered conversation among themselves.

Then one of them addressed Purdham and said, 'Thank you very much. I must congratulate you on your memory. You have confirmed everything that Anderson said.' They had apparently questioned Anderson in Australia beforehand without warning Purdham that they had done so.

Later Purdham was to learn that if there had been discrepancies in the stories or other mistakes made it could have cost the Australian Associated Press many millions of pounds in tax. It was a huge relief for him to know that all those involved in this convoluted affair had behaved with absolute correctness and honour, and that they now had virtual proof that no collusion had taken place.

Purdham had told them that he had lived with this matter for the past five or six years and that it was now part of his normal daily diet.

However, some two or three weeks after his interrogators had returned to Australia, Purdham was telephoned by them and asked if he would swear an affidavit, which would go to the Australian Inland Revenue to prove to them that their suspicions of collusion and any other malpractices were totally unfounded. The affidavit contained what Purdham had said during his three-hour grilling.

He agreed and, without further ado, a dispatch rider brought it down to his home in Angmering, Sussex, for him to sign. The idea was that the dispatch rider would wait a short while for Purdham to sign it in the presence of a lawyer, and then return the document to London straightaway.

But that was not how Purdham wanted to operate. He was not in the business of signing a seventeen-page, closely typed document without reading it most carefully and digesting it, to make sure his words during the interrogation had not been misunderstood or inaccurately reported.

The dispatch rider, no doubt disappointed, went back without the document, and Purdham at once began to study it with what he described as 'a fine-tooth comb'. A few amendments were made and Purdham swore the affidavit in front of a solicitor and, in his own words 'that was that'.

It had been a traumatic period with occasional bouts of infighting. 'It was a very difficult time to keep an even keel with people you had known all your working life,' Purdham said later. And he added with a smile and some considerable relish, 'It's amazing how many free lunches I got.'

28 New Media

THE PRESS ASSOCIATION has always aimed to keep ahead of technology right from its birth. Even in those early days when teenage boys, in their smart uniforms, were dodging in and out of the Fleet Street crowds, speeding telegrams to the post office, the agency was at the forefront of change.

Now, with communications virtually instantaneous from one corner of the globe to another, the PA is still firmly in the vanguard. This has been demonstrated by the arrival on the scene of Ananova, the world's first virtual newscaster, which the Press Association sold to the mobile-phone giant Orange.

But the new-media story really begins in the 1980s, when computers finally arrived in the PA newsroom for the general use of editorial staff. They were a long time coming. While new terminals lay unused, even unpacked in some cases, in the basement at 85 Fleet Street, there was incessant trade union wrangling about their introduction. For some people did not appreciate that computers would make life far more congenial.

However, at 4 p.m. on 12 July 1987, a battery of copytakers – men and women who typed out news stories telephoned in by reporters – moved into the operations room on the fifth floor to await the first call. The first 'on line' story was taken by copytaker Pauline Penney – a weather report from Bexhill-on-Sea. Not a world-beating scoop, but it meant that the agency had at last taken off into cyberspace.

Moments later a sports story arrived, and the agency was now in business on System 55, the name of the computer network it had installed. The first day, thanks to much careful planning, was relatively trouble-free. This introduction of computers involved massive refurbishment, including miles and miles of rewiring.

Although throughout the later years of the twentieth century the technical side of the Press Association was modified and modernised continuously, the new-media explosion was still about to happen. And much of what did happen was to the credit of Mark Hird, a ginger-haired Press Association subeditor who took charge of the operation. He was a man with machine-gun-style Scottish delivery, huge energy and boundless enthusiasm.

It was around this time, in the early 1990s, when the Press Association moved its sports activities to Leeds and acquired a company called Computer Newspaper Services (CNS) in the small market town of Howden in East Yorkshire. CNS specialised in creating page-ready material such as TV listings, finance, weather and sports data. It was produced in such a way that the content could be transmitted straight into a newspaper page. And it meant that newspaper organisations could save an enormous amount of money by taking this material and inserting it into the paper without having to resubedit it.

The secret behind the company's success was some clever software, some clever staff and ideas steeped in the use of the Internet as a development tool. However, the company's entire management team had departed shortly after the PA takeover, leaving it rudderless. It was evident that this new and burgeoning operation required a guiding hand and certainly someone with an entrepreneurial spirit.

That man was Mark Hird. He was summoned to the office of editor-in-chief, Colin Webb, and told there was a really exciting job opportunity in Howden. It was to do with TV listings, finance data and material of that kind. Hird's immediate reaction was that this did not sound like his definition of exciting. But he was urged to go up and take a look for himself. What he saw there amazed him.

The Press Association, by now, owned an astonishing range and mixture of buildings in Howden. They included a bishop's manor, a converted bus garage and a converted restaurant. 'Any door you opened, you found Press Association people beavering away,' Hird said. He walked into the converted restaurant and found it was jam-packed with software developers, all of them wearing jeans and T-shirts, most of them smoking furiously. As they talked to him about the huge potential they saw in the Internet, Hird realised that these were people who could contribute something radically different to the PA. It was an eye-opener for Hird. Like most of the PA staff in London, he had never dreamed that all this innovative work was going on in Howden – or indeed anywhere. Hird returned to the city completely converted. What had seemed a routine, dull job when it was put to him, had, after he had looked at it for himself, turned into an exciting new challenge.

There was no longer the slightest doubt in his mind. 'I'll take the job,' he told Webb. But a lot of Hird's colleagues were mystified why he had decided to uproot himself and his family to undertake what had all the appearances of being a nonjournalistic job in the North of England.

Hird had grasped the nettle. He and his new team were convinced the Internet was going to have far-reaching implications for the media, and that it opened up huge opportunities for the Press Association in particular. But it was important to move fast – and, to his surprise, Hird found he was pushing at an open door. Chief executive Robert Simpson, unlike his counterparts in most other media organisations, was an instant convert to the Internet vision. He told Hird to get on and build the foundations for a completely new business unit, and in particular gave the go-ahead for the launch of the PA's own website – which back in 1994 was one of the first truly dynamic websites in the world. Websites at that stage in the evolution of the Internet were much more static than today, relying on occasional manual updates. The PA's site was a radical step forward, driven automatically from PA's live systems and databases, providing a showcase for constantly-updated news headlines, weather forecasts, sports results and other live data.

The effect was to send a signal to the commercial world beyond the media industry that the Press Association was pre-eminent in the field of live information and a first port of call if you intended to develop an Internet product involving live data. Howden, then, soon became a showpiece for the PA. Influential figures in the media industry and the business world headed north to see what was going on. PA moved to the forefront of the Internet Revolution.

CNS changed its name to PA Data Design and quickly attracted a growing list of clients and partners operating in what became known as the new media industry. Early customers included the big online services AOL and Compuserve, telecoms giants such as BT and software companies such as Microsoft. Traditional media players were slower to dip their toe in the water. One of the first was BBC News, who long before the launch of their own highly successful Internet operations, came to Howden to collaborate with PA Data Design on some ground-breaking Internet experiments including live budget coverage and the Olympics.

The Press Association's great strength in the Internet area was its ability to work to a constant deadline. Almost every other media organisation – including the broadcasters with their precisely-timed news bulletins – had to handle a number of specific deadlines each day. But for the Press Association every second of every day was, and is, a deadline. That was central to the agency's business and meant that it and the Internet were made for each other. What did take the industry by surprise was the entrepreneurial spirit of the news agency. Here was the Press Association, a venerable 127-year-old organisation, moving faster than anyone else and threatening to outsprint the lot. Soon it was difficult to find a major new media service in the UK that didn't use PA to help make their product dynamic, whether it was news, sport, weather, finance, TV or entertainment listings.

By 1997, the new media market was booming and the agency's premises in Howden were beginning to burst at the seams. The PA was simply outgrowing them. The seventeenth-century bishop's manor was creaking with the most modern systems and equipment imaginable. It was time to move on and expand again.

The company was renamed PA New Media and the foundations began to be laid for an even bigger business. Vivienne Adshead, previously the PA Commercial Director, moved over to the New Media team to work alongside Mark Hird. The possibility of moving the whole outfit, lock, stock and barrel, to London was considered. But it was clear that the Press Association was unique in this field in the North, and there was already a talented team in place that would form the nucleus of the bigger business. In London there would be fierce competition for talent as more and more businesses set up Internet operations. So the decision was taken to stay in the North but to move the new media operation thirty miles west to Leeds, where PA Sport was already based. Settled in Leeds, the rapid growth continued, with the number of PA New Media employees growing from ten to eighty in less than two years.

PA New Media's greatest strength was the speed at which ideas were turned into products that could be fast-tracked to the market. Hird constantly told his staff that this was an ideas-hungry business – and that the best ideas, the ones that could make a radical difference to a business, often sounded odd or ridiculous at first hearing. In 1999 one of those odd ideas did just that for PA New Media. The idea came to be known as Ananova, and it resulted in the entire PA New Media business being sold a year later to mobile-phone giant Orange for £95 million.

The idea sprang from an observation that what the PA NewsCentre website lacked was a star, a personality, a front man with whom readers could identify. 'What if we created a virtual character; a computer-generated personality who could read out the news as it breaks.' Simpson, Hird and Adshead loved the idea – and, as they and their teams knocked it around, it evolved into an ambitious plan to create a system that would combine live information, personalisation, webspidering technology, text-to-speech software and real-time animation. The result was Ananova, who burst on to the scene in May 2000 as the world's first virtual newscaster.

She was programmed, with a little help from a Glasgow firm, to be a 28-year-old, five-foot-eight-inch-tall young woman, with a pleasant, quietly intelligent manner that made people feel relaxed when they engaged with her. One of her fortes was sport. She was programmed with an unparalleled knowledge of sporting trivia: everything from who won the FA Cup in 1933 to what percentage of David Beckham's goals come from free kicks. She was launched amid a blaze of publicity, appearing on TV news programmes across the globe as newsreaders debated whether their jobs were under threat. But there was a serious side to Ananova. She had been invented with the technologies of the future in mind – designed for a world where people will use mobile devices to access and act on the vital news and information that's important to each individual.

But it was clear that a different kind of owner was needed to fund and capitalise on this kind of business. The Press Association had an opportunity to realise the value that had been created in the new media business, and it appointed PricewaterhouseCoopers to handle the sale of the business through a structured auction. Orange acquired Ananova Ltd from the PA for £95 million in July 2000.

Robert Simpson, who was until the spring of 2000 chief executive of the Press Association, before being replaced by editor-in-chief Paul Potts, headed up Ananova Ltd until his retirement in July on the date the business was sold.

29 New Beginnings

O
N A CRISP BRIGHT DAY in May 1995, Paul Potts, the deputy editor of the *Daily Express*, strolled across London's Blackfriars Bridge and entered the elegant marble hall of 85 Fleet Street as the Press Association's new editor. Bristling with energy and new ideas, he planned a new beginning for the agency, a new vision that would lead it into the new millennium. But within weeks, instead of being able to put those ideas quickly into practice, he found himself locked in a fight for survival against a rival that had won the backing of his old employer, the *Express*. 'I arrived at PA and the roof fell in,' he recalled later.

UK News had posed a threat to the Press Association for several years, successfully signing many regional customers who were unhappy with the agency's service. But it was in the summer of 1995 that the real threat to the very future of the Press Association emerged. UK News had stepped up its challenge to PA by reaching agreement with Mirror Group and Express Newspapers to supply a national news service to them from the start of the following year. The ensuing battle would take the PA to the brink, and – to steal a phrase from the Duke of Wellington – the outcome was 'a close-run thing'. But the new editor's favourite maxim that every setback is an opportunity led to the creation of a new, leaner, sharper and more customer-focused company as a result of the UK News episode.

Potts, a blunt Yorkshireman with a background on the Sheffield *Star*, used the crisis to launch an overhaul of the agency's editorial operation, injecting fresh Fleet Street talent and promoting from within to create a dynamic atmosphere in which change was taken for granted and welcomed. As he and his editorial team waged a journalistic war, the board and chief executive Robert Simpson confronted the commercial challenge in moves that eventually led to a dramatically reduced tariff for the service.

At one point Simpson, who masterminded the corporate fightback, grimly told journalists, 'It's them or us. There is not enough room in the market for two of us.' Between them Potts and Simpson established an effective double act, with the former addressing the customers, the service and the structure of the agency, while Simpson concentrated on carrying the board and bringing PA into the real commercial world.

The struggle for agency supremacy began as PA moved to its new headquarters at 292 Vauxhall Bridge Road, close to London's Victoria Station. The move took place in the shadow of celebrations to mark the fiftieth anniversary of VJ Day, with spectacular fireworks bursting over Fleet Street as journalists cleared their desks for the last time and headed to the other side of Westminster. But celebrations and the prospect of a new beginning were short-lived, for then came the news that UK News was to go ahead and launch a full frontal assault on the PA's position as the national news agency – thereby rejecting any attempts at compromise or conciliation.

It was particularly difficult because the threat to PA had come from within the ranks of its owners, as the two shareholders in UK News, the Northcliffe Newspapers Group and Westminster Press, also had stakes in the Press Association. In that respect it had the hallmarks and tensions of a civil war. The principal editorial driving force behind UK News was the former *Leicester Mercury* editor Alex Leys, a talented Scotsman whose belief that the Press Association could be taken on and defeated persuaded his masters to give him the green light to go ahead. He argued that the Press Association's monopoly as the national news agency was not invincible and the UK News initiative was able to harness dissatisfaction among customers with the PA. His objective was simple: to replace the PA with UK News. It was to become a fight to the finish, because both sides accepted there was room for only one national agency.

The events that led to the UK News crisis had begun some years earlier when Thomson Regional Newspapers attempted to negotiate a special deal for itself with the Press Association. As part of the negotiations Thomson's threatened to start a news agency in conjunction with Reuters and a sports agency, in opposition to the PA. The outcome was that Thomson's secured a deal with the Press Association that was seen by others as commercially advantageous and therefore caused genuine resentment among other subscribers.

Leys said, 'When Thomson's managed to get this eleventh-hour settlement with the PA, the news naturally leaked to other major groups, including Northcliffe, which thought it would ask for a similar reduction. When Northcliffe approached the agency to negotiate new terms, the impression they received was that the window of opportunity had closed and that they were on the wrong side of it.'

Sir Harry Roche, the former chief executive of the Guardian Media Group, who later became chairman of the Press Association, said that the Thomson deal caused 'a falling out between the customers in the club – and that led to a fundamental change'. The upshot was that Ian Park, who was managing director of Northcliffe, asked a number of his key personnel, Leys included, to meet in London to discuss what had happened and what should be done.

Leys said, 'We posed the question whether it would be possible to construct a venture which would work and, if we did, what would it lead to? You have to remember that the Press Association was an institution which had not particularly been challenged in our working lives. So the respect for its accuracy was natural. How could you build something that could match, on Day One, that sort of perceived skill of the PA?

'But now the truth was slightly different because the Press Association, by then, had become an institution producing a diet of content that it felt it should deliver as the pre-eminent national agency. But the regional press had begun to change its diet and had gone away from the idea of using screeds on government and foreign affairs to local news and, to an extent, the more popular end of the market stories on film stars, pop bands and footballers. All these areas were becoming major players in the thinking of the regional press.'

In November 1992, the UK News idea was given the go-ahead and by February the following year, once the technology and the software had been sorted out, the new agency was ready to launch on a limited scale. It was staffed by a team from Northcliffe and Westminster Press, which had also been denied a settlement with the Press Association. A newsroom had been built and equipped at the *Leicester Mercury*, and Leys told staff, 'We are going to try to prove a point to the Press Association and everyone else that you can run a national news service in a uniquely different manner.'

PA executives were quick to acknowledge that the newly launched UK News service was a success and certainly provided its customers with what they were looking for.

By 1995, the new agency was providing an evening newspaper service to all Northcliffe and Westminster Press titles and to a growing number of other regional evening newspapers. Then came the killer blow when it was announced that UK News had won over the Mirror and Express groups' titles, despite the efforts of Potts to dissuade both his former employers and one of his past editors, David Montgomery, then chief executive of the Mirror Group.

'There's nothing like the thought of the imminent destruction of a century-old institution and one of the most famous editorial names in journalism to focus the mind, especially when you have only been its editor for a few months, and I knew we had a real battle on our hands,' Potts recalled.

Potts, a life-long Sheffield Wednesday fan, declared that the agency must play 'total football' if it was to win back the confidence of its customers. In a matter of weeks his rein-vigorated editorial team was mixing it at the sharp end, covering a whole new range of stories he knew would appeal to the national and provincial market. In the second half of the year there was ferocious journalistic rivalry and behind the scenes both the Press Association and UK News sought to win over major national newspaper groups. It was a question of tariffs, too.

Then at last came the turning point. First the large Thomson Regional Newspapers group (TRN) signed a fresh contract with PA from 1 October 1995, with the chief executive Stuart Garner saying, 'We needed to be happy on two fronts – price and quality of service – and if there were serious doubts about the latter the former was immaterial.' It was a morale-lifting breakthrough with the regional press, to be followed in 1996 by Johnston Press.

Not everyone in the regional press had deserted the PA. The Graham family in Wolverhampton had a long history of involve-ment in the agency, and, with Alan Graham on the PA board, they were crucial champions and core supporters. Alan Graham's passionate commitment to journalistic excellence and his belief in the PA's pivotal role in the media industry gave the executives vital support at a difficult time.

Next it was essential to win over the national customers. Potts recognised that renewing the News International contract, which was due to run out later in the year, was pivotal. The NI stable of *The Times*, the *Sunday Times*, the *Sun* and the *News of the World* was a prize trophy and if he could persuade the new management at Wapping to back the PA the tide would turn. Potts was also counting on the Associated Newspapers titles of the *Daily Mail*, the *Mail on Sunday* and the *Evening Standard* to stick with his improving and more focused service. Although Northcliffe was part of the Associated group, the national editors were not ready to jump ship and sign up to the UK News service. The late Sir David English – editor-in-chief of the *Daily Mail* – deployed all his renowned skills and energy behind the scenes to reconcile the Rothermere publishing empire with the PA. He was a decisive figure in the history of the PA and without his intervention no one would have bet on the outcome.

But there was another key figure in PA's survival without whom the modern PA would probably not exist. Les Hinton arrived to take charge of the Murdoch empire at Wapping in the summer of 1995. As the newly appointed executive chairman and a right-hand figure to Rupert Murdoch, he had plenty to occupy his mind as he rose to the challenge of his new post. But he found time to talk to Potts, whom he had met some years earlier in the United States when Hinton was editing for Murdoch in Boston. He not only gave Potts the time to deploy his case for a new contract, but, as a journalist at heart who had grown up with the PA service, he was interested in the potential and future role of the agency.

He took time to visit the PA operation, listened to the ambitions of the executives and not only agreed a new three-year contract but expressed an interest in an equity stake in the agency. On 25 October 1995, while presenting to customers on changes being made to the service, Potts heard the news he had been hoping for: NI was not only sticking with its contract but in effect backing PA. From then on, with the support of the *Mail* titles, Potts believed the PA would survive.

Announcing the deal, News International's managing director, Doug Flynn, said, 'PA's independence and its commitment to editorial quality make us confident that it will deliver the best service for News International. We have conducted a thorough review of all the options and can see no benefit in moving to an alternative supplier. The Press Association provides the most comprehensive news agency service at competitive prices.' But it was Hinton who had saved the day.

Meanwhile UK News was undergoing its own difficulties. A proposal to restructure the equity to include the Mirror Group and United Newspapers, owners of the Express Newspapers stable, was rejected by Frank Barlow, chief executive of Pearson, the parent company of Westminster Press. That was to be a severe blow to UK News's plans. And so the tide turned. Later in the year both the Mirror Group and Express Newspapers were to sign again with the PA, just weeks before the 1 January date when they should have switched to UK News. The eleventh-hour decision was greeted with relief at Vauxhall Bridge Road, where the sales director, Clive Marshall, said, 'This vindicates the PA's policy of remaining price-competitive while maintaining the highest editorial standards.'

The failure to sign the two national newspaper groups effectively dashed the rival's hopes of providing a national news agency service. There was a further setback for UK News when Johnston Press, the fast emerging regional group, headed by Fred Johnston, also signed up to the PA after tense negotiation during 1996. The deal was clinched by Potts and Marshall only after a series of cliffhanging phone calls with the Johnston negotiator in Halifax while the two PA executives were attending the Conservative party conference in Bournemouth. UK News was to continue for another year but eventually a truce was called – brokered by Sir David English and Sir Harry Roche – and the Press Association bought the agency, with the UK News regional customers returning to take PA services.

It had been a bruising episode, with PA sacrificing £5 million in tariff to remain competitive. But it had been the catalyst for a revolution in the agency's culture, with new executives in place and a new customer-driven agenda. It also led to changes in the ownership of the PA, with News International and Trinity Mirror buying shareholdings in the aftermath.

There is no doubt the fates conspired to rescue the PA. Sir Harry Roche, who was to lead the fightback by harnessing his huge knowledge of the industry and its players, became chairman in the summer of 1995, upon the retirement of the forthright Sir Richard Storey, who had given tremendous service to the PA. But Sir Harry became chairman only because the brilliant entrepreneur David Potter, founder of the Psion computer empire, was not able to accept the board's offer of the post because of business commitments. Never was the adage 'cometh the hour, cometh the man' more applicable than in the appointment of Sir Harry, who had all the skills and contacts needed to guide the PA to safety.

One of his key concerns was that some stability should be introduced to the PA equity structure. Three large regional press shareholders, Westminster Press, EMAP (East Midlands Allied

Press) and Thomson, having sold their newspaper businesses, made it known that they wished to sell their PA shares. After a series of negotiations both Mirror Group and News International purchased shares so that each became a major investor in PA of similar standing to DMGT (Daily Mail and General Trust) and Express Newspapers. Stability was thus achieved. The investments would prove to be shrewd and the changes in ownership, although deeply mistrusted by the regional press, demonstrated the confidence the major groups had in the agency and its new editor. Coincidentally, with the changes in share ownership, negotiations were proceeding with the shareholders of UK News for PA to buy the UK News agency operations. In May 1997, in an exchange of letters between the late Lord Rothermere and Sir Harry Roche, agreement was confirmed and Sir David English was invited to join the PA board.

Sir David joined Les Hinton, David Montgomery and Stephen Grabiner (Express Newspapers) as the representatives of the major shareholders on the PA board. It was a formidable combination, and one that kept the executives on their toes.

The agency now had confidence, security and, above all, the drive needed to transform the business.

As the years unfolded to the end of the century the performance of the agency, both commercially and editorially, fully justified their faith and judgment. Sadly, Sir David did not live long enough to see the full result of his intervention on the agency's behalf.

Sir Harry went on to oversee the reconstruction of the business, the return of Reuter dividends to PA shareholders, the sale of Ananova and the emergence of PA into new-media services, and he encouraged the devolution of the agency away from London and championed the construction of a £5 million purpose-built headquarters for PA's northern operation in Howden, in Yorkshire. In doing so he became the longest-serving chairman in the history of the Press Association and in 1998 was made a knight in recognition of his contribution to the newspaper industry.

The hole in the PA finances was plugged thanks to vigorous activity spinning off from the agency's core services, in particular new media and arts and entertainment listings, and the growing demand for sports data.

But, although the agency became profitable again through these optional services, wire-service customers were reassured that a new customer-friendly PA offering outstanding value had emerged from the rubble. The industry could once again trust the PA and much of the sea change came about because of the intervention of Alex Leys and his lively UK News. Potts readily acknowledged the contribution that UK News had made to the renaissance of the PA and would half joke that he ought to 'send Alex a large cigar and a crate of champagne'.

The chairman, Sir Harry Roche, went on record to declare that for the immediate future news service contracts would not rise faster than the rate of inflation while ensuring that the quality and integrity of the services was maintained. He said, 'In short, our aim is to provide a first-class news service operating at break-even or slightly better and to achieve increased operating profits from our other activities.' Given the precarious state of the agency's finances, even that was an ambitious pledge.

Now came another new beginning for the Press Association. Following the battle against UK News, expansion was rapid in the agency, particularly in the Sports division and in new media. Both these operations had been established in Leeds and by the end of the decade were close to outgrowing their office space.

Located on a purpose-built business park a five-minute drive from the northernmost end of the M1 motorway, the Leeds NewsCentre was within easy walking distance of the city's heart. It was therefore easy to find for the increasing numbers of customers the Press Association businesses based there were attracting.

In the early part of the 1990s Leeds was suffering the same post-recession stop-start development as was plaguing its neighbours in Sheffield, Bradford and even Manchester. Where those cities tried, with varying degrees of success, to regenerate their economies using the twin economic drivers of leisure and sport, Leeds went the hard-headed commercial root. A city that for decades had depended for its prosperity on a West Yorkshire economy centred on coal mining and heavy industry transformed itself in just a few years.

Leeds soon became the corporate headquarters of a number of national and international financial-services companies, and the regional centre of government departments. For the city fathers, the arrival of the London-chic department store Harvey Nichols was the icing on the cake – Leeds had 'arrived' in the big league.

As the city grew, so did the Press Association's presence and the acquisition of another building on the NewsCentre site presented only a partial relaxation of the insatiable demand for space, as new products and business expanded. PA New Media was spun off in the sale to Orange in 2000, but, while that business moved to new premises, PA Sport, still in the News-Centre in New Lane, continued to grow.

The pressure for space in Leeds, where office units were once plentiful, came at a time when other business developments increased the opportunities for the agency's production units to work more closely together. Largely due to historical factors, the Press Association's presence in Yorkshire was located on no fewer than four sites.

With the sale of Ananova, Robert Simpson retired and the chief executive's role was handed to Potts. In the fine record of Simpson's achievements probably his greatest was holding the company together during the incredibly difficult mid-90s, when the board fell out, the agency was at war and the future was bleak. Simpson deployed his Rolls-Royce brain and unrivalled knowledge of the agency business to ensure the PA could enter its third century of service to the media industry.

One of the first decisions taken by Potts and new managing director Steven Brown was to look to the north to build the new PA and particularly to concentrate on building a northern headquarters on one site. The executive team chose the market town of Howden east of Leeds along the M62, which was already home to the listings business, and had a history of links with the PA.

Brown, who had joined the PA as finance director, had played an important part in streamlining the modern PA and was handed the tisk of developing the commercial side of the busines after the sale of Ananova. Potts, Brown and their senior colleagues had always been impressed by the efficiency of the PA listings business in Howden, and by the town's location. No more than five minutes' drive from the M62, it provided easy access from the country's motorway network but retained the charm of a medieval market town.

But, before any location was chosen, it had to pass a Press Association 'health check' for suitability. The site had to have good communication links, not only with neighbouring towns and cities, but also with London. PA's operations should not be unduly disrupted by the centralisation plan – the company needed to ensure that its greatest asset, its people, would see any new site as a positive step with benefits for all. And there needed to be several high-quality universities, colleges and schools within easy reach in order to provide the standard of employee the agency needed to develop its business further.

The scene at last was set for a new building, a new beginning and another challenging chapter in the company's history. With enormous backing and encouragement from the board, the PA vision for a modern, successful and enterprising agency had become a reality and the PA entered the new millennium in its best ever shape.

Epilogue: The Last Word

NEW TECHNOLOGY HAS transformed the lives of millions of people. And equally it has transformed the workings of the Press Association. News speeds round the globe now at the batting of an eyelid.

The days when uniformed PA messengers used to run to the post office with telegrams and (since their journeys were timed by their superiors) run back again are now not only remote in time but remote in conception as well.

Sometimes, trade-union objections deferred the advances of technical modernisation at the PA as well as elsewhere in Fleet Street. But no shop steward, however mighty, could hope to stop the inrushing tide of modern telecommunications. News International's famous moonlight flit to Wapping from Fleet Street doused any last dying embers of opposition.

Modern electronics may have revolutionised the media business in the final decade or so of the twentieth century, but nothing has changed the PA's watchwords, which were born in the gas-lit days of the 1860s and proudly survive to this day.

They are: 'Fast, accurate and impartial.'

Those three words symbolise what a news agency is all about. And, so long as the PA continues to pour out stories, pictures and graphics day after day, night after night, no amount of sophisticated modernisation will alter that simple fact.

Moncrieff: PA's Reporting Legend

By Reg Evans, former Associate Editor, PA News

A MINOR CRISIS in the PA newsroom. The memorial service for Lord Whitelaw, last of the Tory grandees, was due to start in 30 minutes. There wasn't a reporter in sight and they couldn't find a pass.

Then the news desk's prayer was answered: Christopher Wighton Moncrieff CBE walked through the door. Within seconds he was on his way to the service at the Guards Chapel in Birdcage Walk. But even he couldn't penetrate the security barrier without a pass. 'The place was surrounded by the Scots Guards,' he said later.

VIP limos whispered by as he stood pleading with a Guards officer. One stopped. The lady in the back seat took in the situation. She got out of her car and faced the obdurate officer. 'This is Mr Moncrieff of the Press Association,' she told him in the tones of One Who Must Be Obeyed. 'He must be admitted, he's here to report it for the PA.'

The officer melted. As the lady turned towards her car, Moncrieff called out his thanks: 'Much obliged, Madam Speaker.' Then he sped into the chapel.

Betty Boothroyd's instant recognition of the stocky figure, pockets crammed with order papers, notebooks and news-papers, and her desire to help him get his story was typical of the reaction to Moncrieff of politicians of every party and standing, from Cabinet ministers to backbenchers over many Parliamentary years.

To them Moncrieff was and still is PA. A reporter without spin, whose only interest is getting the story, getting it right and getting it out as fast as possible to the media via PA. He's regarded by politicians with respect and affection, to rivals whom he's often scooped but never deceived he's a legend and to successive editors of PA quite simply as their greatest journalistic asset. He stands out among the many fine journalists who have worked for PA, not least because he embodies the qualities of integrity, accuracy, independence and speed to which they all aspired and which mark out the truly committed news agency reporter.

Mrs Thatcher, a great admirer, made him CBE in the 1989 New Year's Honours for services to Parliamentary journalism. Her legendary Press Secretary, Sir Bernard Ingham, says: 'He's unique. There never has been and there never will be another Chris Moncrieff. He's the nearest approach to the 24-hour journalist I have ever known. He's a straight reporter who writes what has happened without any spin unless he's writing his own views in a signed article.'

Derbyshire-born Moncrieff joined PA's Parliamentary staff in 1962, was appointed a lobby reporter in 1973 and chief political correspondent (later political editor) in 1980. When he reached official retirement in 1994, tributes flooded in from politicians and fellow journalists.

Some 123 MPs of all parties tabled a Commons motion congratulating him 'on his tireless devotion to duty, often working 18 hours per day, seven days a week, producing fast, witty and accurate stories' and paying tribute to his 'enormous contribution in reporting politics'. He was profiled by both BBC and ITV.

But the most perceptive comment came from Gordon Brown, later to be Labour's Chancellor of the Exchequer. 'I can't imagine Chris retiring. I suspect reports of his retirement are grossly exaggerated.' Chris had no desire to cultivate his garden or PA to lose his services. The next day he was back behind a PA desk, writing political analysis, backgrounds, obituaries and, inevitably, picking up stories from his vast list of contacts. A new career opened up, too, as a political pundit on TV and radio, where his stentorian, Derbyshire-accented tones made him unmistakable. He's still seen in the Commons lobby. And the flow of stories under his byline never stops.

John Major, Mrs Thatcher's successor, once described Moncrieff as a 'national treasure'. He made the announcement to puzzled Chinese officials after saving Moncrieff from falling off the Great Wall of China. Major recalls: 'Moncrieff emerged from the mist hurtling downhill. His feet were out of control in a way his pen never is . . . He headed irresistibly towards the edge of the Great Wall and the drop over the side. I put out my arm to steady him and the great man was preserved for posterity.

'I thought for this act of mercy he would say thank you. But I misjudged the great man. He stopped, looked up and said, "Can I use this story?"'

Tireless energy makes Moncrieff unique. A close colleague remarked: 'He makes workaholics look like couch potatoes.' In his years as a lobby journalist he was always the first reporter in the House and the last to leave. He urged new MPs, introduced to him by the Whips as part of their introductory tour, to 'ring me any hour of the day or night' (he admitted sleeping only three or four hours). At weekends he produced a stream of political offbeats. And for years his amazingly support-ive wife Maggie, always referred to as 'my good lady wife', was under the impression PA only allowed him two weeks' holiday.

Moncrieff's 'ring me any time' invitation brought him many stories. At 12.30 a.m. one day a highly-placed Labour spokes-man, Denzil Davies, the shadow Defence Secretary, rang him to announce he was resigning and launched a ferocious attack on Neil Kinnock's leadership. Moncrieff's 'PA Snap' flashed up on news-desk screens throughout Britain at 12.41 a.m., with the full story running three minutes later, and was on nearly every front page later that morning. Later Moncrieff came under fire from some morning paper political correspondents who sugges-ted he had taken advantage of the politician's highly emotional state and should have allowed him time for reflection before running the story. Moncrieff was unfazed. He recognised the rush of ethics to his colleagues' heads was because he had scooped them yet again.

Accuracy, speed and balance, the PA imperatives, are sacred to Moncrieff. An immaculate shorthand note – Pitman, of course – means his accuracy has never been successfully challenged. He regards tape recorders as a device for slowing down reporters. His speed at rapping out a 'PA Rush' with the bare bones of a major story, followed immediately by the full version, has often put PA vital seconds ahead of rivals, with the agency story reaching newspaper offices before their own reporters had started dictating. MPs have been keen to oblige as his assistants: he was way ahead of rivals on the leadership ballot which led to Mrs Thatcher's overthrow because a Labour MP was holding the nearest phone open to PA for him.

Moncrieff's style is classic news reporting: the most important fact and best quotes in the first paragraph, the facts stated clearly and simply, quotes in direct speech and any interpretation clearly defined. There's no gloss or slant. Even his closest colleagues have never known Moncrieff's own political views; he probably casts his vote for the candidate or party likely to provide the best stories. He's unfailingly courteous. 'I like to give the impression I agree with everyone,' he says. 'I don't think you get the best out of people by asking them hard questions . . . All I want is to get the stories out.'

In his years as a front-line lobby journalist, Ministers and MPs knew that if they gave Moncrieff a story, within minutes it would reach newspaper, radio and TV newsrooms throughout the country and maybe the world via the PA service. The combination of his own industry, integrity and the PA network brought him many exclusives rarely acknowledged by national newspapers who used them under their own bylines.

Brian MacArthur, the distinguished commentator on media affairs, wrote in *The Sunday Times*: 'Moncrieff is one of the most remarkable journalists in Britain, whose work appears, usually uncredited, in more than 100 papers every day and whose reporting is often incorporated into stories which appear under national bylines. Whether you are reading an evening paper in Bath, Bathurst, Belfast, Bedwellty, Birmingham, Bradford or Brighton, if it is a story from Westminster it will almost always have been supplied by the PA and written by Moncrieff.'

Undisputed master of the political offbeat story, Moncrieff had a repertory company of backbench MPs ready to respond to his call for 'a few of the old well chosen' on a topical issue. They knew they would get publicity – and Moncrieff got his story. Some reached the top: Lord Tebbit, when Moncrieff's own MP for Chingford, met him regularly in the Royal Oak opposite the reporter's modest terraced home. When Tebbit, a former airline pilot, told of the 'Mile High Club' of passengers enjoying high flying sex, Moncrieff had a sure-fire tabloid lead story. The late Tory MP Geoffrey Dickens eagerly espoused Moncrieff's suggestion he take up the paedophile issue in Parliament, although for months Dickens described the deviants as 'Fidopiles'.

Moncrieff has never been known to fawn upon or flatter politicians. And although generally benign, he has his fangs. Holding that Shirley Williams had let him down by denying a story she had given him, Moncrieff bided his time. When Shirley, one of the SDP-founding Gang of Four, was on a whistle-stop train tour he wrote about her tendency to miss the train and the comic song composed by the travelling hacks which began: 'Shirley Williams is my name ... missing railway trains my game.' It made every newspaper.

Described as 'the man with the lived-in face and slept-in suit', he cut a distinctive figure at Westminster and when accompanying Prime Ministers around the world, pockets stuffed with notebooks, bundles of newspapers under his arm. General Al Haig, the United States Secretary of State, broke off in the middle of a news conference on the Falklands crisis to stare incredulously at Moncrieff's crumpled trousers. 'Where did you get those pants?' he asked. 'From a pants shop of course,' Moncrieff replied scornfully.

For many years Moncrieff existed on a diet of draught Guinness. A group of MPs presented him with a framed share in the company to acknowledge his contribution to its profitability. He even managed to smuggle a crate into teetotal Saudi Arabia. In 1983, in a Road to Damascus conversion, he switched to lemonade and food.

His explanation was that to enliven a Labour Party conference in Blackpool he popped into a clairvoyants' gathering for a reading of new leader Neil Kinnock's future. 'Madame Fifi looked at me and said, "I'll tell you this for nothing – if you don't give up the drink you'll be dead within a year." '

Fellow journalists regard Moncrieff with a mixture of affection, respect and even awe. Invited to give the address at a memorial service in St Margaret's, Westminster, for Chris Potter, political correspondent of *The Sun*, Moncrieff decided to tell anecdotes about the stories they had covered together. Soon the congregation was roaring with laughter. A group of Italian tourists, barred from entry because the memorial service was in progress, asked: 'How can that be? Everybody is laughing.' At the end, Kelvin McKenzie, famed *Sun* editor, asked Moncrieff: 'Can I book you for mine?'

Moncrieff is a genuinely modest man, with a sense of his own value. He's been embarrassed but pleased by the praise of his peers. The tribute that almost certainly pleased him most came from David Chipp, the PA editor-in-chief, who promoted him to chief political correspondent: 'A great reporter.'

It was his 'grossly exaggerated' retirement – or more precisely reaching retirement age and stepping down from being political editor – that brought Moncrieff into the public eye.

At the 1994 Labour party conference, TV viewers saw Moncrieff giving the vote of thanks on behalf of the press, regretting that the hacks, who had arrived 'with our fangs drooling for blood', had for once been disappointed. The late John Smith, then Labour leader, was among those convulsed with laughter. And the Labour delegates roared their approval when Moncrieff continued that the portents were that the hacks' blood lust would be satisfied next week in Blackpool at the Tory conference.

Politicians queued up to give what Moncrieff would describe as 'a few of the old well-chosen' about him.

Kenneth Baker, former Tory Home Secretary: 'He looks like a spaniel and acts like a terrier, relentless in his search for news.'

Margaret Beckett, later Labour's Leader of the House: 'Chris Moncrieff and PA are synonymous . . . it's hard to imagine that it can go on without him.'

Sir Edward Heath: 'I've known him all the time I've been in the House. He's absolutely reliable and absolutely accurate. Everybody in the House talks to him.'

John Prescott, later Labour's deputy premier: 'He's got a tremendous capacity for picking up stories. When the rest have gone home, he's still at it . . . and he starts early in the morning before the others have got up.'

Lord Hurd, former Tory Foreign Secretary: 'People who want to get something across plain, straight, totally accurate, no fooling, give it to Chris Moncrieff.'

Neil Kinnock, former Labour leader, recalled receiving a phone call from Chris late one Saturday evening asking for a comment on a Tory Minister's speech about the sex lives of low social groups. 'I said, "It looks like pills for proles." Chris said: "That's it. I've got enough." The next day it was over every newspaper. He's a great maker of reputations.'

Kenneth Clarke, former Tory Chancellor: 'He's the first journalist anyone thinks of when they want to get something across.'

The late John Smith: 'A legend in his own profession, indefatigable, accurate, indestructible and always good fun and great company.'

Malcolm Rifkind, former Tory Scottish Secretary: 'At first he seems a rather crumpled, undistinguished, not terribly impressive figure . . . but then you realise you are dealing with a true professional.'

But although reporting politics has been his life, Moncrieff loves to report anything . . . anywhere. He is one of the few reporters still around who reported the Great Train Robbery. He spent so long away from home on the story that a neighbour, heeding appeals for information about anyone missing from their usual haunts, alerted local police with a tip that Moncrieff might be one of the gang. On his rare holidays at a bracing East Coast resort, he's apt to file offbeat gems culled from local newspapers or casual conversations.

In Parliamentary vacations, Moncrieff was eager to volunteer for any assignment giving a chance of a good story. He did much reporting from Northern Ireland. Going there to report the first anniversary of Bloody Sunday, he booked in, as was his custom, at the Hamill Hotel in Belfast, an old-fashioned and rather seedy establishment across the road from the modern hotel favoured by younger members of the press corps.

One night he was enjoying a late night Guinness with a colleague when two masked men rushed into the hotel bar. 'We've placed a bomb,' they cried. 'You've got 15 minutes to get out.' Unruffled Moncrieff turned to the barman. 'Just time for another pint, then,' he said.

When the bomb exploded an hour later, the hotel was destroyed. Peering through smoke and dust, Moncrieff saw a yawning gap where his bedroom had been. After procuring a new shirt and a toothbrush he just had time to get to London-derry for the next day's anniversary.

Once there, he filed an immaculate account of the events of the day, followed by a beautifully crafted obituary of the Hamill Hotel, much loved by hacks and shady characters through the troubles. Back in Belfast he was contacted by one of the Hamill's maids. She had searched through the rubble and found his travelling bag and gave it to him packed with washed and ironed clothing. Moncrieff, a famously light traveller, was astonished. 'Some of it I'd never seen before,' he said. 'It must have been left by other guests.' He is one of the men that women just love to mother.

From time to time national newspapers have attempted to entice Moncrieff from PA with big money packages. He's always declined. Simon Hoggart, writing in the *Guardian* explained: 'He never went, knowing that the PA which reaches every corner of the British media in minutes was the only place for his talents . . . We are all immensely grateful.'

Index